MISSOURI

An Illustrated History

ILLUSTRATED HISTORIES FROM HIPPOCRENE BOOKS

MISSOURI

AN ILLUSTRATED HISTORY

SEAN MCLACHLAN

HIPPOCRENE BOOKS, INC.
New York

For information, address:
Hippocrene Books, Inc.
171 Madison Avenue
New York, NY 10016
www.hippocrenebooks.com

Library of Congress Cataloging-in-Publication Data

McLachlan, Sean.
    Missouri : an illustrated history / Sean McLachlan.
        p.   cm.
    Includes bibliographical references.
    ISBN-13: 978-0-7818-1196-5 (alk. paper)
    ISBN-10: 0-7818-1196-1
        1. Missouri—History. 2. Missouri—History—Pictorial works.
    I. Title.

    F466.M46 2008
    977.8—dc22   2007039597

Printed in the United States of America.

For Almudena, my wife

and Julián, my son

CONTENTS

ACKNOWLEDGMENTS

One of the most gratifying things about writing this book was the amount of help and hospitality I received from Missourians in every corner of the state. Their love of their history is infectious, and their local knowledge and willingness to help made my task much easier. I would especially like to thank the staffs of the State Historical Society of Missouri and the Western Historical Manuscripts Collection for their patience in looking up obscure documents and answering innumerable questions. Similar thanks must go to dozens of local museums, historical societies, and individuals across Missouri who provided information and photographs. Their efforts to preserve Missouri's past are truly impressive. I would also like to thank Chris and Caitlin of the Lenon-Davis International Youth Hostel of Columbia for their boundless hospitality, the Kneighborhood Knights for chess and conversation, and all my other friends in Missouri for listening to the ramblings of a struggling writer. A very special thanks goes to my wife Almudena. With every book a writer's wife must become a temporary widow. Thank you for your patience, support, and understanding. Another special thanks goes to my son, Julián, who makes life a lot more fun.

CHAPTER 1

THE FIRST MISSOURIANS

For most of its history, the land we now call Missouri had no name. There were no cities, no roads, and no people. The tribe that would give the state its name had not yet arrived. The ecology changed from prairie to woodland, then back to prairie. Strange beasts stalked the land. The dinosaurs came and went, to be replaced around 65 million years ago by the mammals. Human beings would not come until much later.

Archaeologists cannot agree when humans first came to North America. The traditional theory is that they came during the most recent ice age, which lasted from thirty-five thousand to ten thousand years ago.

Ice ages happen fairly regularly. While scientists disagree about their cause, most believe they happen because of the orbit of the earth. The earth orbits the sun once every year, but the path of that orbit changes over time due to the gravitational pull of the other planets. About every ten thousand years the earth is at its farthest from the sun. The tilt of the earth as it revolves around its axis every twenty-four hours also varies. When the earth is far from the sun, and the tilt is more than usual, temperatures become considerably colder for whichever hemisphere is angled away from the sun. A lower temperature means year-round snow at some latitudes. Larger snowfields cool the air, producing more snowfall. As the snowfields expand, their effect becomes greater. Winters become longer and colder, and the snow packs into giant glaciers covering vast areas. As more water is trapped as snow and ice, the water level of the oceans begins to go down.

During the last ice age, giant glaciers covered much of North America. About five percent of the earth's water was locked up as ice. This meant the sea level was 130–160 yards lower than what it is today. A vast land bridge called Beringia, almost a thousand miles wide, connected what is now Alaska to eastern Russia. As the earth's orbit and tilt changed, the

The major ecozones of Missouri, superimposed on a map of the modern counties. Missouri has 114 counties and one independent city, St. Louis. COURTESY MICHAEL O'BRIEN AND W. RAYMOND WOOD.

world came out of the cold cycle. Around ten thousand years ago, or 8000 BC, the glaciers began to recede. Temperatures rose and forests grew. It was the beginning of the Holocene, the environmental epoch we are still in today. Archaeologists believe that before this happened, wandering bands of hunter-gatherers followed the migrations of big-game animals such as mammoths over the land bridge and into North America.

It appears people spread quickly across the virgin continent. There is evidence for people in Alaska by about 10,000 BC, and the first remains of humans appear in Missouri as early as 9250 BC. But the traditional dates have come under fire in recent years. A number of archaeological sites in North and South America show signs of much earlier human habitation. One site even boasts a date of two hundred thousand years ago. These claims themselves, however, have come under harsh scrutiny. Many of the sites are very uncertain, and what some archaeologists call crude artifacts may in fact be naturally broken rock.

But not all of these sites can be discounted so easily. At Monte Verde, in southern Chile, sediments covered up an ancient campsite and preserved it remarkably well, including even the foundation posts of houses and remains of a killed and butchered mastodon. Radiocarbon analysis for the organic material resulted in a date of 10,500 BC. While this is not much earlier than previous theories allow, the fact that this site is far to the south in Chile gives reason for pause. If the inhabitants of Monte Verde had come across the Bering land bridge, they would have had to hurry to get down to South America by that time!

The Monte Verde dates are still controversial, but archaeologists are now rethinking the Beringia theory. While they maintain it was an important corridor for the colonization of the Americas, some suggest that the first Americans got here by sea in small, skin-covered boats, hugging the coastline of Siberia, crossing a narrow stretch of water, and sailing down the West Coast until they found better lands farther south. Since it is known that humans traveled over the ocean to Australia more than fifty thousand years ago, this idea is not so far-fetched.

Whatever the answer to this riddle is, it seems clear that the first significant settlement of Missouri was in what archaeologists call the Paleoindian period from 9250 to 7500 BC. During that time, Missouri was considerably cooler, but as the climate emerged from the ice age, the coniferous (pine) forest that had covered much of the region gave way to deciduous (leafy) forest and tall-grass prairie by the start of the Paleoindian period. The hunter-gatherers at the beginning of this period

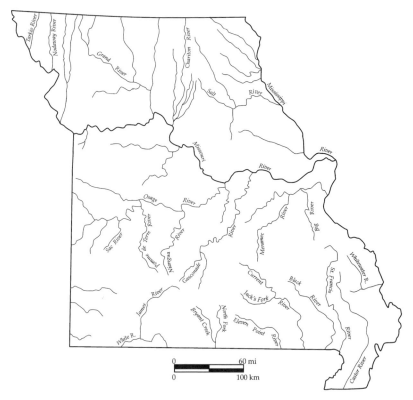

The rivers of Missouri. An easy water supply made it attractive to prehistoric farmers and European settlers. Only the Mississippi and Missouri rivers are easily navigable by large boats, however. COURTESY MICHAEL O'BRIEN AND W. RAYMOND WOOD.

used spears tipped with large points, which became known as Clovis points. The Clovis culture, which lasted in Missouri from around 9250 to 8950 BC, spread across much of North America. The term *Clovis* comes from a town in New Mexico where the distinctive spearheads were first found.

Little is known about these people except that they lived in temporary camps near streams and rivers and followed the animals during their annual cycles of migration. It appears that at first they hunted the large animals left over from the ice age: musk oxen, mammoth, mastodon, camel, and ground sloth. By about 9000 BC, however, these animals became extinct. Archaeologists debate whether they died off because of climate changes or if they were hunted to extinction by the Clovis people, but it is likely that both factors contributed to their demise.

Only the most durable artifacts remain from this time. While the Paleoindians surely must have worked with wood and hide, only tools made from stone and bone have survived the centuries. Besides the Clovis points, which may have been used both for spearheads and daggers, archaeologists have found grinding and hammer stones for breaking up seeds. Stone beads and bone gaming discs show that the people had spare time in which to enjoy themselves and make jewelry.

But their life must have been a hard one. The Missouri and Mississippi rivers flooded frequently because of heavy rainfall and outflow from melting glaciers. Campsites were located mainly on high prairie, where most of the mammals roamed, and away from the floodplain. Melting glaciers uncovered fine dust ground from rocks that blew in great dust storms, carrying particles miles away from river bottomlands.

The first real cultural change appeared in the Dalton phase from about 9000 to 7900 BC. This phase of the Paleoindian period is named after its distinctive points, which are generally longer and thinner than Clovis points and are often serrated. The points are named after the researcher who first made a serious study of them. During this time most of the big ice age mammals had disappeared, and people turned to hunting bison and smaller game. They spent more time in one place and gathered more seeds, sheltering in the region's many caves and rock shelters for protection from the elements. By the end of the period, the emphasis was on trapping and hunting small game and gathering wild food plants. There is also evidence of fishing and collecting shellfish, although this may have been going on in the Clovis period as well.

Missouri's many caves were popular shelters for prehistoric peoples, and their isolated climates often preserve artifacts, such as these pair of prehistoric sandals. University of Missouri-Columbia, Museum of Anthropology.

As people began to have semipermanent base camps and enjoy a wider variety of food, they increased in number. By 7900 BC, humans were everywhere in the state. In the flat, open areas in the Southeast, archaeologists have uncovered seasonal hunting camps with a large number of flint scrapers used for the removal and cleaning of animal skins. Archaeologists believe people went there in the winter, when there were no plants to gather elsewhere and there was less greenery in which the animals could hide. In summer it was hot, buggy, and swampy, making the region less desirable. Deer, squirrel, and cottontail seem to have been the favorite quarry.

Other artifacts show this was a time of technological innovation. The characteristic Dalton point served as a spearhead and also as a serrated knife and saw. Experiments have shown that it was useful in so many ways that some archaeologists have dubbed it "America's first Swiss Army knife."[1]

Another important innovation was eyed needles made of bone. These were essential for making tight-fitting weaves that provided protection against harsh weather and are very similar to ones used by Inuit well into the twentieth century. Hand-woven nets and bags, essential gear for a wandering lifestyle, have survived from the period. There are also tantalizing hints at ritual, such as red mineral paint and pieces of hematite paint stone. These were perhaps used to create pictures on rock, for decorating the body for religious purposes, or simply for beauty.

The climate gradually shifted from cooler, wetter conditions to hotter and drier conditions, and by 5000 BC, much of Missouri was prairie. A new type of culture emerged to deal with these changes, and archaeologists call this era the Archaic period, which dated from 7500 to 600 BC. Archaic sites were located on all types of land, but they concentrated in forests and bottomland near running water. Now that the glaciers had receded and rain came less frequently, people had less to fear from flooding. Most sites were in the open air, but sometimes people made their camps in rock shelters, overhangs, or caves. The population increased, and by the end of the period there were a great many sites throughout the state.

Early Archaic hunting-gatherer groups were small bands, probably extended families, which moved from place to place in search of food.

---

1. Reprinted from *The Prehistory of Missouri* by Michael J. O'Brien and W. Raymond Wood, p. 93, by permission of the University of Missouri Press. Copyright © 1998 by the Curators of the University of Missouri.

In the warm season they hunted in the bottomlands near rivers. In the cool season they wandered the forested highlands collecting hickory nuts, walnuts, and acorns, and hunting deer and other forest animals.

By the end of the Archaic period some groups spent a longer time in one place. The forest was expanding again and there was more food to be had closer to home. Settlement tended to be in larger base camps with smaller specialized camps located further out for hunting or collecting plants. During this more settled time, Archaic Indians started burying their dead in mounds on bluffs above their base camps. They practiced both cremation and inhumation, and some burials received special honors. The bodies were exposed for a time until the flesh decomposed, then the bones were bundled up and buried with stone or bone tools, perhaps the ones the deceased had been famous for using in life. That some individuals were buried with many possessions and others were not indicates that there was some sort of social differentiation.

Artifacts in the Archaic period include carved stone weights tied to atlatls, or spear throwers, to increase their range and force. The elite wore stone gorgets on their chests or throats. Stone axes, bolas, and flat stones for grinding seeds were all common in this period.

A new culture appeared around 600 BC to replace the Archaic. Called the Woodland culture, it lasted to AD 900 and was a time of great change throughout the Midwest. Its beginning was marked by an important innovation—pottery. There had been pottery at some Missouri sites as early as 2600 BC, but it was never very common and died out around 1500 BC. Now it reappeared in the Mississippi Valley, spreading quickly across southeast Missouri. These early pots were simple in form, decorated with lines made with cords on the wet clay. As time passed and people became accustomed to the new medium, the pots began to show more styles and various types of decoration.

Pottery was essential for early people. Without any available form of refrigeration or artificial preservation, pots could store seeds, roots, and other edibles for the long winter months, keeping them safe from dampness and vermin. The Woodland culture made greater use of plant resources than earlier cultures. Many centuries of gathering particular plants had led to what archaeologists call incidental domestication. People were not actually farming, but as they went back year after year to gather plants, they got rid of other plants that competed for water and sunlight. They also favored the more robust specimens of edible plants, encouraging them to thrive. Certain types of plants began to dominate in their local areas. This especially happened with marsh elder and goosefoot, which became larger and more widespread.

By about 250 BC, people used pottery throughout the Midwest, decorating many of their vessels with abstract designs or animal motifs. The process that had begun in the Archaic period sped up as more and more bands settled down and intensified their exploitation of the local area. Permanent settlements began to appear, some protected by earthworks. By 250 BC, incidental domestication and favorable conditions reached a point at which some river valleys could be lived in year-round. Population growth in such areas led to further intensification of gathering. Social stratification increased as well. Burial mounds were accentuated with log crypts for the main burial, and peripheral burials were placed around the edges; some mounds included dry-laid masonry enclosures. Trade goods from hundreds of miles away appeared; copper from the Great Lakes and shell from the Gulf Coast were especially popular. Archaeologists theorize that this evidence shows that tribal systems had developed.

By around AD 750, people were cultivating maize, a practice probably learned from the more complex cultures in Mesoamerica. Maize requires constant care, lessening its usefulness for mobile groups, and the fact that maize became the food of choice shows that at least part of the population stayed put during the growing season. Another technological innovation was the bow, which proved to be a better hunting weapon than spears thrown by atlatls.

While much of Missouri during the Woodland period became more localized, the people living along the Mississippi River valley south of the Missouri River looked outward. Archaeologists have uncovered a concentration of sites there, probably indicating a greater population density as people profited from the abundant fish in the river. Square and circular houses clustered in large groups in these early villages. This was the beginning of the Hopewell culture, an advanced society dating from about 200 BC to AD 400.

The Hopewell, centered in what is now Ohio, was the most stratified and complex society the Midwest had yet seen. The Missouri-Mississippi river valleys were in what archaeologists call the Hopewellian Interaction Sphere, a large area of influence that included Illinois, Missouri, Oklahoma, Arkansas, Louisiana, and Mississippi. Similar cultural developments as far away as New York, Pennsylvania, Michigan, Wisconsin,

Minnesota, and Iowa show that the Hopewell were well known across much of North America.

Hopewell trade networks stretched for hundreds of miles, bringing in meteoric iron, obsidian, and grizzly bear teeth from the plains to the west; imported copper from the Great Lakes; shell from the Gulf Coast; and mica from various regions. Hopewell artisans used these materials to make well-crafted luxury items such as pan pipes, ear spools, and hair ornaments. Burial mounds, some quite large, contained fabulously rich burials, but not all Hopewell people had access to such goods. Many archaeological sites contain no imports, while some have a great many, so it appears that some sort of social elite controlled trade.

One trade route from these early days still survives. A trail dating to the Late Woodland period, or even earlier, crossed the Ozark Highland between the Mississippi and Arkansas river drainages. This path, used by ancient hunters and traders, is now covered along much of its length by Highway 44.

The Hopewell people also made their own luxury goods. Elaborate stone pipes carved in the shapes of animals and humans became popular for the ceremonial smoking of tobacco. Clay figurines, decorated pottery, and flat copper plates in the shape of animals were common. The Hopewell made paint out of red ochre and hematite, and early European settlers around Meramec Spring found prehistoric tunnels where the Hopewell mined for these substances. Bone and stone were carved into beads, buttons, and spindle whorls. There also seems to have been some sort of cup-and-pin game, but the rules are long since lost.

The Hopewell were not able to maintain their rich lifestyle. Trade decreased after AD 100 as the river valleys filled up with people. Trade routes became shorter as the population expanded, placing more emphasis on regular, practical goods instead of long-distance trade for luxuries. There was also a decline in the amount of time and effort dedicated to the Hopewell religious cult. Mounds became smaller and had fewer grave goods. Ceremonial pipes were more often of clay than of stone. It seems the elite lost control of the people and were no longer able to trade for expensive imports. There may have been a cold snap that made it impossible to grow corn. Lack of corn, a plant of ritual importance, may have contributed to the fall of the elite.

Around AD 900, a new culture began to emerge, centered on two large ceremonial and political centers at what are now St. Louis and Cahokia on either side of the Mississippi River. Appropriately, it is known as the Mississippian culture.

One important characteristic of the Mississippian period was the popularity of burial mounds, which dotted the hilltops along every major stream in the state. Depending on the region, they could be rock cairns, a combination of earth and rock layers, or simply a heap of soil. The large amount of pottery found in these mounds suggests that the bereaved left offerings of food and drink for their loved ones to enjoy in the afterlife. Some mounds have even yielded the charred remains of maize, walnuts, and other domesticated and wild foods.

Both Cahokia and St. Louis became large settlements at this time, with a network of dependent villages developing in a radius of thirty to fifty miles. Groups from these centers colonized the upper and central Mississippi valley and lower Missouri valley, building more than a dozen large, palisaded centers across the southeastern part of the state, each associated with smaller, peripheral communities. A secondary center grew up near the modern site of Kansas City.

Since the Mississippians did not use writing, we do not know what they called themselves or their cities. The name Cahokia comes from an unrelated tribe that lived in the region when the French arrived. The site was already a village in Late Woodland times, but it grew rapidly from AD 1050 to 1200 in the Mississippian period, when it became the largest settlement in what is now the United States, with a population of around twenty thousand. The city featured more than one hundred large earthen mounds, many of which survive to this day. Some of these were not burial mounds but artificial hills on which the elite lived. Monk's Mound, named after some Trappist monks who lived there in the early nineteenth century, is 100 feet high with a base measuring 1,037 by 790 feet; it contains about 22 million cubic feet of soil, making it the largest in North America. At its summit stood a large rectangular building, probably the chieftain's house, overlooking a large plaza in front of the mound. Other houses were arranged in plazas between the mounds.

In another mound, dubbed Mound 72, archaeologists discovered the burial of a man in his forties who had been laid out on a bed of twenty thousand shell beads in the shape of a bird. Several hundred arrowheads lay around the burial. There were more than 250 other burials in this mound, some missing heads or hands, indicating that they may have been human sacrifices in honor of this important man. Radiocarbon dating puts the burial at about AD 950.

The "Birdman Tablet" found at Cahokia. Mississippian art often shows influences from Mesoamerican cultures. COURTESY CAHOKIA MOUNDS STATE HISTORIC SITE, PHOTO BY PETE BOSTROM.

A Mississippian ceramic figurine depicting a woman sitting on the back of a serpent and apparently cultivating its back with a hoe. The serpent's tail rides up the woman's back and turns into a vine of gourds or squash. A similar creature is known from various historic tribes as the Underwater Monster, and is a fertility symbol. COURTESY CAHOKIA MOUNDS STATE HISTORIC SITE.

Reconstruction of Cahokia circa AD 1150–1250, when the city was at its height.
COURTESY CAHOKIA MOUNDS STATE HISTORIC SITE, PAINTING BY WILLIAM R. ISEMINGER.

The market at Cahokia. This and other large settlements were important centers for long-distance trade. Goods from across North and Central America were available here, as well as more common items such as locally grown food and local handicrafts. COURTESY CAHOKIA MOUNDS STATE HISTORIC SITE, PAINTING BY MICHAEL HAMPSHIRE.

Reconstruction of the central plaza of Cahokia, with Monk's Mound in the background. COURTESY CAHOKIA MOUNDS STATE HISTORIC SITE, PAINTING BY L. K. TOWNSEND.

Community life at Cahokia, showing the chief's house atop Monk's Mound, and the homes of common people on the level ground. COURTESY CAHOKIA MOUNDS STATE HISTORIC SITE, PAINTING BY MICHAEL HAMPSHIRE.

One of the most intriguing finds at Cahokia is a ring of red cedar posts that was rebuilt several times from about AD 900 to 1100. For a person standing at the center, the posts align with sunrise at the winter and summer solstices and the spring and fall equinoxes. Archaeologists have dubbed this circle Woodhenge after a similar structure in England. Agricultural societies needed to know the dates of the solstices and equinoxes to calculate the best time for planting and fertility rituals. On the equinoxes, the sun rises due east and seems to be coming out of the front of the nearby Monk's Mound. Other posts may have aligned with other celestial bodies to mark now-forgotten festivals.

Around AD 1100, the people of Cahokia built a two-mile-long stockade surrounding the central part of the city. The labor required to cut and position an estimated fifteen thousand to twenty thousand logs, each twenty feet high, hints at some serious threat. The inhabitants rebuilt the stockade three times over the next two hundred years and fortified it with regular bastions like the castle walls of medieval Europe.

St. Louis was another important urban center, second in size only to Cahokia. In the early nineteenth century, traces of this once-great city still survived, and many people called St. Louis "Mound City." There were at least twenty-five mounds, and weathering and the spread of the more modern city had probably destroyed many others even by that period. Early excavators found burials equipped with arrowheads, shell beads, and copper masks. Sadly, all but one of these mounds disappeared during the city's expansion in the nineteenth century.

The Mississippian period coincided with an important event. For the first time, agriculture became the primary occupation for large numbers of people. Farmers grew corn, beans, squash, sunflowers, gourds, and other plants. Fishing and collecting mussels also contributed to the food supply. A steady food supply made the urban centers possible.

Long-distance trade reappeared as people settled into a more secure way of life. The salt springs near St. Louis provided an important commodity to export in exchange for the same luxury goods the Hopewell had craved. Other exports included fine pottery vessels, and whatever was in them, and high-quality flint from the large mines near the Crescent and Meramec rivers.

The towns, especially the major centers, were far more elaborate than anything that had come before. Houses varied in shape and were made of a latticework of wood covered with thatch and hide. The larger ones were cigar shaped and had roofs supported by a line of posts

Sunrise on the Fall Equinox at the restored Woodhenge, Cahokia. This circle of wooden posts aligned with important celestial events and helped the prehistoric residents schedule their planting and rituals. COURTESY CAHOKIA MOUNDS STATE HISTORIC SITE.

The chief at Cahokia greeting the sun. Courtesy Cahokia Mounds State Historic Site, painting by Michael Hampshire.

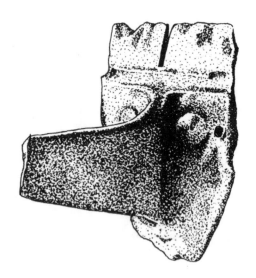

The "Long-Nosed God," an enigmatic copper ear ornament from Big Mound, the largest Mississippian mound in what is now St. Louis. Similar ornaments have been found along the Mississippi river valley and the southeast United States. Courtesy Michael O'Brien and W. Raymond Wood.

down the center. At the Cagle Lake site in Pemiscot County along the Mississippi River, a fire preserved a mid-to-late Mississippian period house, providing a rare look at prehistoric architecture. The house was nearly square, the walls supported by large posts of red mulberry wood. Smaller posts were placed between the larger ones, and the whole wall was covered with cane mats and daubed with wet clay, which, when dried, made a watertight seal.

Some villages imitated Cahokia and featured large plazas surrounded by mounds. The chieftain lived atop one mound, and the town center usually featured a large, flat-topped temple mound. Archaeologists believe a house atop these mounds held the remains of the dead and served as a center of ancestor worship. The cult of the ancestor seems to have been important, with cemeteries located adjacent to or inside the village. As in earlier periods, commoners were buried with few possessions, while the elite were exposed to the elements until they decomposed, after which their bones were bundled up and provided with rich grave goods. These burials often included vessels with sculpted heads or in animal-like shapes, prompting archaeologists to suggest these may have been clan symbols. Some vessels show humans with distinctive hair styles and face decoration, giving us a glimpse at prehistoric fashion.

Copper ceremonial objects became very popular. The holiest of these were copper plaques carefully wrapped and preserved in medicine bundles. These and other artifacts show a remarkable consistency in subject matter, showing hands, weeping eyes, snakes, suns, and birds. These cult symbols are also seen in the rock art of the period.

Like at Cahokia, residents of more than a dozen settlements in southeastern Missouri, mostly along the Mississippi, fortified their towns, usually with simple ditches and earthen palisades. This process started around AD 900 and continued until the sites were abandoned around AD 1350–1400. Cahokia itself began to decline after AD 1200 and was abandoned by 1400. The reasons for this decline are uncertain, but disease, depletion of resources, and social upheaval are all possibilities. No one knows what happened to the people or where they went; it is assumed that they spread out and either founded or became absorbed into other tribes.

As the great cities along the Mississippi declined, the Oneota culture emerged. Some archaeologists believe that this culture developed into either the historic Osage or Missouri tribes. Other researchers maintain it was the ancestor to both tribes, and still others argue it was related to neither. Regardless of whether they are the direct ancestors to historic

Head pots from Pemiscot County. These ceramic heads are found almost exclusively in northeast Arkansas and the Bootheel of Missouri and date to AD 1400–1700. Note the pierced ears and lines suggesting tattooing or scarification. CHERRY COLLECTION, COURTESY MICHAEL O'BRIEN AND W. RAYMOND WOOD.

tribes, the Oneota culture greatly influenced the cultural development of the region.

The Oneota spread across the eastern plains and Great Lakes and can be traced by their distinctive artistic style. They appeared on the Upper Mississippi in Wisconsin around AD 900 but did not spread to Missouri until AD 1350. Pottery during this time shows a great increase in the variety and amount of decoration and an extensive palette of paints. Some pots had faces or bodies. Bowls often had decorated rims in the shape of fish, bats, birds, deer, opossums, turtles, and catlike monsters. Some vessels looked like gourds or conch shells, while others took the shape of human heads, showing tattoos and decorative scars.

As with the Hopewell, the Mississippian and Oneota cultures eventually declined. The large, fortified villages were abandoned in the fourteenth century in much of the Mississippi valley. Some archaeologists say that southeast Missouri was mostly empty by 1350, or populated by small, dispersed groups that left little trace. Changes in the weather may have caused this disruption, as there is some evidence for drier conditions that adversely affected maize cultivation. Once again, the loss of this vital crop led to disaster.

This disruption was short-lived but had permanent consequences. There was a new emphasis on hunting and gathering and a general stabilization of the population. By 1400, small settlements reappeared. While the people of Missouri seemed to be rebounding from the disintegration of their urban centers, they did not have time to create another elaborate civilization before the disastrous arrival of the Europeans. The tribes of this period were the same ones the first Spanish and French explorers would meet upon their entry into Missouri.

Missouri gets its name from the Missouri tribe, who, at the time of European contact, lived at the confluence of the Missouri and Grand rivers. They share a culture with the Otoe and Iowa tribes and today are known as the Otoe-Missouria. All three tribes traditionally spoke the Chiwere-Siouan language, although it is fast dying out in favor of English. The Missouri called themselves the *Mintache*, meaning "those who reached the mouth of the river," and called the river they lived on the Missouri, meaning "(people having) dugout canoes" or "(people having) wooden canoes." The French thought it meant "Great Mud," which developed into the Anglo expression "Big Muddy," and called the Mintache the Missouri. Eventually the word came to mean the river, the people, and the entire state.

Like other tribes in the area, the Missouri combined the cultivation of beans, corn, squash, and pumpkins with hunting and the collection of wild plants. They lived in villages of large, round earth lodges made of a wooden latticework covered with sod, and a floor sunk into the earth with a fire pit at the center. Each earth lodge housed an extended family.

Twice a year the Missouri went west to the plains to hunt bison, living in tepees they brought with them. Every morning during the hunt a few hunters would go out to find buffalo. When they spotted them they put tobacco on the ground as an offering and asked the buffalo for help in the hunt.

Men were responsible for hunting and fighting. While the Missouri were not a warlike people, warriors were admired as a middle class between the chiefs and the common people and also acted as police. They carried clubs and spears and took scalps from the enemies they killed. With the arrival of the French they soon acquired guns.

Women did the farming and owned the produce and all family property; they even had claim to any animals their husbands killed. Men owned only their personal possessions. Older relatives arranged marriages for their younger kinfolk through the exchange of gifts, especially horses, between the two families. Most marriages were monogamous, but occasionally a man would also marry one or more of his wife's sisters. The birth of a child was considered a great event to be celebrated with a host of rituals. The baby would be given a name on the fourth day, and each name had its own song, which the child would be taught once he or she could talk. The entire family raised the children, and there was an especially close relationship between a boy and his mother's brother, who was supposed to teach him all the important things about being a man. Grandparents who were no longer able to do their share of manual labor acted as the primary caregivers. When someone died, the entire village would go into mourning for four days. Close relatives would mourn for longer and would sometimes mutilate themselves.

The Missouri had several clans, each with its own rituals and duties within the greater tribe. For example, the Bear clan headed the fall buffalo hunt and the Buffalo clan headed the spring buffalo hunt. Other clans had other responsibilities. A hereditary clan chief headed each clan and conferred with other clan chiefs on important matters at a council. The chief of the Bear clan was considered the supreme chief, although none of the chiefs had authoritarian power, and agreements were usually made by consensus, not decree.

days to seek a vision. Then there were seven days of dances and rituals before the men could go off to war.

In the northwest corner of Missouri and much of northern Kansas lived the Kansa, who had a culture similar to the Osage. By the late seventeenth century they lived on the Missouri River, just upstream of the Missouri tribe, and in an area of northwest Missouri and northern Kansas. Like many tribes in the region, they cultivated the prairie and hunted bison on the plains. All able-bodied people would go on the hunt, sleeping in tepees big enough to house a dozen people. Dogs accompanied the hunt to drag travois with the people's possessions. These would also be used to carry back meat and hides when the hunt was done. The hunt would be led by a hunt leader, elected by the chiefs of each band, who also commanded a group of warriors authorized to act as police along the way. The elderly and infirm stayed behind to tend fields of squash, beans, and corn. Everyone would return in late summer for the harvest. After harvest they would go on a second hunt on the plains and then split up into small groups to hunt deer on the prairie during winter. When fur became a valuable commodity to trade with the Europeans, the Kansa dedicated most of their winter to trapping beaver and otter.

Their clothing was similar to the Osage, as were their houses, except for a unique circular building made of wooden beams covered with hides, bark, or reed mats. These could be up to sixty feet in diameter and could shelter dozens of people. A sunken floor allowed for an earthen bench around the inside wall for seating. Early European settlers commented that from a distance these structures looked like haystacks.

The Kansa were more peaceful than the Osage, but they often raided other tribes while out on the plains and had an intense rivalry with the Plains Apache and the Pawnee. The warriors carried spears and, when they became available, guns and metal tomahawks. For protection they had only a round shield adorned with the scalps of fallen enemies. They painted these shields with designs depicting visions they had seen during their traditional period of isolation and fasting at puberty.

Girls started doing household chores from an early age, while boys were raised to be independent and aggressive. Both would get married shortly after puberty, often in their early to mid teens. Courtship was arranged by the families and was very public. Mothers would dress up their daughters in their finest clothing and stroll through the village to be seen. An interested family with an eligible boy would visit, and the two families would exchange gifts of blankets and horses. The girl would don her finery again and go to the boy's house, whose female relatives would dress her in clothes they had made and send her back with more gifts. Then there would be a feast at the wife's home. As with the Osage, a man could also wed his wife's younger sisters.

Like other tribes, the Kansa had sacred bundles used for various rituals. The bundles' magic would keep the tribe healthy and safe. Dances were also an important part of Kansa religion, especially the war and scalp dances.

Each village was led by an elected chief, and there was a hereditary chief for each clan. Clan chiefs could be women if the previous chief died without a son.

By the beginning of European contact, people had been living in what is now Missouri for thousands of years. It was a rich land, well watered and with abundant game. Each tribe had its own traditions and unique culture, but they all shared the same general lifestyle and a deep connection with the land. Sadly, that connection would be severed with the coming of the French, Spanish, and British.

CHAPTER 2

THE SPANISH AND THE FRENCH
(1541–1803)

By the end of the sixteenth century, the Indians of Missouri came into their first direct contact with Europeans. The first known European expedition to the region was by the Spaniard Hernando de Soto in 1541. Spain had recently created a vast empire in Central and South America, at a time when France and England had only tiny settlements on the east coast of North America. Now the Spanish became interested in expanding their territories to the north.

De Soto was an experienced explorer, having been an officer in Francisco Pizarro's conquest of Peru in 1530, after which he returned to Spain laden with gold. As a reward for his service, the king named him governor of Cuba and all the lands north of Mexico. Not content with merely administering these dominions, he set out in 1539 with a force of six hundred to explore much of what is now the southeastern United States. In 1541, the explorers became the first Europeans to see the Mississippi River, approaching it from present-day Tennessee. They followed the river all the way up to present-day Arkansas and perhaps as far as the Missouri Ozarks.

The people of the region had never seen Europeans before, and their first contact was a warning of things to come. De Soto claimed he was a god and plundered villages, seized food, and enslaved Indians. Various tribes fought back, and many of de Soto's men were killed, but the diseases the Europeans brought began to spread throughout the region. The locals did not have any immunity to illnesses such as smallpox and cholera and died in large numbers. De Soto himself died of a fever in 1542, and his assistant threw his body into the river to keep the Indians from learning that he was not immortal as he had claimed. The surviving Spaniards, now reduced to half their original number, struggled south to Mexico empty-handed.

At the same time, Francisco Vásquez de Coronado, governor of the province of Nueva Galicia in New Spain (now Mexico), was exploring the region to the west. While less bloodthirsty than de Soto, he also inadvertently spread diseases that ravaged the indigenous population. With 340 Spaniards and hundreds of Indian allies and slaves, he set out from Mexico in 1540 and marched through the Southwest, eventually getting as far as Kansas, where he met the Wichita tribe. The expedition sighted buffalo and met dozens of different tribes, greatly expanding Spanish knowledge of the region. But the explorers were disappointed when they found that the objects of their quest, the fabled Seven Cities of Cibola, were not made of gold but were just simple pueblos inhabited by the Zuni in what is now New Mexico.

These twin disappointments lessened Spain's interest in North America. From then on the empire concentrated its efforts on the wealthier regions of the Caribbean and Central and South America. The Indians, however, had been irrevocably changed. Diseases had decimated the population and seriously weakened many tribes.

There were cultural changes, too, as the Indians became interested in the material goods the Spanish brought. Metal tools and ornaments were especially popular since the Indians knew little about working in metal. Soon shipments were making their way through Indian middlemen into the Missouri region. Runaway horses from Mexico drifted northward until they reached the Great Plains, where they found a perfect habitat, and their numbers increased rapidly. The Plains Indians were delighted with the new arrivals and domesticated them. Soon tribes that had spent many long weeks trudging across vast grassland could ride at top speed, hunting buffalo and attacking their enemies.

By the late seventeenth century, the French and English had made inroads into North America. England colonized much of the Atlantic coast, while the French had large holdings in both the Caribbean and eastern Canada. The settlements themselves were rather small, but fur traders and missionaries ranged far and wide. French explorers were less bellicose than the Spanish. While de Soto and Coronado fielded small armies, the French generally traveled as individuals or in little groups, getting to know the local cultures better and usually staying on friendly terms with them.

The French were intrigued by the many stories of a vast river the Indians called the "Mesippi" to the south and west of their holdings in Canada. De Soto's account was not widely known, so the French had no idea where this river led. The colonial government in Canada sent Louis Joliet to find out.

Unlike many explorers of his day, Joliet was actually born in the New World, probably at Beaupré, Quebec. He made his living as a trader among the Indians and knew their customs well. He joined with Jesuit missionary Jacques Marquette and five woodsmen and set out from St. Ignace (in present-day Michigan) in 1673. After a month they reached the Mississippi, following it south as far as the Arkansas River. Marquette named this river "Akansa," meaning "people of the wind," another name for the Quapaw tribe. The name would eventually evolve into "Arkansas." By this point it became obvious that the Mississippi emptied to the south in Spanish territory, so they turned back. Joliet returned home, while Marquette stayed among the Indians to convert them, but he died within two years.

Joliet's account caused great interest among French officials, but communication was slow in the underpopulated and far-flung empire, so it was not until 1682 that another French expedition, led by René-Robert Cavelier, Sieur de La Salle, explored the Mississippi to its mouth. To La Salle's relief, he found the Spanish had not established any settlements there, and so he was able to claim the entire river for France. He named the new land Louisiana, in honor of his king, Louis XIV.

It took some time for the French to exploit their new territory. Fur traders ventured into the area, but few left any records. The first permanent European settlement on the Mississippi was at Cahokia, on the eastern bank of the river near present-day St. Louis, founded in 1699 by priests from the Seminary of Quebec to convert the Tamaroa and Cahokia tribes.

In 1718, the commandant general of Louisiana, Jean-Baptiste Le Moyne, Sieur de Bienville, established the trading post and town of New Orleans at the mouth of the Mississippi. The site had easy access to the sea and was in a good position to control the river trade, so it soon became prosperous.

Over the next two decades the French tried to expand their influence in the Mississippi valley, searching for valuable metals and attempting to open up trade with the Spanish to the southwest. Both of these efforts failed, but a settlement at Kaskaskia, on the eastern bank of the river seventy miles south of Cahokia, became an important center for trade. The government established Fort Chartres between Cahokia and Kaskaskia to oversee the region, and settlers founded several other hamlets.

René-Robert Cavelier, Sieur de La Salle, planting the French coat of arms near the Gulf of Mexico in 1682, proclaiming and naming Louisiana for his king, Louis XIV. Used by permission, State Historical Society of Missouri.

Some settlers made their living through farming, but trade with the Indians proved more lucrative. The French traded manufactured goods and alcohol for furs and slaves. Some unscrupulous traders actually encouraged warfare among the Indians to increase the supply of captives for the slave market.

The fur trade was an important aspect of Upper Louisiana's economy from the very beginning. Back in Europe, fur hats were all the rage and fetched high prices. The most popular were made of felt created from the wooly underfur of beavers, of which the Missouri River seemed to have a limitless population. Bison and deer skins were useful for making leather goods, and the meat from these animals provided a major source of food for settlers and Indians alike.

Frustrated by the failure to develop either mining or trade with the Spanish, the French government granted the development of the region to the Company of the West, a mercantile venture founded by a charismatic Scottish gambler named John Law. The ambitious investor soon expanded it into the Company of the Indies and dreamed of reaping huge profits from the unknown lands. He funded mining expeditions along the river and discovered several veins of lead on the west bank of the Mississippi, prompting the company to send Philippe François Renault to establish a mine. In 1720, he set out from New Orleans with a team of miners and black slaves and started digging near the Meramec River. They hit a major vein, and within five years the mine was producing 1,500 pounds of lead a day. This is an impressive figure, considering that the early "mines" were simply trenches cut into the ground, with workers tossing up dirt, rock, and lead ore. The ore would then be melted down in simple furnaces. The veins were so rich, however, that a little primitive technology was all that was needed to make the mines profitable.

Development had now reached the point at which more serious control was deemed necessary. The Company of the Indies did not like having unauthorized traders competing for their profits and stirring up the Indians, so it sent Etienne Véniard, Sieur de Bourgmont, a veteran explorer and trader, to take over military operations along the river.

Bourgmont was an enthusiastic supporter of Louisiana development and had lived among the Missouri tribe for several years, marrying the daughter of a chief. His travels along the Missouri River were the first recorded explorations by a white man. He wrote that the region was "the finest country and the most beautiful land in the world; the prairies are like the seas and filled with wild animals; especially oxen, cattle, hind and stag, in such quantities as to surpass the imagination."[1] In 1723, he and his men founded Fort Orleans along the Missouri River in present-day Carroll County.

This fort acted as a trading post to dominate commerce with the Indians and to push unauthorized traders out. It was also a potent symbol of French presence in the region, designed to keep the Spanish from expanding from the southwest. At that time, France, Spain, and England were the three major powers in the world. They had fought numerous wars in Europe, and it was obvious that the New World would become another battleground.

Once the construction of the fort was well underway, Bourgmont set out to establish a formal treaty with the Indians. He traveled west, exploring the region, giving out gifts, and signing treaties with local tribes. This brought a measure of stability to the region and strengthened the company's position as the sole trading venture.

Bourgmont returned to France in 1725, bringing several Indians with him, including a Missouri chief, the daughter of another Missouri chief, an Osage, and an Otoe. They were feted in Paris, where they fascinated the French by performing dances at a Parisian opera house and hunting stags on the king's estate. The daughter of the Missouri chief was baptized at Notre Dame and married Bourgmont's sergeant. While they all appeared to enjoy themselves, they insisted on returning to Missouri, laden with gifts and telling strange tales of what they saw. One of the warriors commented that the perfume French women wore made them smell like alligators.

Despite living on a little-explored frontier, the French organized their trading system as well as they could. Theoretically, the right to trade was limited to a few merchants called *congés* ("licensees") who owned grants to territories that could be posts, rivers, or regions. The congés granted licenses to *voyageurs* ("travelers"), who supplied their own trade goods and boats. The voyageurs hired *engagés* ("hires") who signed up for fixed terms, usually one to three years, to do the manual labor. Expeditions usually set out in the fall and stayed in Indian villages through the winter to take advantage of the best beaver season. They competed with independent trappers called *coureurs des bois* (literally, "forest runners"), who

---

1. Reprinted from *The Osage in Missouri* by Kristie Wolferman, p. 4, by permission of the University of Missouri Press. Copyright © 1997 by the Curators of the University of Missouri.

were often lawless and traded alcohol to the Indians for slaves. Merchants would occasionally risk going into the trading business without congé rights. The land was large and open, and the Indians proved willing to trade with anyone who gave a fair price, so the authorities had difficulty getting people to obey the law.

Few European women came to the early settlements, and the French men were not averse to marrying Indians. Within a generation or two, many of the "French" settlers were actually of mixed ancestry. Like Bourgmont and his sergeant, these men learned the local languages and respected Indian customs. While some retained their French identity and Catholic religion, others moved off into the countryside and became almost indistinguishable from their fellow tribesmen.

Despite the expansion of trade, the Company of the Indies never made a profit and abandoned Fort Orleans in 1729. The settlements on the eastern bank of the Mississippi did well, but the region to the west still could not support a permanent European population. The Company gave up its charter for Louisiana in 1731, and the national government took over again.

Meanwhile, population pressure caused by white expansion east of the Mississippi had tragic effects on the Osage and Missouri. The powerful and warlike Sac tribe, who found their lands in Illinois shrinking due to settlement, raided to the west. In 1730, a large Sac war party attacked the Missouri village near the abandoned Fort Orleans, killing almost three hundred tribesmen and prompting the Missouri to move to the Osage lands for protection.

The next attempt at founding a permanent French presence in what is now Missouri proved to be a lasting success. Saline Creek on the west bank of the Mississippi, about seventy miles south of the mouth of the Missouri, had a salt spring and a good supply of lead. In the days before refrigeration, salt was vital for preserving food, and this creek had been an important source since prehistoric times. Frenchmen from the east bank visited this area frequently, and in the early 1730s some came to settle and establish farms. The town became known as Ste. Genevieve. The first years were tough ones. The town was situated on the flood plain and was often soaked, leading the inhabitants to call the place *Misère,* meaning "misery."

The French, being mostly from Canada, copied the architecture used there and built square or rectangular houses of usually only a single story, although some added basements or attics. The walls consisted of vertical logs set into the earth and plastered in a style called *poteaux-en-terre*. A sharply angled "hip" roof channeled rain away from the house. The roof extended past the walls and created a sheltered porch that often ran all the way around the building. The earliest roofs were thatched, but these were soon replaced with wooden shingles. Generally, buildings were put together with wooden pegs since iron implements were not made from local ores in the eighteenth century and metal was quite expensive to import. Other manufactured goods were also expensive, so immigrants customarily brought along doors and windows from their old houses.

Each lot was surrounded by a palisade of vertical logs to keep out the animals that strayed unattended around town. The tops of the logs were sharpened to dissuade unwelcome two-legged visitors as well. Since the lots clustered close together, it was easy to seal off the narrow lanes between them and make a complete wall around the town in case of attack. Within these palisades the family would do much of their work. In addition to the house, there would be a yard, garden, barn, an outside kitchen with a built-in oven (fires were common, so it was wise to do the cooking away from the house), and perhaps a henhouse and milk house. Less prosperous farmers or engagés who only stayed in town part of the time often made do with a simple square cabin.

Ste. Genevieve did well as a center for fur trading, and many residents made extra income digging for lead and salt. Farming and hunting were important as well. There was plenty of game about, and the French enjoyed hunting—so much that officials complained that they neglected their fields.

The next settlement proved even more successful. In 1763, a new governor took over in Louisiana. His name was Jean Jacques Blaise D'Abbadie, and he was determined to advance the fortunes of the backward territory. He granted a short-term monopoly to New Orleans merchant Gilbert Antoine Maxent, giving him exclusive rights to trade along the west bank of the Mississippi and up the Missouri River. Maxent went into partnership with fellow merchant Pierre de Laclède, whom he sent north to establish a trading post.

Laclède and his young stepson, Auguste Chouteau, sailed upriver to Fort Chartres in search of a suitable site. They found one just south of the juncture of the Missouri and Mississippi rivers. With its favorable location and good docking area it could easily control the Missouri River trade. It also had the advantage of being on high ground, which

A turkey shoot. Early settlers relied on hunting for a major portion of their food supply, and made many of their tools and clothing from fur, leather, bone, antlers, and feathers. USED BY PERMISSION, STATE HISTORICAL SOCIETY OF MISSOURI.

meant settlers wouldn't have to deal with the floods that eventually forced the residents of "Misère" to move their entire town uphill. Early the next year, Laclède sent Chouteau and a team of workmen to start building. Despite being only fourteen years old, Chouteau managed the team well and soon had a large tract of land cleared and several log cabins set up. He also started work on a stone building, the first in Missouri, to house the company office. Laclède named the new town St. Louis, after Louis IX, a famous king of medieval France.

Meanwhile, rivalry between the British and French led to war in 1754. The British owned most of the east coast, but the French controlled Quebec and were trying to contain westward British expansion with an arc of inland forts from Nova Scotia to New Orleans. Both sides used Indian tribes to do much of the fighting, and the conflict became called the French and Indian War. It spread to Europe in 1756, where it was called the Seven Years' War. There the fight was over the control of Germany, which at that time was made up of several independent states. The British Empire and her German allies fought France, Spain, Russia, Sweden, and their German allies. The British got the upper hand when they took Quebec in 1759. Sweden and Russia withdrew from the fighting in Europe, leaving Spain and France to be quickly defeated. In 1763, as Laclède planned his expedition to establish St. Louis, the Treaty of Paris ended the conflict. The British acquired all of France's New World territories east of the Mississippi, except for New Orleans, and acquired Florida from Spain.

The region of Louisiana did not fall into British hands. Just before the end of the war, the French gave Louisiana to Spain as compensation for their imminent defeat and as an incentive to give up before that defeat got any worse. The British understood that the transfer of Louisiana was hastening the end of the war, so they did not demand it in the Treaty of Paris; thus, Louisiana became part of the Spanish empire.

Back in Louisiana the French had not heard the news, but they could see which way the war was swinging. Many French on the east bank of the river decided to join Laclède in St. Louis, reasoning, quite correctly, that if the British got control of the east bank they would not get the west. But what they could not know was that they were moving to a Spanish territory, not a French one.

When the news finally came it caused some consternation among the new arrivals, but it also led to another wave of immigration to the west bank of the river. The French feared being ruled by their former enemy, and since Spain and France were both Catholic countries, they felt more at home among Spaniards than Englishmen.

The British arrived in Illinois in October, 1765, and took over the French outpost of Fort Chartres. The French military command post moved to St. Louis, further adding to its importance. In two years, St. Louis had turned from being an uninhabited spot on the river to the center of Upper Louisiana.

Short of money and personnel after the war, the Spanish took some time to take over Louisiana. The first Spanish governor, Don Antonio de Ulloa, did not arrive in New Orleans until 1766. His government had not supplied him with a sufficient number of men, so he decided to keep the acting French commander in power and work through him.

Now that the transfer of power had actually taken place, the French resented being handed over to the Spanish crown, and they resented it even more when Ulloa tried to make the French freewheeling style of trade conform to the more organized Spanish model. The Spanish system operated on established trade centers with licensed traders, and a law forcing the importation of Spanish wine in preference to French wine must have hit close to the Gallic heart. When Ulloa tried to make all fur traders use Spanish vessels, New Orleans rose in revolt. The French deposed Ulloa and forced him to flee after he had ruled for only four years.

The rebellion didn't last long. Soon a Spanish fleet appeared with Ulloa's successor, Alexander O'Reilly, an Irishman employed by the Spanish crown. Realizing that further resistance was hopeless, the French grudgingly accepted Spanish rule.

O'Reilly set about consolidating Spanish control over Louisiana. He had more manpower than his predecessor and wasted no time using it. Since St. Louis was a two-month trip (in good weather) upriver, he decided he needed a lieutenant governor there to act on his behalf. He assigned Captain Don Pedro Joseph Piernas to the position.

Laclède had picked his site well and St. Louis prospered. It was the first elevated area below the Mississippi, Missouri, and Illinois rivers where it was possible to land boats. This made it a natural meeting place and preserved the early inhabitants from the muddy and flooded conditions that the citizens of Ste. Genevieve had to endure. There was also good timber and building stone in the area. Laclède predicted it could become "one of the finest cities in America."[2]

---

2. Peterson, p. 3.

The majority of the early settlers were French Canadians who tended to live close together, as they did in Ste. Genevieve. From the start, St. Louis was a compact cluster of houses surrounded by fields and pasture. There was a public plaza centered on the riverfront and regular streets and blocks in a grid formation three streets deep along the river. The plaza had a landing area for boats and doubled as a market. Residents called it either *Place Publique* or *Place d'Armes*, or simply *la Place*.

The administration marked out blocks for houses, and any new settler could get land for free on the condition that he build upon it within a year and a day. Once developed, the owners could resell. Blocks for the company headquarters and a church were set aside from the start. The houses themselves were in the typical French style found at Ste. Genevieve. Laclède lived in a fine stone house, which contained his treasured library of philosophical works by Bacon, Locke, and Descartes.

The area outside of town was a commons for pasture and logging. Everyone could use it and shared responsibility for its upkeep. The settlers fenced it off in 1782 to keep out wild animals, but it gradually expanded, and within a few years the fence extended to seven miles. Individuals were assigned a section for which they were responsible. They had to write their name on it and repair it by grain planting time, fixed at April 15. Even as late as the 1820s, the people of St. Louis were using the old French commons as a source of timber. Some of that area is still preserved today as Lafayette Park.

Farmland was divided using Old World methods. Each farmer received his plot as a thin strip so that everyone would have a bit of waterfront, bottomland, and high ground with trees. In St. Louis each farmer got a field measuring an arpent (192.5 feet) wide for each lot they had in town and a standard forty arpents (about 1.5 miles) long. The Spanish government allotted extra land to settlers with families and required all settlers to raise three different crops on their land to ensure diversity in the food supply.

Maize and wheat were the main crops, but farmers also grew tobacco, hemp, rye, buckwheat, flax, oats, barley, beans, pumpkins, watermelons, muskmelons, and cotton. Soon, apple and peach orchards appeared. Many of the citizens, however, were more interested in the fur trade than farming, and the village often found itself without enough flour. The French referred to St. Louis as *Pain Court*, meaning "short of bread." In lean times local Indians often gave them gifts of bread and corn.

An early settler making hominy, a coarsely ground corn meal boiled with water or milk. Originally an Indian recipe, it became a staple food on the frontier. USED BY PERMISSION, STATE HISTORICAL SOCIETY OF MISSOURI.

Other facilities developed quickly. By 1766 there was a watermill to grind grain and smaller mills turned by horses. By 1771 there was a billiard hall, and perhaps to offset its influence, the townspeople decided in a town meeting on Christmas 1774 to build a new church to replace the original temporary one. Everyone fourteen years old or older had to contribute to its construction. Auguste Chouteau had been that age when he first started work on the city; on the frontier, children were expected to work and adulthood responsibilities came early.

While the land was fertile and the fur trade plentiful, not everyone prospered. There are records of debtors fleeing out of reach to the British side of the river in the dead of night. The French also had to deal with British competition for the fur trade. The northern route via British-controlled Lake Michigan was actually the better one because the colder climate meant fewer furs would spoil or become infested with vermin than if they were sent down the river through the humid swamps around New Orleans. Because of this the British could offer higher prices.

But once again the struggles of other nations affected the frontier. Some of the British colonies in North America became increasingly unsatisfied with British rule. The thirteen colonies had gone through significant changes in the previous century. A population boom made them viable states in and of themselves. The British Crown had maintained a laissez faire attitude, but the massive costs of the Seven Years' War led to stricter enforcement of taxes and the introduction of new ones. The colonists, used to being left alone, resented the increased role of government. They also did not like that the Crown kept them from settling in Indian lands west of the Appalachians.

Matters came to a head in 1775, when the colonies rebelled and launched the American War of Independence. As battles raged in the east, both sides looked to the Mississippi as a potential supply route. Spain and France remained officially neutral, but as rival empires they naturally wanted the British to lose. In 1778, the French began to support the rebels with arms shipments. Spain followed suit the next year.

In the summer of 1778, a rebel leader named George Rogers Clark led a band of Virginia militiamen to capture Kaskaskia and Cahokia. According to Clark's account, they took both by surprise and with no losses. He proudly wrote that in Cahokia "hozaing for the Americans rang through the wole town."[3]

---

3. Parkin, p. 3.

Clark set up a local civil government, the first in the Mississippi valley, and got himself on good terms with the new Spanish lieutenant governor and commandant in St. Louis, Captain Don Fernando de Leyba. Soon guns, ammunition, and provisions were sailing upriver to the rebels under the "neutral" Spanish flag.

In February of 1779, Clark was on the move again. This time he led his men on a long winter march through flooded prairie to attack Vincennes, a fortified British settlement far to the east on the Ohio River. Struggling through icy water that at times rose to their chests, Clark's men made it to the outpost and completely surprised the British troops, who had assumed that an attack would be impossible in such foul weather. The rebels captured the outpost and sent the local British governor to Virginia as a prisoner.

But the threat from the British was far from over. Patrick Sinclair, the British lieutenant governor, had orders to invade the northern part of Spanish Louisiana. He organized the Indians in his region, including the Sac and Fox, the Winnebagoes, the Sioux, and other tribes and promised them rich plunder. To European civilians who wanted to fight he offered exclusive trading rights on the Missouri.

On May 2, 1780, the hastily organized army set out, led by Emanuel Hesse, a hunter eager to make his fortune. Sinclair could spare only a few soldiers, but their numbers were swelled by Indian warriors and European civilians hungry for loot until there were about 750 men on the march, a greater number than the entire population of St. Louis.

Rumors of the invasion reached St. Louis through sympathetic Indians and Leyba's agents. Despite being so ill that he had to have a subordinate write all his letters, Leyba was determined to fight.

He had little to work with. His garrison was tiny and the fortifications almost nonexistent. Leyba complained that the area's only fort, situated at the mouth of the Missouri River, was a fort "only in name"[4] and requested men and supplies from Governor Bernardo de Gálvez in New Orleans to build a bigger one. But the governor had sent most of his troops to take the British forts and towns in Florida and had no men or money to spare. Leyba would have to defend St. Louis with what he had at hand.

The commandant did some quick thinking. He called in troops stationed at the fort and at Ste. Genevieve and alerted the militia. This

---

4. Parkin, p. 5.

brought his strength up to 29 soldiers and 281 armed civilians, as well as several cannon. Leyba decided to use local labor to construct strong defenses for the town. He envisioned four stone towers on the corners of the town connected by trenches. He estimated it would cost one thousand piastres and managed to raise six hundred from concerned citizens, donating the remaining four hundred from his own pocket.

He erected the first tower, called Fort San Carlos, on high ground, where its cannon could cover the main northern approach to the town. The spot is now at the intersection of Walnut and Fourth streets. All this, however, cost time and money. Leyba realized he would not finish before the British attacked and would run out of money even sooner, so he switched to a cheaper plan—he had a trench dug all around the town. It would have to suffice.

Scouts reported Hesse's army closing in. The attackers must have been confident. St. Louis, they had heard, had no fortifications and almost no soldiers. On the May 26, 1780, they arrived.

That morning, sixty-seven-year-old Pierre Raimond Quenel was fishing at the mouth of Cahokia Creek when he was startled by a noise and saw his old acquaintance Jean Marie Ducharme standing on the other side. Ducharme lived on the British side of the river and had been charged with illegal hunting a few years before. "Come over," Ducharme called, "I have something in particular to tell you." Quenel noticed some Indians hiding in the nearby bushes. "No," he responded, "'though old and bald, yet I value my scalp too highly to trust myself with you."[5]

Quenel got into his canoe and hurried back to St. Louis to warn Leyba. The commandant thanked him for the information and promptly threw him in jail so he could not start a panic.

Leyba hurriedly collected his men and sent the women and children to hide in the governor's mansion. Leyba's illness had worsened, but he insisted on commanding the men himself and had someone push him to the tower in a cart. At one in the afternoon, the attack began.

Suddenly a large force of Indians burst from the tree line to the north of the town and, according to Leyba's account, attacked "with an unbelievable boldness and fury, making terrible cries and terrible firing."[6] The defenders opened fire. From the tower came the boom of cannon.

---

5. Parkin, pp. 18–19.
6. Parkin, p. 22.

The Indians stopped in their tracks. They had been told they would be facing only a few panicked soldiers, not a determined force equipped with cannon. They retreated to the tree line and kept up a steady fire at the defenses. Leyba extolled his troops from where he lay, telling them to hold fast. A middle-aged woman named Madame Rigauche grabbed a knife and pistol and joined her husband in the trench, shouting encouragement to her fellow townsfolk and firing at the Indians.

For two hours the defenders held their ground. Eventually the attackers realized they would not be able to take the town without a bloody frontal assault, so they took out their frustration on the surrounding countryside, burning fields, looting farms, and killing or carrying off anyone unlucky enough to be left outside the fortifications when the attack came.

While Hesse attacked St. Louis, Ducharme led an attack on Cahokia. There the townsfolk hid in a small fort and stone house and lost only four or five killed and five captured before they forced Ducharme's men to withdraw. The attempt to conquer the Mississippi River valley had failed.

But the victory did not come cheaply. Twenty-one men lay dead in and around St. Louis, seven of them slaves who had been working the fields when the attack came. Many more area residents had been wounded or captured. Farms for miles around were looted or burned. Only four Indians were confirmed killed, and no British troops or traders are reported to have died.

Leyba's illness worsened. On June 28, the victor of the Battle of Fort San Carlos, the westernmost battle of the American War of Independence, passed away. The king of Spain posthumously promoted him to lieutenant-colonel.

Governor Gálvez sent Francisco Cruzat to replace Leyba. The new lieutenant governor wasted no time stabilizing the situation. He made peace deals with several local tribes, helped by a supply of provisions he brought with him from New Orleans, and built a stockade around the town. He also sent a retaliatory mission upriver to destroy the British fort at St. Joseph, Michigan. There were no more threats to St. Louis. The following year, British general Charles Cornwallis surrendered at Yorktown, ending major military operations in the war. In 1783, the Treaty of Paris formally recognized the thirteen rebellious colonies as the United States of America.

But Britain was still able to harass the Spanish. The British had more money to spend on gifts for the Indians, so it was a simple matter to get young warriors to raid Spanish territory. The Spaniards found themselves increasingly unable to control the Mississippi north of the Missouri River and decided to concentrate their efforts on trading with the tribes along the Missouri.

The end of the war did nothing to stabilize Spain's position. In fact, it made it worse. The British were still hostile, and the east bank of the Mississippi was now part of the new nation of the United States of America. More and more Americans settled in the region, and many wanted to move into the more sparsely populated lands on the west bank.

Spain's initial reaction was to close off the area to Americans. In 1784 they blocked all American trade on the Mississippi. The new American government quickly protested this limitation on their expansion, and American settlers stated they would trade on the Mississippi one way or another. Taking the hint, Spain modified its stance and allowed Americans to trade on the river once they paid a duty. They also allowed Americans to settle in Spanish territory. In exchange for a loyalty oath they received free land, no taxes, and the right to trade. Part of the loyalty oath included professing the Roman Catholic faith and promising to raise any children as Catholics. This rule does not seem to have been much enforced, however, as there are numerous references to Protestant preachers from the American side of the river coming over to give sermons; also, a few Jews are known to have lived in the colony. The local Spanish authorities wanted settlers, not converts, and generally ignored the commands of the central government when it proved convenient to do so.

The most famous of these early settlers was Daniel Boone, who arrived in 1799. The frontiersman is reputed to have become disenchanted with Kentucky because it was getting too populous, exclaiming, "Too many people! Too crowded! Too crowded! I want more elbow room!" Boone wasn't alone in wanting "elbow room." There was a popular saying on the frontier that "When you see the smoke of your neighbor's chimney, it's time to move."[7] Another factor might have been his large debts. His son, Daniel Morgan Boone, scouted out the area west of St. Louis, and they received a large land grant from the lieutenant governor in St. Louis. They settled along the Femme Osage River, and

---

7. Botkin, p. 276.

in 1800 the older Boone became the syndic, the chief administrative official, for the area.

Another American interested in Missouri was Colonel George Morgan, a merchant and veteran of the War of Independence. He made a deal with Spanish authorities to bring a small group of colonists to found a village on the west bank of the Mississippi, which he named New Madrid. While he ended up moving back to the United States to settle in some lands he inherited there, many of his colleagues stayed and the village prospered.

The Spanish also encouraged Indian immigration. The Osage were causing a great deal of trouble, trading or raiding as the mood suited them. The Europeans did not understand the limited authority of the chiefs and assumed that if a chief made a promise of peace he could control all the hotheaded warriors in his tribe. In 1787 the Spanish brought the Shawnee and Delaware tribes into the territory to act as a buffer between them and the warlike Osage. This failed to stop the raids, however, and in 1793 the situation had deteriorated so much that the Spanish actively recruited several tribes to gang up on the Osage. The Sac, who were the Osage's biggest nemesis, took special delight in attacking the Osage's weaker allies, the Missouri. In 1796 a large group of Missouri was nearly wiped out in a Sac ambush while canoeing down the Missouri River. The survivors fled to the west, some going as far as the Otoes in Nebraska to find safety. The result of this union is still noticeable today, as the modern name of the two tribes is the Otoe-Missouria.

The Spanish also used trade to pacify the Osage. In 1794 the new governor, Francisco Luis Hector, Baron de Carondelet, sent Auguste Chouteau to build a fort and trading post next to their main village along the Osage River. He gave Chouteau exclusive trading rights with the tribe, and, in return, the Frenchman named the new post Fort Carondelet in the governor's honor. The fort was not entirely successful at stopping the raids, but it did increase Spanish influence over the Osage. The Spanish also ordered all Indian slaves freed in order to reduce the intertribal raiding that stirred up the frontier on a regular basis. Like Spain's other attempts to bring order to the far-flung settlements, this effort met with limited success since raiding was up to individual warriors or small groups, not the tribe as a whole.

To satisfy the Americans' continued calls for more trading rights, the Spanish Crown signed the Treaty of San Lorenzo with the United

States in 1795, allowing free navigation along the Mississippi. They also revived attempts to bring in American immigrants. This time the reaction was more positive. Land on the eastern side of the river was getting scarce, making Louisiana a tempting place to move. Within a decade, three-fifths of the population would be American in origin.

Spain's liberal immigration policies led to a quick expansion of population. Most of the newcomers were Americans, but French Canadians still moved into the territory, along with small numbers of other nationalities. Several new villages sprang up, including St. Charles, Carondelet, and Florissant near St. Louis, and Cape Girardeau downriver. small, independent farmsteads spread across the countryside. While the French typically lived in villages and farmed communally, Americans preferred to live out on their own. Few ventured far from the rivers, and soon the banks of the Mississippi and lower Missouri were studded with small farms. There were still no roads, and the river was the only means of communication.

While the face of Louisiana began to change, the government was fated to change hands once again. Napoleon envisioned a rebirth of a French colonial empire in the New World and convinced Spain to give up Louisiana in exchange for some lands in Italy. This sounded like a good deal to the Spanish government, which had failed to make a profit in the region. Spain's minister of foreign affairs complained that, "Louisiana costs us more than it is worth."[8] The two nations ratified the agreement with the Treaty of San Ildefonso in 1800.

As with the previous transfer of power, communications and transport kept the treaty from being put into effect for quite some time. The formal transfer of Louisiana to France did not happen until 1803.

The Spanish had little cultural influence on Upper Louisiana. Few Spaniards moved there permanently; Spanish officials tended to stay for a few years and then leave. But the Spanish left an enduring legacy. They were successful at meeting major threats from the Indians and British and encouraged the development of trade. Their rule also saw a boom in European settlement. When they took over the territory in 1770, there were only about a thousand Europeans in the area. By 1804 there were more than ten thousand. Thanks to the Spanish, the Americans would soon gain a viable new territory.

---

8. Reprinted from *The Osage in Missouri* by Kristie Wolferman, p. 46, by permission of the University of Missouri Press. Copyright © 1997 by the Curators of the University of Missouri.

CHAPTER 3

TERRITORIAL DAYS

(1804–1821)

The French kept Louisiana for less than a month. In a ceremony in New Orleans on December 20, 1803, they transferred the territory to the United States for $15 million, less than 3 cents an acre for 827,987 square miles of land. The price included $11,250,000 for the land and $3,750,000 to honor claims by American settlers against France. This massive land sale, now known as the Louisiana Purchase, occurred through a unique set of circumstances and radically changed the future of the United States.

Napoleon had signed the Treaty of San Ildefonso with Spain because he wanted to create a strong French empire in the New World to replace the one lost to the British. Meanwhile, the Spanish, who had controlled New Orleans until the French arrived, abolished the trading privileges the Americans had previously enjoyed in order to increase their own profits.

President Thomas Jefferson saw these moves as a threat to American expansion, so he sent James Monroe to Paris to help the U.S. minister to France, Robert Livingston, negotiate a solution. The original plan called for one of four outcomes: the renewal of trade privileges, the purchase of New Orleans, the purchase of land for the Americans to build their own port, or the purchase of New Orleans and Florida.

In the meantime, Napoleon's political situation changed. A slave rebellion in the Caribbean colony of Santo Domingo and a wave of yellow fever wiped out the French army there, and Napoleon feared another war with England. He made Monroe and Livingston a different offer: either buy the entire Louisiana territory or nothing.

The American diplomats were taken aback, but the deal was too good to pass up. It would double the size of the fledgling United States.

Despite what is shown in this oft-reproduced early drawing, the transfer of the Louisiana Territory to the United States was greeted with caution by French and American settlers alike. USED BY PERMISSION, STATE HISTORICAL SOCIETY OF MISSOURI.

Not waiting to hear from Jefferson for fear that Napoleon might change his mind, they signed the treaty.

Jefferson had mixed feelings when he heard about the acquisition. The Constitution did not authorize the president to buy land, but he could make treaties. While some in Congress worried that such a vast expansion could lead to chaos and encourage the expansion of slavery, most generally liked the idea of cheap land won without war and approved the measure, deciding to call it a treaty instead of a purchase. Thus, the greatest single expansion of U.S. territory was made legal.

The Senate's approval was understandable. Americans were insatiably hungry for land. In 1790, the United States had a population of four million. By the time of the Louisiana Purchase that number was approaching seven million. Most of the existing land had been claimed, and Americans clamored for more. Many had already crossed the Mississippi, and the region the United States had bought was becoming increasingly Americanized.

Although the official handover took place in New Orleans, there was a separate ceremony in St. Louis on March 9 and 10, 1804. One of the witnesses who signed the transfer document was Captain Meriwether Lewis, personal secretary to the president. He and Lieutenant William Clark, younger brother of war hero George Rogers Clark, were camped nearby, waiting for spring before heading out on what was to be called the Corps of Discovery. The purpose of the expedition was to look for a water route connecting the Atlantic and Pacific. They hoped the Missouri River might be the first link in such a route.

As they waited, they became friends with the Chouteau family and other French settlers, who helped get them bargains on provisions and provided welcome hospitality before their trek across the continent. Both explorers would later become prominent figures in Missouri politics, and the time they spent with the Creole residents of St. Louis made them sympathetic to their interests in the controversies that were to come.

The Corps set out on May 14 with a crew of soldiers, engagés, frontiersmen, and Clark's slave, York. Some of the crewmen had been up the river before. They had also learned a great deal from the experience of the Mackay and Evans expedition, which had been sent by the Spanish government on the same quest in 1795. Mackay and Evans only reached as far as present-day Nebraska, but their notes and maps proved very useful. Despite this, Lewis and Clark had tough going right from the beginning. They found their fifty-five-foot-long keelboat unsuited to the unpredictable currents, sandbars, and hidden driftwood of the Missouri River. The keelboat hung up several times on submerged logs and sandbars, and the explorers were grateful for their two pirogues—large, flat-bottomed canoes cut from logs. Just ten days into the trip, Clark complained that one section near St. Charles was the worst stretch of river he had ever seen. He would continually repeat that assessment as he came upon even more dangerous parts of the river, and his diary reads as a litany of "worsts." It was probably for the best that he didn't know he was navigating the longest river in the United States.

It must be remembered that the Missouri River at that time looked very different from how it does now. Careful management throughout the twentieth century, much of it by the Army Corps of Engineers, has freed the river of many of its dangers, but in the nineteenth century it was clogged with dead trees and branches, some piled up into mounds of dangerous spikes, and also contained treacherous sandbars and whirlpools. The Corps of Engineers straightened many of the sharp bends in the river, making it shorter and more navigable.

The Corps of Discovery, however, had to deal with the river in its natural state. One tense moment came about three miles upriver from Arrow Rock, a bluff overlooking the river and named for the large amount of chert (flint) found there that the Indians used to make arrowheads. On June 9, 1804, as they passed the mouth of Blackbird (now Richland) Creek, Clark noted, "Current exceeding strong. . . . Struck her bow and turn the boat against some drift and snags which [were] below with a great fierce; this was a disagreeable and dangerous situation, particularly as immense large trees were drifting down and we lay immediately in their course, ---- some of our men being prepared for all situations, leaped into the water, swam ashore with a rope, and fixed themselves in such situations, that the boat was off in a few minutes. I can say with confidence that our party is not inferior to any that was ever on the waters of the Missoppie [Mississippi]."[1]

Despite these troubles, the expedition persevered. Lewis recorded numerous plants and animals previously unknown to Americans. Clark, drawing on his considerable frontier experience, acted as the expedition's mapmaker. Their extensive journals, and those of some of their men, read like an encyclopedia of discoveries. Lewis and Clark had the added responsibility of announcing to the Indian tribes they met along

---

1. Moulton, pp. 288–289.

the way that they were now part of the United States. They handed out trade goods and peace medals bearing the image of Thomas Jefferson on one side and two clasping hands on the other, promising trade with the tribes in return for peace, although their promises of guns were a rather short-sighted way to ask for it. Of equal interest to the Indians was the slave York, the first black man most of them had ever seen.

Missouri acted as a testing ground for the Corps of Discovery on its long journey to the sea. They learned to handle their boats in the river's tricky waters and began to work as a team. Two men who drank too much and flouted orders were sent back. The rest proved worthy and continued on. Lewis and Clark proved to be well matched for command. Lewis held the rank of captain, while Clark was beneath him with the rank of second lieutenant. This was rather uncomfortable for Lewis because Clark had been his superior officer during their army days, so they referred to each other as "captain" and made decisions together, so their men never knew they did not have the same rank.

While finding a route to the Pacific was the nominal reason for the expedition, seeing what was along the way was equally important. The Corps brought along vocabulary lists that they filled out each time they came across a new language among the tribes. These became handy phrase books and dictionaries. Even more useful was Sacagawea, a Shoshone woman who acted as translator. Amazingly, she traveled with her newborn baby and her white husband, Toussaint Charbonneau. The baby must have made for some welcome diversion, but the journals agree that the husband was nothing but a lazy and unreliable burden, although he could cook up excellent bison sausages.

The natural resources of the new territory also came under study. The Corps gathered seeds and plant samples and described any new species they came upon, cataloging 122 animal species and subspecies and 178 plant species, including the now familiar grizzly bear, California condor, the western red cedar, and eastern cottonwood.

Through all this danger the Corps lost only one man, Sergeant Charles Floyd, who died of "bilious colic," probably appendicitis. Several others came close to death in various mishaps, and all suffered from illness at one time or another, but they managed to return to St. Louis without serious injury.

Jefferson hoped that once the expedition reached the Missouri's headwaters at the Rockies, they could pass over the mountains and find another river heading straight to the Pacific. While the route was not as easy as he hoped, the group did make it to the ocean and gathered an immense amount of important data on the Indian tribes and natural resources of hitherto little-known areas. Their epic twenty-eight-month, eight-thousand-mile journey through harsh winters and unfamiliar peoples was not only a boon to science, but it inspired many more Americans to expand into the vast country and discover easier ways to get to the Pacific.

Back in St. Louis the territorial government was hard at work sorting out America's new western frontier. It had a large task ahead. The United States had to organize a new government, make treaties with the Indians, and manage the flood of immigration. The population in 1804 was about ten thousand; by 1810 it had doubled. There were several growing settlements in the territory. St. Charles, twenty-four miles across prairie and woodlands up the Missouri River from St. Louis, had four hundred people, mostly French. Towns such as Florissant and Cape Girardeau expanded, while individual farms appeared on or near the banks of major rivers.

The first task was to set up a governmental structure. The federal government divided the territory along the 31st parallel, with the southern part called the Territory of Orleans and the northern part, including what is now Missouri, called the Territory of Upper Louisiana. Jefferson originally wanted to forbid Americans from living in Upper Louisiana and use it as a place to resettle Indians from east of the Mississippi. The reality on the ground, however, dictated otherwise. There were already several settlements in Upper Louisiana, and the Louisiana Purchase only encouraged the steady migration from one side of the river to the other.

To oversee the Territory of Upper Louisiana, Jefferson appointed Captain Amos Stoddard. Oddly, when Stoddard arrived there was no French official on hand to transfer the area to the United States. They had never formally retaken Louisiana from the Spanish, so they told Stoddard to act on their behalf. He received the territory in the name of France as a French official on March 9, 1804, with Captain Meriwether Lewis and important members of the community standing as witnesses. The next day he presented it to himself and the area became American territory.

Stoddard reassured the American and French residents that they would have full rights as American citizens, but they remained wary about what changes would come. They had enjoyed life under the

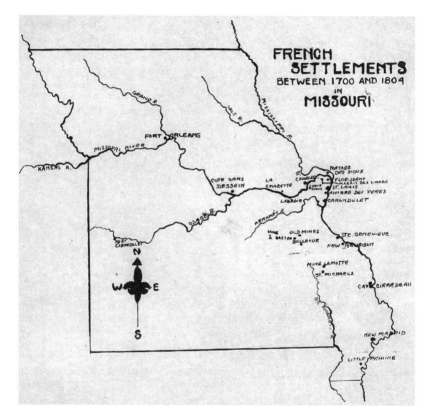

French settlements in Missouri. While the French population remained small, they founded many of Missouri's important towns. Note that all of them are either on a major river or in the mining region in the southeast of the state. USED BY PERMISSION, STATE HISTORICAL SOCIETY OF MISSOURI.

Spanish system, where the government left settlers alone and did not tax them. To help ease the transition, Stoddard kept the old Spanish system pretty much intact. He took over all the civil roles once run by the Spanish lieutenant governor, and Major James Bruff took over the military duties. While Spanish soldiers were replaced with Americans, Stoddard kept most of the old civil officials in office.

One of the main issues in the territorial years was land claims made during the Spanish period. Large swaths of land along the rivers had been claimed as private property by various residents, especially rich French families in St. Louis and Ste. Genevieve, and they expected the U.S. government to honor those claims. Unfortunately, some land was claimed by more than one person, and a large number of claims appeared to be forgeries. American officials found it difficult to decide which ones were valid because they did not understand the Spanish legal system and the vast majority of claims had not been fully processed. In Spanish times, the claimant had to go to New Orleans to get the deed approved, and few people bothered to make the long trip. In the free and easy times under the French and Spanish, this had not been an issue, but now it caused no end of headaches.

Even Daniel Boone got caught up in the legal tangle. The Spanish had granted him 8,500 acres, but he never got his paperwork in order. Due to his fame, Congress granted him a tenth of his land in 1814, but creditors back in Kentucky took it away from him.

Nathan and Daniel Morgan Boone followed in their father's footsteps by becoming frontier leaders. They started manufacturing salt from a salt spring in Howard County, boiling away the saline water in big cauldrons and shipping the salt to St. Louis and other settlements. The spring and eventually the whole area became known as Boone's Lick or Boonslick, a "lick" being the name for a saline spring where animals would lick the salt from the rocks. The Boones cut a path from the salt lick to St. Charles. While it began as just another path through the woods, like those of the Indian tribes, after 1815 the Boone's Lick Trail became an important thoroughfare for migrants headed westward and developed into Missouri's first real road. Their famous father spent his waning years with them near present-day Defiance.

The Stoddard regime lasted only seven months, after which Upper Louisiana came under the control of the Indiana Territory. In his short time in office, Stoddard did his best to work with the locals, but the switch made little difference in the short term. Most local officials stayed on and Upper Louisiana retained its own laws, thus avoiding the delicate issue of slavery, which was legal in Upper Louisiana but not in Indiana. One lasting change was that the boundary line with the Territory of Orleans was changed to the 33rd parallel, a boundary that would eventually become the southern boundary of Missouri.

The main trouble came when the federal government declared no land claims made after the Treaty of San Ildefonso, October 1, 1800, would be honored. Anyone living on such a claim had to leave. The government also decided it had the authority to make agreements with tribes to settle in the territory.

The St. Louis elite immediately organized against the transfer. Not only would they be governed from distant Vincennes in Indiana, but many of their land claims would be rejected and they would have to share space with the Indians. They were not even sure they would be allowed to keep their slaves since the government made no specific mention of the institution one way or the other. Auguste Chouteau and other prominent St. Louis residents led the protest movement and called for representatives from the area to come into town to meet Indiana territorial governor William Henry Harrison, who was coming for a visit. Before Harrison arrived, the delegates, made up of leading French and Americans, drafted a petition asking Congress and the president to revoke the handover. They pointed out they had been promised full citizenship and deserved their own territorial government. They also asked for guarantees on slavery and the consideration of all land claims.

When Harrison finally arrived on October 12, 1804, he received a warm welcome and was entertained in Auguste Chouteau's mansion. Harrison enjoyed his time in St. Louis, and when one of the delegates went to Washington with the petition, he sent along a letter of support. This led the federal government to declare that Upper Louisiana was now the Territory of Louisiana. It also repealed the law about land claims and opened up all claims for consideration by a newly formed land commission.

The territory became self governing on July 4, 1805, under the governorship of Brigadier General James Wilkinson, a close friend of Vice President Aaron Burr. As usual, Auguste Chouteau entertained the new leader in his mansion and managed to get Wilkinson to favor the interests of the territory's most established residents.

It did not take long for Wilkinson to become embroiled in the land claim issue. The most contentious area was around Ste. Genevieve, where competing claims for rich lead mines caused bitter rivalry and even some violence. A leading figure in these disputes was John Smith T, who added the *T* to his name after his home state of Tennessee, so not to have such a common name. He got involved in a dispute with local chief justice Moses Austin over an area with a productive lead mine. When the local army commander, Major Seth Hunt, sided with Austin and tried to evict Smith T, the Tennessean successfully appealed to Governor Wilkinson. This led to Hunt's removal, making him a longstanding enemy of the governor. Hunt soon gathered allies, mostly American newcomers who resented the previous residents claiming the best land for themselves. The three territorial judges were so incensed by Wilkinson's management of the affair that they refused to recognize his authority to name officials. Wilkinson called every judge and justice of the peace in the district of St. Louis, men who were predominantly Frenchmen whom he had appointed, to rule on this. Not surprisingly, they overruled the legislature, although a minority of Americans loudly complained about Wilkinson's methods.

The controversy was not helped by the board created to review land claims. Of the three board members, one was his nephew and another a close friend. They wanted to confirm the largest claims, while the third member opposed them. Because of this infighting, they made little progress on the issue.

The new government also had to deal with its Indian neighbors. Jefferson had already started a system of "factories" with tribes east of the Mississippi, and he soon expanded the policy to the west. A factory was a trading post where Indians could exchange furs for European goods such as cloth, metal tools, coffee, and sugar. The idea was to provide an honest price and cut out unscrupulous traders who cheated the Indians or sold them alcohol. These practices had caused a great deal of resentment and violence in the past. Another reason for the factory system was to try to "civilize" the Indians by bringing them into a commercial system upon which they would become dependent. For this reason, factories often included smithies and farms where the Indians could learn European trades.

In 1804, the Sac and Fox tribes signed a treaty with the federal government ceding all the land between the Illinois and Mississippi rivers, as well as some land west of the Mississippi, to the United States. In return they received a factory, lessons in farming, a smithy, and a thousand dollars a year and were allowed to stay on the land until it was

Members of various Indian tribes would often come to trading stores like this one to exchange furs for manufactured goods. USED BY PERMISSION, STATE HISTORICAL SOCIETY OF MISSOURI.

sold. They would not stay long, and soon the Sac and Fox added their numbers to the influx of displaced tribes pushed into Missouri. The Indians' factory was at Fort Belle Fontaine, four miles up the Missouri River. Wilkinson also sent explorer Zebulon Pike to scout out places to build more forts. The British were still siphoning off much of the Indian trade, and Wilkinson wanted them stopped. He refused to grant trading licenses to British citizens, but the federal government did not fund the new forts and the British continued to trade with local tribes. Wilkinson also suspected them of encouraging the Sac to fight the Osage. The violence even encompassed white settlers, and several of them were killed.

Because of the large number of complaints reaching Washington and the lack of progress in the territory, the federal government ordered Wilkinson to take command of the troops in the Territory of Orleans. The government did not explicitly remove him from office, but the demands of his new duties and the distance from his old ones precluded him from having any real influence in St. Louis. He left in August of 1806 and never returned. He left behind a lasting division between the old residents, who held large Spanish land claims, and the new American settlers, who wanted to speculate in land.

The Corps of Discovery returned to St. Louis on September 23, 1806, to much fanfare. The town did not have a newspaper at the time, but the *Western World* of Frankfort, Kentucky, reported in its October 11, 1806, issue that a great crowd showed up to see the boats come into town and were

> united in celebrating their arrival by a splendid dinner at Christy's Inn, on the 25th, which was succeeded by a Ball in the evening. The respectable number of persons who attended both the dinner and the ball, given on the occasion, together with the unanimity which prevailed throughout the company, cannot but be esteemed an honorable testimony of the respect entertained for those characters who are willing to encounter, fatigue and hunger for the benefit of their fellow citizens: but what is not due to those who penetrate the gloom of unexplored regions, to expel the mists of ignorance which envelope science, and overshadow their country?

The dinner was accompanied by seventeen toasts to the various political figures, the territory and nation, and to the "fair daughters of

Louisiana – May they ever bestow their smiles on hardihood and virtuous valor." After Lewis and Clark went to bed there was a final toast to "Captains Lewis and Clark – Their perilous services endear them to every American heart."

Lewis and Clark's return helped Jefferson solve the political controversy surrounding Wilkinson. He replaced the unpopular governor with Lewis, while Clark became a brigadier general in command of the territorial militia as well as Indian agent to all the tribes west of the Mississippi except the Osage, for whom Pierre Chouteau was still responsible. Like Chouteau, Clark understood the Indians and the "Red-Headed Chief," as they called him, became popular with them.

Lewis was not eager to take up his new duties and left most of the responsibilities to Clark and the new territorial secretary, Frederick Bates, while he spent a considerable amount of his term back east taking care of family and business matters. Bates has been portrayed by many historians as a difficult man. He did not like the French Creoles and could not accustom himself to their culture. He also thought their influence was too great. While he did not get along with many of the territory's longstanding residents, he worked more than his boss on the problems facing the new territory. Bates wanted to get rid of the factionalism of the Wilkinson era and acted against the biggest troublemakers on both sides. He removed Smith T from the various local offices he held, but he was unable to untangle the land claim issue, and the arguments and disputed mining continued as before.

The St. Louis junto, as people called the French and American elite, realized their position was in jeopardy, and not just from Bates. The new immigrants were predominantly Americans of modest means, and the junto saw that they would soon be in the minority. The junto tried to swell its ranks by making ties with wealthier newcomers, especially lawyers.

Lewis finally returned to St. Louis in March of 1807, and his attention was soon taken up with Osage attacks on the frontier. Settlers had moved onto Osage land in violation of the peace treaty, so the Osage no longer felt bound by it either. In retaliation, Lewis cut off trade with the tribe. He then told other tribes the Osage were no longer protected by the United States and encouraged them to attack. Lewis also had to stop trade on the Lower Missouri and Upper Mississippi because the Sac were dealing with the British, and the Kansa, Pawnee, and other tribes were meeting with the Spanish to open up trade to the southwest. This threatened American hegemony over Indian affairs.

The government decided to expand its economic control by building Fort Osage three hundred miles up the Missouri River from St. Louis. The Osage, threatened by their enemies and suffering under the trade sanctions, took the bait and asked Clark for a treaty. In exchange for a reinstatement of protection and trade, they gave up their lands east of a line running from the fort south to the Arkansas River. White men were forbidden to hunt in the remaining Osage lands. The Osage got to trade at the fort and were provided with a smithy, a mill, and $1,500 a year.

Clark was a shrewd negotiator. The Osage had gradually become accustomed to having American goods, and they especially needed the smithy and mill. The treaty, which required them to give up two hundred square miles of their ancestral land, was a serious blow, but they had no choice but to sign. American settlers were fast encroaching on the land, and the ban on trade was impoverishing the tribe.

Fur traders began to look further up the Missouri River for new areas to exploit. The animal population had dwindled in the old areas, and the competition from government factories made matters worse. Leading traders formed the St. Louis Missouri Fur Company to send expeditions up the Missouri River, where the Corps of Discovery had reported plentiful game. The first expeditions got underway in the spring of 1809.

The fur company was a joint venture between the Chouteau brothers and other important businessmen, the most prominent of them being Manuel Lisa, a Spaniard from New Orleans who moved to St. Louis in the 1790s and successfully challenged the Chouteaus' near-monopoly on the fur trade. After they pooled their resources, Lisa became a driving force behind the company, personally leading expeditions up the river and making alliances with the Indians. He even took a wife, named Mitain, among the Omaha people, despite the fact that he was already married to Mary Hempstead Keeney back in St. Louis. Mary, perhaps suspicious of her husband's long absences, came along on one trip, but Lisa was able to send Mitain off into the wilderness before the two met.

The territory developed in other ways as well. American merchants opened shops in the large towns, gradually pushing out the old French traders. Brick buildings appeared next to wooden *poteaux-en-terre* homes. English was heard alongside French in the streets. At Lewis's prompting, the printer and former Irish rebel Joseph Charless moved to St. Louis and started the *Missouri Gazette*, the first American paper west of the Mississippi. The weekly paper cost three dollars per year and carried international, national, and local news, as well as advertisements. One early issue reported on a July 4th celebration in St. Charles. A large number of people gathered at a house in the center of town and listened to a Mr. John Heth give a speech indicative of the political feelings of the time:

"Our independence, liberty and our safety are founded on our constitution, a work of unpresident wisdom of our political sages, and which 'tis our indispensable duty to support: it's also our indispensable duty to support with dignity, the small branch of the great tree of liberty, which we have the honor to bear in Louisiana."

Heth also called for unity between the established residents and newcomers and led seventeen toasts to the country, constitution, various politicians, and "the fair daughters of America." The paper continued by saying, "The day was spent in mirth and glee among the youth, whilst the veterans of '76, drank in the sweet effusiencs of the patriotic drought, which seemed to add fresh vigour to their decayed constitution, at 8 o'clock they repaired to the ball room and spent the night on a similar enthusiasm of the day without a desenting voice."[2]

The paper also carried advertisements. Since many items were scarce on the frontier, shops would print an announcement when they got a major shipment and list the goods they had for sale. Other ads were of a more personal nature.

"Whereas my wife Polly has seen proper to leave my bed and board, I hereby forwarn all persons from crediting of her, as I am determined to pay no debt of her contracting. Thomas Beavers."[3]

This was not the only announcement of its kind. The *Missouri Gazette* reused the wording of this ad several times, changing only the names of the wife and angry husband. It appears that some women took advantage of the freer society on the frontier to leave unhappy marriages and start a new life.

At this time Louisiana was a first-class territory, the least organized of the three classes of territory the government recognized. There was little infrastructure and only a basic government. Public offices were few, roads almost nonexistent, and letters had to be sent by private messenger. Residents began to think that upgrading to second-class status, with its more organized government, would help build the infrastructure the increasing population demanded. Second-class territories also

2. *Missouri Gazette*, Aug. 3, 1808.
3. *Missouri Gazette*, Aug. 17, 1808.

got a delegate in Congress. While the representative would not be able to vote, he could inform the national government about issues facing the territory. Mr. Heth had called for advancement in his July 4 speech, but he had also admitted that the time was not yet ripe. Others disagreed and pointed out that the Territory of Orleans had already been advanced.

Some were not so enthusiastic, including the influential editor of the *Missouri Gazette*. Charless said taxes would go up and the governor would enjoy more power and less accountability from Washington. The legislature was currently being paid with federal funds, but second-class territories had to pay their officials themselves. Not to be dissuaded, advocates of advancement sent a petition for an upgrade in status to Congress in early 1810, but it was not acted on.

The board reviewing land claims met regularly and finally began to make rulings late in 1808. Despite this, by early 1810 they had confirmed or rejected only about 15 percent of all claims. Smith T and other large claimants formed a committee to press for second-class status in the hope that more government and increased rights for citizens might speed up the process.

Governor Lewis became distraught over the constant turmoil in Louisiana, a territory he never wanted to govern. Matters became worse when he learned the federal government was not going to pay for some of his expenses. Threatened with bankruptcy, he headed to Washington to plead his case. Always a moody man, he plunged into a deep depression and died on October 1, 1809, in Tennessee, an apparent suicide.

Bates took over as acting governor until President Jefferson sent Kentucky politician and soldier Benjamin Howard to take the post. Howard arrived in St. Louis to a host of problems and rising tensions with the British. The British Empire was still at war with Napoleon, and their navy had run short of men. The Royal Navy frequently stopped American ships and took men to work as sailors. The British claimed they only took British deserters, but a large number of Americans were taken as well. Also, any American ship trading with the French was considered fair game for confiscation. On land, the British had been getting various Indians on their side, including the influential and charismatic Shawnee leader, Tecumseh. The British had influence over many tribes along the Upper Mississippi and helped them resist American expansion. Tensions between settlers and Indians increased, as did tensions between the British and American governments, and by 1811 Britain and the United States were on the brink of war.

That year the frontier settlers had another worry, this time natural. Early in the morning of December 11, 1811, the residents of New Madrid were awakened by a violent shaking of the ground. They fled outside into the cold and huddled there all night as the earth trembled under their feet. Although cold and frightened by the trees tumbling down around them, they did not dare return to their shaking houses.

The tremors lasted all night. At dawn came another quake. Witnesses said the ground rolled like a heavy sea and was split by great rifts that belched clouds of sulfurous vapor. Later that morning an even stronger quake created thirty-foot waves on the Mississippi. Tremors continued in the weeks to come. Boats sunk in the raging waters and the towns of New Madrid and Little Prairie, with a total population of about a thousand people, had to be abandoned. The biggest quake came on February 7, 1812, and opened deep cracks running for miles through the flattened woods. It also tore rifts in the riverbed that created waterfalls that sucked up boats and made a stretch of the Mississippi next to New Madrid run backward for a few hours. This quake was so strong it split stone houses in St. Louis, two hundred miles away, toppled chimneys in Cincinnati, four hundred miles away, and was even felt in the nation's capital, a distance of almost eight hundred miles.

Meanwhile, Howard and Clark were organizing the militia and fortifying outlying settlements against a possible Indian attack. On November 7, 1811, Indiana governor and future president William Henry Harrison led a force against Tecumseh's younger brother, known as the Prophet for his vision that the Indian warriors were bulletproof. Harrison soundly defeated the force, making the Prophet flee in disgrace and greatly hurting Indian morale, but this did not end the raids. In February of 1812, Indians killed nine members of a single family in the St. Charles district.

These problems strengthened the push for second-grade status. Many felt it would help them get their troubles heard in Washington and increase funds for defense. The measure passed Congress and President Madison approved it on June 4, 1812. That same year, the Territory of Orleans became the state of Louisiana. In order not to have two Louisianas, the government renamed the Territory of Louisiana as the Territory of Missouri.

Then, on June 18, 1812, the United States declared war on Great Britain. Missourians feared the British would send Indians against them, as they had during the War of Independence. Their fears proved well founded when several tribes, including the Shawnee, Winnebago, Kickapoo, Potawatomi, and Miami, declared war on the United States. It was rumored that other tribes would soon join them.

In its early stages, the war did not go well for the Americans. The British captured Detroit without firing a shot, and an American invasion of British Canada ended in disaster. The beleaguered federal government had few resources to spare for the exposed frontier. Only a couple hundred soldiers guarded the region, assisted by an unreliable and poorly trained militia. Locals in St. Louis dug trenches and fixed the old Spanish fortifications.

Much of the work in preparing the territory for war fell to the inexhaustible Frederick Bates, because Governor Howard spent an inordinate amount of time back in his home state of Kentucky, reportedly scheming for a seat in the Senate. When Howard's term was up in 1813, he did not ask to continue, instead becoming a brigadier general and taking command of the troops in Missouri and Illinois. President Madison asked William Clark to become territorial governor.

Frequent and vicious Indian raids made the outlying settlements uninhabitable. Many settlers fled to local forts or more populated areas. Howard reinforced the garrison at St. Louis and sent troops up the Illinois and Missouri rivers on a successful campaign against the hostile tribes. Clark led a raid five hundred miles up the Mississippi to Prairie du Chien at the confluence of the Wisconsin and Mississippi rivers. The men started building a fort at the site and Clark returned to St. Louis. He was lucky that he did, because the British and their Indian allies took the fort a month later.

An especially large raid occurred in the summer of 1814, when a group of Sac and Fox passed through the Boonslick region. Residents fled to homemade forts while the Indians plundered houses, stole horses, and terrorized the region for several months. Settlers caught alone outside were killed or taken away as captives. The *Missouri Gazette* for August 13, 1814, tells a typical story of one of these raids:

> A few days ago, a barge belonging to Messrs. M. Lisa & Co., which was ascending the Missouri to their trading establishment, were induced to stop at Mackay's Saline, (commonly called Boon's Lick) as the country was overrun by the Indians and all the inhabitants were in Forts. The crew . . . reports that

on the south side of the Missouri, the Indians had taken all the horses and were killing the cattle for food; that on their arrival at the Saline, the people of Cole's fort were interring a man just shot by the Indians. On the north side near Kincaid's fort a man was killed in a flax field.

Fortunately for the territory, the war ended with the signing the Treaty of Ghent on December 24, 1814. This treaty was basically a return to the status quo. The British Empire had defeated Napoleon in Europe, so even though the British did not give up the right to kidnap sailors from American ships, they no longer needed to. The land taken by both sides was returned to its previous owners, except for a few islands off the coast of Maine that remained in British hands. Canada remained a British colony and became fully independent in 1867. Tecumseh had been killed in the fighting, but the British still had influence over the western tribes. Some continued their raids until a delegation including Clark and Auguste Chouteau distributed twenty thousand dollars in gifts to tribal leaders to induce them to sign peace treaties. Missourians resented bribing their enemies, but peace was restored for a time.

The war years seriously hurt the territory. The economy declined and immigration stopped. The St. Louis Missouri Fur Company, unable to send expeditions up the Missouri River during those dangerous times, went out of business.

That all changed after the war. The population pressure that had caused the first rush of immigration had not gone away, but had been building. Now that the frontier was safe again, more people entered the territory than ever before. In the five years after the war, Missouri's population more than doubled. Most of the settlers came from southern states such as Kentucky, Tennessee, Virginia, and North Carolina, causing Missouri's slave population to rise as well.

Laws governing blacks, both free and slave, became much harsher under American rule. Unlike French and Spanish law, blacks could not testify against whites in court. Laws limiting how much a master could physically abuse his slave were revoked. Most Missourians at the time approved of the institution of slavery, and the minority who opposed it learned to keep their opinions to themselves. A prominent exception was Joseph Charless, who, remembering the oppression in his home country, editorialized against the spread of slavery. He would not be the last immigrant to draw parallels between the plight of blacks in the United States and the peasants of Europe.

Many of the immigrants moved beyond the two rivers and spread inland. New counties had to be named, new courts and land offices established, and the government spread along with the population. Villages cropped up everywhere, especially in the rich lands of the Boonslick region. Franklin was founded in 1817 and became the county seat for Howard County, growing to a population of one thousand by 1820. Immigrants to the region were so plentiful that the federal government opened a land office in Franklin in 1818 to deal with all the new land claims. Within two years there were twenty thousand people in the region, using slave labor to farm hemp and tobacco in what came to be called "Little Dixie" because of the region's imitation of the Southern plantation economy. Other areas of Missouri had smaller farms, and typical plantations of the Deep South, with their hundreds of slaves, never gained a foothold in Missouri.

While people settled in all parts of the state, Little Dixie became the most popular destination. Franklin's newspaper, the *Missouri Intelligencer*, reported in 1819, "During October it is stated no less than 271 wagons and four-wheeled carriages and cars passed near St. Charles bound principally for Boon's Lick. It is calculated the number of persons accompanying these wagons . . . could not be less than 3,000."[4]

The rough hills of the Ozarks attracted the least number of immigrants. With richer lands still available, only the hardiest, or most solitary, settlers moved there. The most famous of these were the four Yocum brothers—Solomon, Jacob, Jess, and Mike—who arrived around 1818. They would found the famous Yocum clan, which became an influential family throughout the history of the Ozarks. The brothers hunted and traded along the many rivers until settling in the James River valley in the early 1820s. At that time it was the territory of the Delaware tribe, which had been relocated there from the east. The Yocums illegally sold them liquor in exchange for the silver coins the Delaware received from the federal government. To hide the fact that they were breaking the law, they melted the silver down and cast their own "Yocum dollars." By 1831, the federal government had moved all the Delaware tribe to Kansas, but by then the Yocum fortune had already been made. Yocum dollars were actually purer than federal silver dollars and remained valid currency in the back hills for decades. The Yocums became one of the major landholding families in the Ozarks, and the legend of their "silver cave," which they had told people was the source of their silver, has attracted treasure hunters ever since.

The advancement to second-class status led to the creation of a territorial House of Representatives. Each region elected one seat for every five hundred people; this territorial House of Representatives gave the president a list of eighteen names, from which he chose nine to form a Legislative Council as an upper house. A delegate from the territory sat in Congress but did not have a vote. The territorial governor, appointed by Congress and approved by the president, had veto power over the legislature, and so politics remained very much under the influence of the federal government. The new legislature's dominant faction was the old junto of established interests and large land claimants.

The new legislature tried to solve the shortage of roads by requiring local authorities to build them. They did not provide county governments with funding but authorized them to draft men to work a certain number of days on roadwork without pay. Transportation, however, remained a problem. The rivers were the main means of communication, but keelboats and canoes were slow. It was not until 1817 that a steamboat, the *Zebulon M. Pike*, dared ascend the tricky waters of the Mississippi as far as St. Louis, thereby ushering in a new era for the city and the territory as a whole. The first steamboats were primitive affairs, but the technology advanced rapidly. A trip between New Orleans and St. Louis on a keelboat took months; a good steamboat made it in less than a week. It did not take long for merchants to realize that the rewards of quick trade outweighed the risks, and by the 1830s there were more than five hundred steamboats docking in St. Louis every year. By the 1850s, that number had risen to three thousand. Products became cheaper and visitors more numerous. The eastern part of the Missouri territory began to lose its frontier feel.

Travel up the Missouri proved more dangerous, as Lewis and Clark had discovered, and while the steamboat *Independence* reached the new town of Franklin in 1819, travel on the Missouri developed more slowly. Steamboats had to be specially designed for the Missouri's shallow waters, and their captains needed time to fully learn the hazardous route involving sandbars, tricky currents, and sunken logs.

The federal government started selling public land in 1818 to meet the voracious appetite for new settlement areas. By then, many of the

A family of settlers in their log cabin. Most activities were conducted outdoors, since the inside of log cabins was usually cramped. USED BY PERMISSION, STATE HISTORICAL SOCIETY OF MISSOURI.

Spanish land claims had either been accepted or rejected, but some of the bigger claims remained unresolved. Sales of public lands went quickly, and property values soared as speculators rushed into the area to make a quick fortune. Buyers had to take at least 160 acres at two dollars or more an acre. Land near towns or that had already been cleared went for much more, but the government offered easy credit.

Industry developed more slowly. Agriculture, fur trading, mining, and land speculation remained the biggest money makers. Most industry supplied local needs such as metalwork, woodworking, and brick making. The first ironworks opened in the Arcadia Valley near Ironton in 1815 or 1816, near the incredibly rich veins of ore at Iron Mountain and Pilot Knob.

Lead mining helped southeast Missouri develop quickly. Settlers and investors came to the area to open new mines, and as the population grew there was a call for the creation of new counties. Washington County was created out of part of Ste. Genevieve County in 1813. Moses Austin and Judge John Rice Jones donated fifty acres to create the county seat, a small town called St. George near the existing town of Mine-a-Breton. In 1826, the two towns merged into the present-day town of Potosi. In 1818, Jefferson and Madison counties were created, also using land from existing counties. Their county seats were Herculanium and Fredericktown, both important mining centers. When local lead mining suffered a setback, the county seat of Jefferson County moved to Hillsboro in 1838. As mining spread west of the river, St. Francois County formed in 1821, with a county seat at Farmington.

With the rise in commerce, merchants called for the establishment of a bank. Auguste Chouteau and Manuel Lisa helped found the Bank of St. Louis, which opened its doors in 1816, issuing their own paper currency to land speculators. The ability to print its own money proved too tempting to the bank's management, and it made commitments it could not meet. Furious stockholders forced the bank to shut down. It reopened briefly but finally failed in 1819.

Chouteau and Lisa had distanced themselves from the bank early on and opened the Bank of Missouri in 1817 in Chouteau's basement, continuing the French tradition of doing business out of the home. It, too, lent more than it could back up with hard currency and failed in 1821.

It is interesting to note that many of the leading businessmen in this period were French. The large influx of Americans after the Louisiana Purchase was mostly to unsettled areas, and St. Louis remained a

A $3 bill issued by the Bank of Missouri in 1817. Each note was signed by bank president Auguste Chouteau and cashier Lilburn Boggs. USED BY PERMISSION, STATE HISTORICAL SOCIETY OF MISSOURI.

predominantly French-speaking town. Only about a third of its inhabitants spoke English as their native language, although many of the French could do business in English. The French influence would be slow to fade.

Other groups came to St. Louis, too. A Philadelphia merchant named Joseph Philipson is the first Jew known to have settled in the city. He and his brothers had already invested in lead mining and fur trading, and Joseph decided to move to St. Louis in 1807 to oversee the business personally. He operated a store in the downtown business district, which at the time consisted of a few dozen stores on Main Street, where the Gateway Arch stands today. There he sold food, clothing, musical instruments—basically any goods a person could want in an area with few stores and limited contact with the outside world. He also became one of the city's first brewers. The Jewish community grew slowly at first, but by the 1840s there was a sizable number of Jews in St. Louis. While religious gatherings had been going on for some time, the first formal religious organization was the United Hebrew Congregation, started in 1841.

The development of a more sophisticated economy increased the need for education. Most families were too poor or too rural to consider sending their children to school, but educational institutions were on the rise. Churches ran some of them and taught religion in addition to the basic subjects. Teachers also set up their own private schools. Ste. Genevieve had a primary school during the Spanish and French period, and in 1807 it raised almost three thousand dollars to create a public school, but it struggled from lack of funds and soon closed. The Mine-a-Breton Academy (later called the Potosi Academy) fared better. It started in 1817, receiving help from the legislature, which provided a special four thousand dollar grant from lottery funds. Even at this early time, there was a desire for separation of church and state in public schooling; the legislature provided the money on the condition that no student or teacher would be discriminated against on the basis of religion. While most schools were for boys, there were a few girls' academies as well, many of which were simply "finishing schools" designed to raise girls to be capable housewives. Most girls, unfortunately, received little education at all. This was the case for a great number of boys, too, and many adults at that time were illiterate.

For those who could read, the choice of newspapers was limited to the *Missouri Gazette* until 1818, when Thomas Hart Benton established the *St. Louis Enquirer.* Newspapers opened in Franklin and Jackson the next year. The editors of the *Missouri Herald* in Jackson interspersed their news with calls for social development.

> *The independence of mind,* (says an intelligent and philosophical writer) *lays the foundation of the independence of nations.* There is as much truth as eloquence in the observation. History is abundant in the testimony which it bears to the accuracy of this political aporism. An *ignorant and uninlightened people* sunk in the shade and degradation of *moral and intellectual debasement* can never be FREE. A general diffusion of knowledge is the only source from which public spirit draws its essence of vitality—the only foundation of rock on which a nation's liberty can rest.[5]

People could also get access to some of the large private libraries that, in a tradition dating to French and Spanish times, were open to visitors. Another option was the offices of the *Missouri Gazette,* which opened a "Reading Room and Punch House," combining two relaxing activities. For those interested in anthropology, Clark displayed mementoes of the various tribes he had met on the Corps of Discovery and other trips in an "Indian Museum" in St. Louis.

As with roads, the territorial government was reluctant to raise taxes to fund schools or other basic infrastructure. The rise in government offices did, however, add expenditures that led to higher taxes, although Missourians still paid considerably less tax than people in full states.

The shortage of roads and other amenities did not stop religious individuals from making the trek into the territory to spread the word of God. The United States was in the midst of the Great Awakening, a massive upswing in religious feeling. The disorganized and somewhat lawless frontier seemed ripe for conversion, and Protestant churches soon sprang up in the formerly Catholic colony. The first was the Bethel Baptist Church, a simple log cabin near Jackson, in 1806. The Baptists became one of the most successful of the Protestant faiths in the new territory, and by 1816 they had seven churches and enough parishioners to found the first association of Missouri Baptists, known as the Bethel Association. At that time, the Baptists were concentrated in the south-

---

5. *Missouri Herald,* Aug. 13, 1819.

eastern portion of the territory, but they would soon spread across Missouri, largely through the efforts of the Reverend John Peck, who ranged all over the territory, making converts, founding churches and schools, and writing guides for immigrants. He became a familiar face to backwoods settlers and city dwellers alike, riding the length and breadth of the territory and preaching to both whites and blacks.

Another important early missionary was the Reverend Salmon Giddings, a Presbyterian sent by the Missionary Society of Connecticut to preach on the Missouri frontier. He founded a dozen churches, including the First Presbyterian Church of St. Louis in 1817, the first formal Protestant religious body in the city. That same year he organized the Presbytery of Missouri, the first organization of Presbyterian churches west of the Mississippi. His congregation included many men who would become instrumental in Missouri's early development as a state, including its first governor, Alexander McNair, and its first senator, Thomas Hart Benton.

Despite being of different denominations, Peck and Giddings were good friends. This was typical of feelings on the early frontier, where doctrine took a backseat to faith, and people would go to whichever church was available. While Peck created Baptist churches and Giddings Presbyterian ones, it should not be assumed that all their parishioners had been brought up in those faiths. To many early Missourians, going to a church—any church—was more important than worrying about its denomination. In the many villages that had no church, the faithful of various denominations gathered together in private homes, or outdoors, for informal ceremonies.

Missourians would not have to wait long for a choice in churches, however. Other denominations were making their influence felt in Missouri. In the early 1820s, Elders Thomas McBride and Samuel Rogers of the Christian Church traveled from village to village, making converts and camping out when they could not find a log cabin for shelter. A Methodist preacher named John Clark had been sneaking over at night from Illinois to preach in Missouri when it was still a Spanish colony, and his successors took advantage of the new religious freedom to send missionaries. The Episcopal Church became influential in early St. Louis with the foundation of Christ Church at the corner of Second and Walnut streets in 1819. Other denominations would soon follow.

The arrival of Protestant missionaries did not seem to hurt the Roman Catholic Church. It remained the church of choice among the

Going to church in territorial days. Note that everyone in the family is walking with bare feet and the wife appears to be smoking a corncob pipe. USED BY PERMISSION, STATE HISTORICAL SOCIETY OF MISSOURI.

Creole population, whose numbers would be augmented in early statehood by Irish and German immigrants. St. Louis got its first bishop in 1818 in the person of Father Louis William DuBourg, a Frenchman who fled the French Revolution and ended up in New Orleans. He started work on a cathedral and established a seminary at Perryville that same year, also sending numerous priests to outlying villages and to the Osage. Aiding him in his work was Sister Rose Duchesne, a French nun in the Society of the Sacred Heart of Jesus, who opened the first free school west of the Mississippi, in St. Charles in 1818. This and other schools that she founded soon failed due to lack of finances, but she was more successful at creating a free school in Florissant in 1819. She founded several more schools, including one for orphans and another for Indians, which closed down when the federal government forced her students to move to a reservation further west. She spent most of her years in St. Charles, working among the poor.

Now that the population was growing and vast areas of the hinterland were being cultivated, Missourians began speaking about statehood. Missouri became a third-class territory in 1816, allowing direct election of the Legislative Council. Statehood was now only one step away.

The 1816 territorial election saw a serious challenge to the St. Louis junto by a faction of American newcomers who opposed the big land claims, hoping to benefit from speculation if those holdings opened up to public bidding. The main contest was between those who aspired to be the next territorial representative. On one side stood Rufus Easton, the incumbent and leader of the American faction, and on the other was John Scott, the junto's candidate. The elections went to Scott by a mere fifteen votes. Easton cried foul, pointing out that Scott's ally, Governor Clark, had accepted late returns submitted by Scott himself. The debate ended up in Congress, and after much discussion they agreed with Easton and ordered another election. Again Easton lost, and again there were charges of fraud. The government confirmed Scott, however, and he stayed in power for the rest of the territorial period.

This second election caused tempers to flare. When Charles Lucas, a supporter of Easton, claimed that Thomas Hart Benton, a Scott supporter, had failed to pay his taxes and was therefore ineligible to vote, Benton called him a "puppy." Lucas challenged him to a duel. The two met on Bloody Island, a sandbar near St. Louis that was a traditional place for duels since it was outside of territorial jurisdiction. Anytime two men faced off there, a crowd would gather on a prehistoric burial mound in St. Louis to watch. From a distance of thirty feet Lucas and Benton fired at each other with single-shot pistols. Lucas missed and Benton shot him dead.

Scott and Clark both urged the government to declare Missouri a state, and the junto faction added its support. This was an issue both sides could agree on. The territorial legislature submitted to Congress a formal request for statehood in December of 1818, but the issue stumbled over the national debate on slavery.

There were twenty-two states in the Union at the time, divided equally between those that allowed slavery and those that did not. With a population of sixty-six thousand, of which ten thousand were slaves and only a few hundred were free blacks, everyone realized Missouri would have to be admitted as a slave state. This caused worry among Northern senators because it would upset the balance in the Senate.

In the U.S. House of Representatives, where the number of seats is based on population, the more populous free states held a majority that would not be upset by Missouri's admission. The House approved the territory's application but added an amendment proposed by New York Representative James Tallmadge restricting the importation of new slaves and requiring that children of slaves born after the bill's passage be declared free at age twenty-five. When the bill came to the Senate, Southern senators rejected it because of the Tallmadge Amendment, and even the two senators from Illinois voted against it because they owned indentured servants, a form of bonded labor for white debtors that they were afraid would be endangered by restriction on slavery.

At the following session of Congress another bill for statehood went through the House. Antislavery politicians attached an amendment forbidding both slavery and indentured servitude. Missourians' hopes for statehood seemed bound for failure again, until the Senate offered a compromise. Maine, where there were no slaves, was applying for statehood. Why not make Maine a free state and Missouri a slave state? The balance would be maintained.

The issue went back and forth between the Senate and the House until a further amendment was added banning slavery in the Louisiana Purchase north of 36° 30', the southern border of Missouri, with the exception of Missouri. The Missouri Compromise, as it came to be known, was formally accepted on March 6, 1820. Maine entered the Union as a free state, Missouri as a slave state, and the American West was given a border between slave and free.

CHAPTER 4

EARLY STATEHOOD

(1821–1854)

In May of 1820, Missourians went to the polls to elect representatives for the state constitutional convention. In keeping with the laws of the time, only white men aged twenty-one or older were allowed to vote. Each of the twenty-five counties had at least one representative, more for the more populous counties, for a total of forty-one. As with the territorial legislature, most of them were wealthy businessmen or lawyers. Only two had been born in Upper Louisiana.

At a meeting in St. Louis they agreed on a constitution forming a state legislature called the General Assembly with counties getting one representative for every five hundred people. A governor and lieutenant governor would serve for four years, and the governor was limited to only one term in office. The governor had the power to appoint many important state posts, although the state treasurer was appointed by the General Assembly. An independent judiciary with a supreme court was set above the local courts.

The constitution also tackled the issue of slavery, stipulating that the state government could not free slaves without the master's consent or prohibit newcomers from bringing their slaves into the state. It also prohibited free blacks from entering Missouri.

The U.S. Congress balked at this last resolution, citing the law that no state could limit the movement of free citizens. While the constitutional convention did not remove the clause, it promised not to enforce it, a promise it broke in 1825 and again in 1847. The delegates formally adopted the constitution on July 19, 1820.

The next month Missourians went to the polls again, this time to vote for their first state officers. There were no real political parties, but voters remained divided between those who supported or opposed the St. Louis junto. The race for governor became a battle between the old

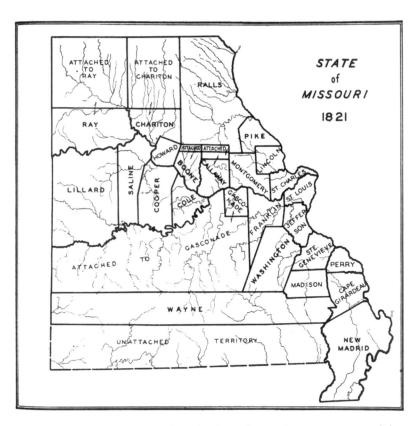

Missouri counties by the time of statehood. As the population grew, most of these broke into two or more smaller counties. Used by permission, State Historical Society of Missouri.

friend of the Creole population, William Clark, and Alexander McNair, whose tenure as land administrator had favored newcomers and opposed the recognition of large Spanish land claims. McNair crisscrossed the state and gave countless speeches during his campaign, while Clark spent much of his time caring for his sick wife in Virginia. The explorer relied on his old ties to win, but the time of the junto had passed. Too many newcomers had arrived for the Creole families to control politics anymore. McNair defeated Clark by a margin of nearly three to one. While Clark continued on as Indian Agent, his power had begun to wane.

William Ashley, another anti-junto politician, won the lieutenant governorship. John Scott, who had been territorial delegate to Congress, was elected to the U.S. House of Representatives. The majority of seats in the General Assembly also went to anti-junto candidates. Despite this, the assembly elected David Barton and Thomas Hart Benton to the U.S. Senate. Both of these prominent lawyers had ties to the junto, but their popularity, personal influence, and force of personality won them their positions and made them influential politicians for many years to come.

By the time Missouri was officially proclaimed the twenty-fourth state on August 10, 1821, the General Assembly had already started on the task of building a state infrastructure. They were meeting in the Missouri Hotel in St. Louis, an inappropriate venue for a state government, so they chose to move to St. Charles because of its proximity to the state's largest city and the fact that the town had offered a free building. This was only a temporary measure, however, and the legislature debated where to put a more permanent capital. Lieutenant Governor Ashley hailed from Potosi and wanted his town to be chosen. The thriving town was busy building a courthouse, but many in the General Assembly wanted a more central location. It finally picked a site on the Missouri River near where it meets the Osage River. They named the new town after Jefferson, the man who had gained Missouri for the United States. The City of Jefferson, later Jefferson City, was laid out in 1822, and the government moved there in 1826.

At first Jefferson City did not have much in the way of facilities. The town's tavern became a popular meeting place for officials since the drinks made it inviting and there were not many other places to meet. There is an old story about a novice legislator who applied for board and lodging there, thinking he would be treated as a VIP. The story goes that after he finished his meal in the dining room, a simple place with a dirt floor, he asked to be taken to his quarters. The proprietor said he would give him room 15 and led him around back to a row of tents. In front of one was a board painted with the words ROOM 15. Faced with these conditions, it was not long before government officials built homes for themselves.

Unfortunately for the new state, it began its existence during the country's first economic depression. The Panic of 1819 was brought on by a slump in exports and the collapse of many unregulated banks that lent money to high-risk ventures and failed when their creditors defaulted. Migration into Missouri slowed as easterners found they did not have the money to move. Many Missourians went bankrupt, and land prices fell as buyers became scarce. Both Missouri banks failed. Paper money, lacking any precious metal to back it up, became almost worthless.

Many Missourians called for the creation of a state bank based on sounder principles than those of the previous two. While the General Assembly did not want the responsibility of running a bank, they did provide some debt relief and created a state loan office. Many businessmen said the state loans were not adequately backed and refused to accept them, and political opposition led to the closing of the loan office. The St. Louis state circuit court declared the loans unconstitutional because only gold and silver, not paper, were legal tender. Debtors decided that since the loans were illegal, they were not required to pay them back. The debate ended up in the U.S. Supreme Court, which ruled in favor of the debtors.

Because of their vast natural resources, both Missouri and the nation recovered from the Panic of 1819, but the depression left a lingering distrust of banks and paper currency that would affect economic policy for years to come.

Missourians were also unhappy with the state constitution, a constitution for which they had not been able to vote. They felt the governor and courts had too much power, and the General Assembly too little. The two thousand dollars minimum salary for judges and the governor, at a time when forty dollars could buy a horse, also raised some eyebrows. The General Assembly quickly lowered it.

During this time there was an increasing split between Missouri's two senators. Although Thomas Hart Benton was a wealthy man, he appealed to popular tastes and supported the populist movement of Andrew Jackson, a Tennessee politician who called for greater power for the electorate and local governments. Jackson became a major voice for western concerns against the entrenched interests of the older states. Benton likened his political movement to the philosophy of Thomas Jefferson, who had envisioned a nation of independent farmers living without the constraints of wage labor or big government run by the rich. David Barton, on the other hand, was more of a Federalist, advocating a strong national government, an idea popular with the urban elite but less so with the common man on the frontier. Missouri's one representative, Scott, was closer to Barton in his beliefs.

Benton gained popularity by leading the push to abolish the factory system, claiming the trading posts had outlived their usefulness and created unfair competition for the big fur traders. Popular sentiment was against the factories, since people resented using government money to support the Indian tribes. The last factory closed in 1822.

Most of the long-disputed Spanish land claims were resolved with a ruling against the large claimants in 1824, which stated that the Spanish official who had granted those claims had exceeded his authority. Decisions on a few claims remained pending; the last one did not get settled for another half century, but by then the issue was no longer a major one.

At this time a trade route developed with Santa Fe in northern Mexico. The Spanish had banned the trade, but when Mexico became independent in 1821, the route opened up. The first trading mission headed out that same year, and commerce quickly grew after that. First Franklin, then Independence, and the appropriately named Westport became jumping-off points for caravans. Missourians shipped out cloth and manufactured goods and brought back silver, furs, and livestock. The caravans generally left in May and returned in September or October. Mexican merchants came in the other direction and some settled in western Missouri, founding a Hispanic community that would see a remarkable growth in the latter years of the following century. Within a decade the Santa Fe trade was worth a hundred thousand dollars a year.

One early visitor described Independence as follows:

> The town of Independence was full of promise, like most of the innumerable towns springing up in midst of the forests in the West, many of which, though dignified by high-sounding epithets, consist of nothing but a ragged congeries of five or six log-huts, two or three clap-board houses, two or three so-called

hotels, alias grogshops; a few stores, a bank, printing office, and barn-looking church. It lacked, at the time I commemorate, the last three edifices, but was nevertheless a thriving and inspiring place, in its way; and the fortune made here already in the course of its brief existence, by a bold Yankee shopkeeper who had sold sixty thousand dollars' worth of goods here in three years,—was a matter of equal notoriety, surprise, and envy. It is situated about twenty miles east of the Kansas River, and three south of the Missouri, and was consequently very near the western frontier of the state. A little beyond this point, all carriage roads ceased, and one deep black trail along, which might be seen tending to the southwest, was that of the Santa Fe trappers and traders.[1]

One of the most successful businessmen in Independence was Hiram Young, a former slave who bought his freedom by whittling and selling yokes for teams of oxen. Setting up a workshop in 1851, his yokes became big sellers to the caravans headed for Santa Fe and for settlers headed out onto the plains. Since teams of oxen pulled most wagons, and a caravan could have more than a hundred wagons, it was not long before Young became a rich man. Within a decade, his workshop employed more than a dozen people and produced thousands of yokes a year, as well as several hundred wagons.

The western trade and the brisk business in outfitting settlers and merchants led to the creation of an important city at the junction of the Missouri and Kansas rivers. A small settlement named the Town of Kansas appeared there in the late 1830s and was chartered as a city in 1853. Kansas City, as people began to call it, became a boomtown in the 1850s when it emerged as a major outfitting center for immigrants to the new Territory of Kansas.

With the economy on the mend, voters felt satisfied with the status quo and the 1824 election created little interest. Barton and Scott returned to office. Benton had a longer term and did not have to run. Frederick Bates, who had served so well in territorial days, became governor.

The presidential election proved more interesting. The Federalist camp supported John Quincy Adams. More popular with Missourians

---

1. Latrobe, vol 1, p. 128.

were Andrew Jackson and Henry Clay. None of the three candidates got a majority, and the decision went to the House of Representatives to choose between the two frontrunners—Jackson and Adams. Scott, as Missouri's sole representative, faced a tough decision. More Missourians had voted for Jackson than Adams, but Clay received more than both of them in Missouri and put his support behind Adams. Should he go with the candidate who received more votes, or the candidate who was supported by the person with the most votes? Benton publicly called on Scott to vote for Jackson, but Scott ended up choosing Adams, as did the majority of the House. Many Missourians felt their representative had betrayed them.

They vented their anger in 1826 when there was a special election for governor following the death of Governor Frederick Bates. The Barton/Scott faction supported one candidate, while Benton and other Jacksonian politicians supported another. The backlash against Scott's federalism helped give the seat to the Jacksonian candidate, John Miller. Scott lost his seat to Edward Bates, who shared his politics but not his unpopularity. Benton retained his seat in the Senate.

Governor Miller pressed for a number of populist causes, including cheaper sales of public lands, the establishment of public schools, and other public improvements. He had little success in these ventures because of resistance from the General Assembly and lack of funds, but they gave him popularity.

The congressional elections of 1828 advanced the Jacksonian camp still further. Bates was defeated by Spencer Pettis, a favorite of Benton's. The General Assembly also ended up with a majority of Jackson men and created a united front to support Jackson's second attempt to become president. Barton's supporters threw their weight behind Adams's reelection campaign. The two sides were not calling themselves political parties yet, but they were beginning to appear as such. Jackson advocated cheap land and an abolishment of the electoral college, which he saw as an undemocratic barrier between the people and the candidates. The Clay/Adams philosophy thought the best course for the nation would be to have a protective tariff on foreign goods and a steady program of internal improvements. They also supported the national Bank of the United States, which Jackson's supporters mistrusted. Jackson won the White House in 1828, and in the next decade the populist Jackson supporters would eventually develop into the Democratic Party, while the Federalists became the Whig Party.

Assailed on all sides by Jackson men, Barton did not seek reelection to the Senate in 1830. The Jacksonian candidate, Alexander Buckner, took his place, but once elected he did not follow their policies, choosing to support the tariff and national bank. The Jacksonians suffered another setback when Spencer Pettis was killed in a duel. Pettis, like other Jacksonians, bitterly opposed the national bank. When he questioned the honesty of the president of the bank, the man's brother, Major Thomas Biddle, whipped him while he lay sick in bed. Once he recovered, Pettis challenged him to a duel. Tradition of the day ruled that the man who had been challenged had the right to choose the weapons and circumstances of the duel. Biddle was nearsighted, so he chose pistols at five feet. Not surprisingly, neither man survived. Several candidates came forward to take Pettis's place, all describing themselves with the popular term "Jackson men," magic with the voters, yet their policies differed. The Jackson "party" was more of a spectrum of ideas than a party, and the split ticket helped the Federalists get their candidate elected to the office. Fearing more splits, the Jacksonians held their first state convention and began to organize as a tangible political party with an ordered set of policies.

This put them in a good position for the election of 1832, when their candidate for governor, Daniel Dunklin, won. Jackson won reelection to the White House. Now an organized political body, Jackson's supporters would dominate Missouri politics for many years to come.

On the state level, the government passed only a few populist measures, such as the election, rather than appointment, of county judges. The legislators were more concerned with limiting the role of state government and protecting states' rights against the federal government.

More action happened during the governorship of Lilburn Boggs, elected in 1836 under the newly named Democratic Party, a name picked by Jackson's supporters to reflect their principles. Boggs advocated internal improvements, working with the General Assembly to pass charters granting land to companies that promised to build the state's first railroads. The charters were set for a limited term, could be repealed, and their stockholders were held liable if they failed to do the work. Unfortunately, the Panic of 1837, an even worse depression than the Panic of 1819, wiped out the companies before they built any tracks.

Given the need for more stable capital investments, the Democrats modified their opposition to state banks. The General Assembly chartered the Bank of the State of Missouri in 1837, with the state owning half the stock. The bank was limited by law to conservative practices, could only issue a set amount of banknotes, and was under close state control.

Like the previous one, the Panic of 1837 was fueled by an overextension of credit, issuance of too many notes not backed by precious metals, and land speculation. At first the conservative policies of the Bank of the State of Missouri, helped by the influx of capital from immigrants and strong tobacco and lead markets, mollified the depression's effects in Missouri. But the demand for currency became greater than the state bank could meet, and soon several cities and companies issued their own notes. Missouri got sucked into the national depression. Many people lost their jobs and went bankrupt. As with the previous panic, Missouri and the rest of the nation bounced back within a few years. The vast amount of money to be made from the frontier guaranteed that.

The Panic of 1837 left many out of work. Employers took advantage of a desperate workforce by cutting wages as much as 75 percent for some jobs. This led to an organized labor movement promoting strikes and collective bargaining. They had some success raising wages, but unions would not become a significant power in Missouri politics until after the Civil War.

As the population rose, Missourians continued to expand westward. The original state line was set at a north/south line from the confluence of the Missouri and Kansas rivers. This left a fertile area called the Platte region between the border and the Missouri River as territory for the Sac and Fox tribes. Since rivers were looked upon as natural boundaries, it made sense to most Missourians to ask the federal government for that land. Congress agreed in 1836 and gave the tribes $7,500 and land in Kansas. The Platte region became part of Missouri officially in 1839, and land-hungry settlers followed quickly thereafter. Soon farms and small towns sprung up all across the Platte Purchase.

Other areas of Missouri were filling up, too. In the far southwest of the state, on the border between forest and plains, settlers from Tennessee, Kentucky, and Arkansas founded the town of Neosho in 1839 to be the seat of Newton County. Neosho was named for an Indian word meaning "clear or abundant water" and was well endowed with several fine springs. While at that time there were only Indian trails and a few scattered farms, the town would become a crossroads for the region.

Farther to the east in the Ozarks, settlement was gradually increasing, although the rough landscape meant that the region would never have the population of most other parts of the state. Many of the settlers in the Ozarks came from hill country in Tennessee and were accustomed to the backwoods lifestyle. Their relative isolation and fierce independence created a distinct culture, traces of which still survive. Ozark residents became known for a hardy lifestyle necessary to survive in the tough backwoods, as well as a combination of rowdiness and deep religious feeling. While they lived on isolated farms and liked it that way, communal festivals and religious gatherings were common. Loyalties tended to be for the South, but the people considered themselves a breed apart and not really part of any state or region except their own.

While newcomers swelled the population of all regions of Missouri, "Little Dixie" along the central Missouri River still got the greatest number, and towns there grew quickly. This area was encompassed by Howard County, created by the territorial legislature in 1816. Soon the population grew enough to necessitate a division into smaller counties. Howard County was soon dubbed the "mother of all counties," because it created a total of thirty-nine counties in central Missouri. Boone County, created in 1820, was home to the prosperous town of Columbia, which leapt from being a village in the wilderness to a center of commercial and legal life in less than twenty years.

Columbia started its life as Smithton in 1819, but a lack of ready water forced the villagers to move across the Flat Branch River, at which point it took on the name Columbia, after the county seat of Adair County, Kentucky, from where many of its residents originated. The circuit and county court both met there, initially under a sugar maple arbor since there was no building. Hamilton Gamble, who would later be governor, acted as circuit attorney. The first business was Gentry's Tavern, which also housed the post office, but by 1822 there were two grocery stores, four dry goods stores, another tavern, and a jail. The main street was called Broadway and was a hundred feet wide so that a carriage could turn around on it. Residents soon found other uses for the wide, straight track, and started a tradition of Saturday horse races. In 1822, the Boone's Lick road was rerouted so it could go through town, bringing stagecoach traffic and connecting the town directly to Rocheport, Franklin, and the Santa Fe Trail. This caused a sharp increase in the number of businesses, and by 1824 the town had enough money to build a brick courthouse. With so many people coming to conduct business or legal affairs, Columbia soon became a hub, with roads leading to many Boone County towns.

Missourians were for the most part tolerant of other religions, but in the 1830s they became swept up in a surge of anti-Mormon feeling that took hold of the nation. The first Mormons to settle in Missouri came to the sparsely populated Jackson County in 1830. Joseph Smith, the founder of the Church of Jesus Christ of Latter-day Saints, visited the following year and declared it the new Zion, a refuge from persecution for his flock. Soon large numbers of Mormons moved into the county.

The Mormons' ideas seemed strange to other Missourians. They believed Indians should be treated as equals and that slavery was a sin. They also tried converting the whites, insisting the Book of Mormon was as important as the Bible. The previous residents did not like their new neighbors with their unfamiliar faith and proselytizing. They also saw them as a political threat because they worried that the rigidly organized Mormons would vote as a bloc. Soon there were incidents of violence against the newcomers.

Matters came to a head in 1833 when *The Evening and the Morning Star*, a Mormon newspaper, ran an article explaining to free black Mormons how to emigrate to Missouri, an intolerable affront to the original Jackson County residents, who were mostly from the South. They organized a vigilante group of five hundred men, burned the newspaper's office, and demanded that the Mormons leave. The newcomers had little choice but to sign a document saying they would all be gone by April of 1834.

The Mormons appealed to the courts for help, but the local law did nothing to stop the repeated and deadly raids on Mormon settlements. Governor Dunklin and some newspapers denounced the attacks, but they did little else.

The deadline passed, but the Mormons remained. Attacks were on the rise. Dunklin called out the militia, but they took the side of the old settlers, disarming the Mormons but not those who preyed on them. Facing annihilation, the Mormons fled to Clay County.

At first the locals welcomed the refugees, but as it became apparent they intended to stay, the whole process repeated itself. By 1838, the Mormons had moved to Caldwell County, created by the General Assembly specifically for them. But the Mormons proved to be too numerous and started spreading into neighboring counties. Violence flared on both sides as Mormons and locals alike created vigilante groups to burn and plunder. DeWitt, a Mormon town, and Gallatin, a non-Mormon town, both became depopulated.

Governor Boggs finally sent in the state militia in late 1838, telling them the Mormons "must be exterminated or driven from the state if necessary for the public peace."[2] He, too, had fallen under the spell of anti-Mormon propaganda. The Mormons had no choice but to surrender. The militia confiscated their property and arms and arrested their leaders. The entire community of about fifteen thousand was forced to leave Missouri and trudged to Illinois in the middle of winter. The Mormon leaders bribed their way out of custody with money and whiskey and fled to Illinois as well.

Mob violence was not always directed at the Mormons; it was a common form of "justice" in a state that was not fully settled but no longer quite a frontier. Criminals often received summary judgment at the end of a rope, and disputes were often settled by gunfire, either in formal duels, like the ones held on Bloody Island on the Mississippi near St. Louis, or in less organized gunfights and brawls. As with all regions in the vanguard of the country's expansion, people arrived before police and resorted to their own means of law enforcement.

Even the more urbane residents of St. Louis were not above mass lawlessness. The Reverend Elijah Lovejoy published the *St. Louis Observer*, a religious paper that opposed slavery. A St. Louis mob destroyed it and Lovejoy moved to Alton, Illinois, hoping to find safety in a free state. There he ran the *Alton Observer*, the only abolitionist paper in the region. Proslavery men had already destroyed Lovejoy's printing press three times, and on November 7, 1837, another mob decided to make it four. Some sources say that proslavery men from St. Louis poled across the river that night to help destroy the hated paper. They surrounded a warehouse where Lovejoy and his followers hid out with the press. The two sides exchanged shots; Lovejoy took five bullets and fell dead. The mob broke up his printing press and dumped the pieces into the river. The Northern press railed against the deed, and Lovejoy became the first martyr for the abolitionist cause. Blood had been spilt over slavery, and many realized it would not be the last time.

While tensions rose over slavery and religious differences, Missouri got into a strange dispute with its new northern neighbor, the Territory of Iowa, created in 1838. Congress had originally drawn Missouri's northern border at the latitude of the Des Moines River rapids, set by a surveyor at 44° 44' 60". When a new survey delineated the Territory

---

2. McCandless, p. 110.

of Iowa, the surveyors found there were no rapids on the Des Moines. They suggested putting the line nine miles south along the boundary used to delineate the old Territory of Missouri in Indian treaties. They also suggested an even more southerly line, where the Des Moines flowed into the Mississippi. Governor Boggs insisted on the more northerly line from the original survey, but the Iowans, of course, disagreed. A Missouri sheriff tried to collect taxes in the disputed area and got hounded back south by local farmers. When he tried a second time, a sheriff from Iowa arrested him.

The issue escalated when a Missourian cut down three bee trees in the district. This was illegal in Iowa, beehives being considered a communal resource, and the Iowa government gave him a fine, but he had already fled back into Missouri. Missourians spread wild rumors that the Iowans were raising a militia to fetch him, so Boggs called up almost eight hundred militiamen. This caused the Iowans to make the rumor true and really call out their militia. Peacemakers on both sides stopped any more foolishness and submitted the issue to the federal government, which decided in 1851 to set the boundary at the old Indian treaty line.

The two Panics made the debate over currency a central issue in the 1838 elections. The Democrats were divided between the more rural group led by Benton, who supported "hard" money, gold and silver coin or paper money backed by precious metals, and the more urban commercial class who lived off of speculation and needed "soft" money, notes that had value because everyone agreed they did. The Whigs backed soft money. While Benton won again on the Democratic ticket, he won by a narrower margin. The Whigs were getting more organized and popular by taking advantage of splits among the Democrats.

The dispute between the "Hards" and the "Softs" created deep splits within the Democratic Party. The Softs tried to get the state bank to issue paper money, while the Hards tried to rid Missouri of all out-of-state paper currency and any printed illegally within the state. The Hards had the upper hand and limited the use of paper money in state business, but a general shortage of currency meant it was still popular with the common people.

The Whigs came into national prominence in the general elections of 1840 by advocating soft money and large state-financed improvements to infrastructure. This brought them a great deal of support from an expanding middle class who wanted to see Missouri grow like the older states to the east. The Whig presidential candidate, Indian fighter and former Indiana governor William Henry Harrison, won the White House. Harrison gave a two-hour inauguration speech in bad weather and developed pneumonia. He died after only thirty-one days in office and was replaced by his vice president, John Tyler. A strange rumor arose that Harrison died because of a curse from his old enemy, Tecumseh. Supposedly, the Shawnee leader had made the curse as he lay dying in battle, stating that all presidents elected in a year ending in zero would die in office. This had indeed been the case until Ronald Reagan, who was elected in 1980, survived an assassination attempt. George W. Bush, elected in 2000, appears unconcerned.

On the national scene, the admission of the Republic of Texas into the Union in 1845 fomented fierce debate in Congress. Northern politicians did not want such a vast region to be admitted as a slave state. Some worried about Mexico's reaction, since only a few years before, the Texans had fought a bloody rebellion to break away from Mexico and founded a short-lived republic. The Wilmot Proviso, which would outlaw slavery in any area taken from Mexico, passed the House but got hung up in the Senate, where Benton joined in the fight against it. Benton could not tolerate such a violation of the Missouri Compromise and warned that the increasing debate over slavery could break up the nation. Although he was against the Wilmot Proviso, he took a middle ground in the debate, reasoning that the government should proceed slowly to avoid a conflict with Mexico, which would dry up the Santa Fe trade, Missouri's main source for silver. He also said that the federal government had the authority to decide on the slavery issue. These were not the words proslavery people wanted to hear, and he found himself unpopular with both sides. Eventually Texas was admitted as a slave state and Benton's fears of a war with Mexico came true. The Mexicans were upset at what they saw as the theft of a rebellious province. The two countries also argued over where the border should be. When President Polk ordered General Zachary Taylor to lead troops into the disputed area in 1846, the fighting started.

The war proved controversial. Many in the North saw it as a callous bid to expand slavery, which was legal in Texas but not in Mexico. Supporters pointed out that the Mexicans declared war first. These arguments mattered little to Missourians, who generally supported slavery and got caught up in the war fever. Many had relatives in Texas, and they also bridled under the tariffs Mexico enforced on the Santa Fe trade.

Missourians soon formed the First Missouri Mounted Volunteers, led by Colonel Alexander Doniphan, a six-foot-six, muscular lawyer from Liberty who drank, swore, and played cards with his men. They gathered at Fort Leavenworth in June of 1846, a rough mob with no uniforms, little training, but a lot of enthusiasm. The men joined up with other units to form the "Army of the West" under the command of General Stephen Kearny, a cavalry officer married to William Clark's stepdaughter. The army marched all the way to Santa Fe and took it without firing a shot. Kearny stayed there to become the military governor of the New Mexico Territory while Doniphan continued south.

The Missourians marched across northern Mexico fighting several battles, usually while outnumbered, and won them all. At the end of the war they ended up at the port of Matamoros and sailed to New Orleans and up the Mississippi to St. Louis. This vast, circular victory parade made them the most famous unit of the war. In one year they had marched 3,500 miles and sailed another 1,000, the longest march in American military history.

American troops took Mexico City after a hard fight, and the Mexicans had no choice but to sign the Treaty of Guadalupe Hidalgo in 1848, giving the United States Texas to the Rio Grande, as well as California, Nevada, Utah, Arizona, New Mexico, and parts of what are now Colorado and Wyoming.

The war had not distracted the people from the issue of slavery, and the debate raged across the nation. In Missouri, it took the form of an anti-Benton campaign. The Speaker of the House for the General Assembly, Claiborne Jackson, proposed a set of resolutions ghostwritten by Missouri Supreme Court Justice William Napton that denied the federal government had any right to dictate whether a new territory was to be slave or free. That, he said, was up to the people (meaning white people) of the territory to decide. He supported the Missouri Compromise but also said that if Northerners tried to take the Southern states' rights, Missouri should help to defend them, an ominous statement. He went on to say that the role of Congress should be limited solely to the issue of fugitive slaves fleeing from one state or territory to another. The Jackson Resolutions quickly became law. This was a challenge to Benton's support of federal power over slavery and his opposition to the spread of slavery to the western territories. As a populist who advocated that elected officials should always obey the will of the people, he was caught in a bind similar to Scott's during the presidential election of 1824. The

General Assembly, elected by the people, was telling him to switch positions and support the very ideas he thought endangered the Union. Benton tried to circumvent this problem by calling for a popular vote against the resolutions. He traveled the state, telling the people that Missouri should not aid those who sought civil war and that the North had no intention of abolishing slavery, only limiting its spread. His detractors gave speeches everywhere he did. During this time he lost some of his most important constituency, Southern Hards who liked his monetary policy but could not stand his attitudes on slavery. Missouri's other Democratic senator, David Rice Atchison, was a strong supporter of the Southern cause and fought him continuously in the Senate. Atchison was a quick-witted lawyer who became senator in 1843 at the age of 36, making him the youngest senator from Missouri to date. He was an enthusiastic supporter of the annexation of Texas and the expansion of slavery. When the Democratic Party became split over the Jackson Resolutions, Atchison led the proslavery wing of the party against Benton's moderates.

The public split helped the Whigs win three of the state's five congressional seats in the 1850 elections. They also gained more seats in the General Assembly than either Democratic faction. With Benton's Senate seat up for election, a fierce struggle broke out over whether the long-established senator would remain in office. After much acrimonious debate, the assembly elected Henry Geyer to take his place. Geyer was a Whig whose opinions on the Jackson Resolutions and federal power over slavery were vague; this got him votes from both parties. The whole affair seemed to be more about ousting Benton than about finding his replacement. The Whigs also promised anti-Benton Democrats important posts such as the management of the State Bank, a victory for the Softs.

Benton was down, but not out yet. In 1852, he won a seat in the U.S. House of Representatives. His two-year term would be his last in any office, but he remained a fighter to the end, giving speeches to large crowds across the state.

On the national level, the U.S. Congress also struggled with the slave issue. California wanted to enter the Union as a free state, and Southern Congressmen worried this would upset the balance of power. The Compromise of 1850 settled the issue by allowing California to be a free state and banning the sale of slaves in the District of Columbia (a delicate issue since it was under federal control). It also passed a harsh fugitive slave law, denying slaves the right to trial by jury or to testify on their own behalf. Even more significant, it allowed slavery in the rest of the territories taken from Mexico, even those north of the 36° 30' line, thus eroding the Missouri Compromise.

Despite these political battles, everyone thought Missouri had a bright future. Even though it was on the frontier, everyone knew the nation would keep expanding westward, and Missouri would be at the center of that expansion. It was easily accessible from the north and south via the Mississippi and from the east along the Ohio River.

The chief occupation in Missouri throughout the nineteenth century was farming. When Missouri became a state, about 85 percent of the population worked farms, mostly small ones run by a single family. There were few large plantations like in the Southern states. Tobacco, grain, fur, and lead were the main exports.

With local supplies running out, most fur during early statehood came from lands to the west. Large companies, such as the Rocky Mountain Fur Company, founded in St. Louis in 1822, bought and shipped the majority of furs. The days of the individual trapper paddling down the Missouri to St. Louis to sell his catch were over. Further loss of supply and changes in fashion led to a serious decline in the trade by the 1850s.

At statehood, Missouri had about sixty-six thousand people, mostly concentrated along the Mississippi and Missouri rivers. The majority lived on farms, but St. Louis had five thousand people in 1820 and Ste. Genevieve almost two thousand. Franklin, which had only been founded three years before, had one thousand. Cape Girardeau, Jackson, Potosi, and St. Charles all had more than five hundred each.

An unprecedented level of immigration soon changed the face of the state forever. In its first thirty years of statehood, Missouri's population increased tenfold. At first these newcomers settled along the major rivers, but they soon expanded into all parts of the state. The Ozarks, with its rough hills and less fertile soil, had the slowest development, but there were concentrations of population at mining regions such as the Arcadia Valley. Most immigrants came from the South, mainly Kentucky, Tennessee, and Virginia, and some brought slaves with them. The census of 1850, which counted 682,000 people in Missouri, found that more than 87,000, or 13 percent, were slaves. Newcomers from Northern states tended to settle in the cities and land north of the Missouri River, while those from the South favored rural areas in all parts of the state, especially "Little Dixie" counties along the central Missouri River.

Slaves had no rights and in 1847, it even became illegal to teach blacks to read or write. That same year the state passed a law forbidding free blacks from entering Missouri. This was in violation to the original agreement that led to statehood in 1820, but Congress made little objection.

In addition to settlers, Missouri attracted its share of explorers, adventurers, and tourists. One of them was a Prussian lawyer named Gottfried Duden. Arriving in 1824, he bought a farm in what is now Warren County and lived there for three years. Impressed with the fine soil and political freedom, he returned to Prussia and wrote a book encouraging Germans to move to Missouri. Germany was not a country at the time (it would not become so until 1871) and was made up of a patchwork of warring and often oppressive states. Duden's book described Missouri in such glowing terms that thousands of Germans were soon buying tickets across the Atlantic.

The problem was that Duden's account was not terribly accurate. Duden was not used to manual labor, so he had Americans clear and farm the land for him while he spent his days writing and traveling. He was also blessed with unusually mild weather during his stay. When the first settlers arrived, they found themselves unprepared for the tough life on the frontier. Many were idealistic university students who could recite the Latin classics but knew nothing about farming, leading their neighbors to dub them "Latin farmers." Still, in Missouri Germans could own their own farms, while at home they had to farm the great estates of the nobility, so they stuck it out.

The German community in Philadelphia organized a German Settlement Society in 1836 and bought 11,300 acres on the Missouri River as a colony. They named it Hermann, after an ancient German warrior who fought the Romans. The colonists found that the land was not ideal for farming but produced excellent grapes, so they set up vineyards. The wine became so popular that by 1848 the people of this "Little Germany" produced ten thousand gallons a year and held their first annual Weinfest.

The Irish came to Missouri, too. They had been trickling in since the French and Spanish periods, attracted by a region where Catholicism was no barrier to advancement. Several became prominent merchants. The Potato Famine in the late 1840s forced huge numbers to flee their homeland. These Irish came from poorer farm counties and could not buy land like the Germans, so they moved to settled areas

Established in 1847 by German immigrants, the Stone Hill Winery became one of the leading wineries in the state. It is located in Hermann in Gasconade County, home to several large wineries. COURTESY STONE HILL WINERY.

and took jobs as day laborers or on steamboats. Many worked their way up to become shopkeepers and merchants like their predecessors.

While the Irish spread out across the state, mingling with other ethnic groups, the Germans tended to live in close communities in the countryside or in St. Louis. Many were Catholic and, along with the Irish, strengthened the church in Missouri. More came, especially to St. Louis, after the failed 1848 revolution across Central Europe. They were joined by a smaller number of Hungarians, who were also affected by the revolution and, like the Germans, were German-speaking Catholics.

While they were eager to live in Missouri, the Germans held on to their own distinct culture and language. Their beer halls stayed open on Sundays and both men and women mingled in Turner clubs, a combination of gymnasium and adult learning center. Having fled oppression at home, Germans had a low view of slavery. Slavery was almost unknown in Europe, and the newcomers loudly criticized the institution. Cultural and linguistic differences, and the growing influence of Germans in state politics, led to the creation of the Missouri branch of the American Party, a national movement of white Anglo-Saxon Protestants against immigrants, especially the poor and Catholics. With their motto "Only Americans shall rule Americans," they tried to reduce the influence of foreign elements. Many called them the "Know-Nothing Party" because of their secretive nature. If an outsider questioned them about their activities, they would say they knew nothing.

This anti-immigrant reaction flared into violence during the 1852 St. Louis city election. A group of Germans seized a polling station in Soulard Market to keep the Know-Nothings from voting. This caused a furor, and five thousand Anglo-Americans marched on the city center to take it back. In the ensuing riot, one person was killed and a German tavern was torched. The Know-Nothings did not win that election, but they did get their candidate, Washington King, into the mayor's office three years later. King forced the German and Irish bars to close on Sundays, but both groups had become too entrenched for him to hurt them seriously. The Know-Nothings, as with other "Americanist" parties in the United States, would not last long.

The bulk of Missourians remained Anglo-Saxon Protestant farmers. Many lived in quite primitive conditions far from town. Luxuries were few, and leisure activities usually confined to communal events such as barn raising and roadwork. These activities were called "bees" and were as much social events as communal labor. They often turned into parties after the day's work was done. Newcomers lived in tents or neighbor's homes until they could build a log cabin. Once they made enough money, they would replace it with a bigger house of brick or wood and outfit their farm with better equipment. While the large land speculators made the news, many farmers engaged in this practice on a smaller scale. Villages dotted the landscape, serving as agricultural centers where crops could be processed and sold and manufactured goods could be bought.

The most popular crops were corn, grain, tobacco, and hemp. Missouri became the second biggest producer of hemp in the United States from 1840 to 1860, growing a quarter of the national total. Used for rope, sails, bags, string, and medicine, it was an important cash crop. The harvesting, which required the laborious task of breaking the tough stems to get at the fiber, was done by slaves, so the industry was nearly wiped out by the Civil War. Hemp continued to be grown in Missouri on a smaller scale until a government reaction against its recreational use as marijuana caused it to be banned in 1937.

Farmers also raised cows, sheep, pigs, chickens, and, most famously, mules. Mules came to Missouri from Mexico over the Santa Fe Trail.

With careful breeding, Missouri mules soon gained the reputation as the best in the world for their strength and endurance, and they became a major export.

White expansion quickly led to the removal of the last Indians. While there were only a few thousand left in the state, the General Assembly asked the federal government to remove them to make room for white settlers. Several treaties followed, in which various tribes gave up land in exchange for small payments and new land to the west. These treaties, like the ones before, were signed by tribal leaders who did not necessarily have the authority to do so. Some Indians refused to move and got forced out by posses led by local sheriffs. The last tribal lands were signed away in 1832, and by the end of the decade all Indians were gone. The people who had first settled the land of Missouri would have no more influence on its development.

At the same time that the last native Missourians were being removed from their land, the federal government put the Cherokee people on a forced march from their homeland in the southeastern United States to a reservation in the Indian Territory, now called Oklahoma. They passed through Missouri in groups of a few hundred to a few thousand from 1837 to 1839. The winter of 1838–1839 was especially fierce, and the poorly equipped Cherokee suffered badly. It is not known exactly how many died along the way, but their route became known as the "Trail of Tears." It was the largest and most systematic forced removal of a native people in U.S. history.

White settlements in Missouri grew rapidly, helped along by improvements in shipping technology. By the 1840s, steamboats were a common sight on the Mississippi and Missouri, getting faster and bigger as innovators altered the boats to the specific challenges of the rivers. By the 1850s, they were going as far as Kansas City. Steamboats carried passengers as well as freight, and the most expensive cabins were often quite luxurious. The boats proved a fast, comfortable, and relatively cheap way to travel. They were not always safe, however. Boiler explosions, sunken logs, and fire could destroy a boat if the pilot and crew were not careful.

The state's other rivers were narrower, so steamboats were mainly limited to the Mississippi and Missouri. This was unfortunate, because the state's few roads were usually little more than dirt tracks. The term *road* certainly did not have the same meaning as it does today. The General Assembly defined a road as any cleared path with crossings over

A corn husking bee. In rural areas any large job became an excuse for a social get-together. At a husking bee, if a boy found a red ear of corn he could demand a kiss from the girl of his choice. USED BY PERMISSION, STATE HISTORICAL SOCIETY OF MISSOURI.

The Sharp-Hopper Cabin, built in 1835, is a rare example of an early log cabin. Originally located three miles north of Harrisonville in Cass County, it has since been moved into town and is a living history museum. COURTESY CASS COUNTY HISTORICAL SOCIETY.

A rope walk, where workers twist long strands of hemp into rope. Hemp was an important material for rope, string, paper, clothing, and medicine before it was banned because of its recreational use as marijuana. USED BY PERMISSION, STATE HISTORICAL SOCIETY OF MISSOURI.

The steamboat "Grapevine" being loaded at Washington, Franklin County. Towns like Washington thrived on the river trade. Even though the Pacific Railroad put a line through the town in 1855, local farmers still used steamboats to ship tobacco and other crops to market for a few more decades. Courtesy Washington Historical Society.

streams and tree stumps no taller than one foot. This, of course, meant that travel by road could be slow at the best of times and simply impossible in bad weather. The state began to provide some funding for road building in the 1830s, but progress remained slow.

One interesting solution was plank roads, made by laying parallel lines of heavy timbers end to end, then nailing oak planks crossways between them to create a solid surface. An eight-foot-wide plank road connecting Iron Mountain with Ste. Genevieve opened in 1851. Along its forty-two-mile length were several sawmills to replace the planks, which wore out quickly under the strain of heavy ox carts laden with lead ore. Since the road was only wide enough for traffic to go one way, carts headed eastward were given right of way since they were carrying the ore. The lighter carts carrying supplies and settlers westward had to make way.

While it seemed a good idea at the time, plank roads quickly turned out to be a bad investment. Weather warped the planks, and even under the best conditions people were in for a bumpy ride. Considerable investment kept the plank road between Iron Mountain and Ste. Genevieve open for a time, but similar projects failed throughout the state.

Railroads seemed the obvious answer, but they required a large amount of investment, and the early companies had a bad habit of going out of business before finishing or even starting construction. A few lines opened in the 1850s, mostly connecting inland towns to water routes, and the state had sunk a tremendous amount of money into failed projects. By 1860, there were only about eight hundred miles of track.

Communication became easier with the arrival of the telegraph. The difficulty of stringing a wire across the Mississippi delayed its arrival for a few years until the St. Louis and Louisville Telegraph Company erected tall poles on both banks in late 1847 or early 1848. The line linked to a network crisscrossing the United States, so someone in St. Louis could send a Morse code message by relay to any major and most minor cities. By the late 1850s, most large towns in Missouri were linked into the network, but the system was unreliable as storms, floods, and repairs could stop the line for days, even weeks. The wires were not grounded, so if they got hit by lightning the charge could run all the way down the line to the telegraph office, blasting the operator right out of his chair. The long wire across the Mississippi attracted birds, and sometimes so many sat on it that the wire would break under their weight.

The St. Louis levee in 1855, when the steamboat river trade was at its height. While St. Louis had the busiest levee, the riverfront at all major towns on the Mississippi and Missouri were often this crowded. USED BY PERMISSION, STATE HISTORICAL SOCIETY OF MISSOURI.

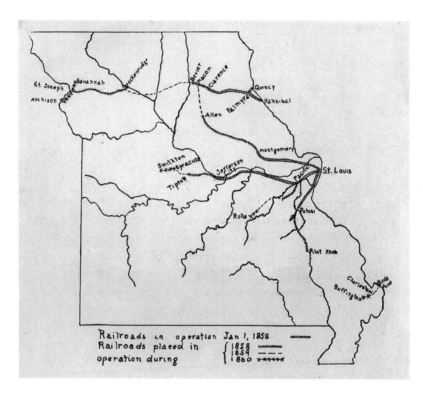

Railroads built before the Civil War. Note that most radiate from St. Louis, which acted as the state's major port. USED BY PERMISSION, STATE HISTORICAL SOCIETY OF MISSOURI.

As with roads, schools were a county responsibility. Significant state funding did not appear until the 1850s, except for a small amount of money set aside for a public university in Columbia, in prosperous Boone County. It opened its doors in 1839 and is the oldest state university west of the Mississippi. It was not the first university, however. St. Louis Academy, founded in 1818 by the bishop of Louisiana, became the first private university west of the Mississippi when it was chartered by the state in 1832. Now known as St. Louis University, it is still open and even has a campus in Madrid, preserving the link between Spain and its former colony. Other private universities followed in the 1820s and 1830s.

Because of this lack of government funding, churches became vital to the early Missouri educational system. The Catholic Church already had several schools in place by the end of the territorial period, and the Protestants were busy building schools of their own. The Protestant denominations were especially successful at founding colleges, providing higher education to generations of students who otherwise would have had to leave the state. The Baptists founded William Jewell College at Liberty in 1849, among many others. The Columbia Female Academy started in 1833 in a Presbyterian church and became Columbia Female Baptist Academy when the Baptists took over management in 1856. A little more than a decade later it changed its name to Stephens College and is still open, now the second oldest female college in the country. George and Mary Sibley, leading Presbyterians, founded Lindenwood Female College at St. Charles in 1829. It is now known as Lindenwood University. Another Presbyterian college opened in Fulton in 1851. Originally called Fulton College, it is now Westminster College. Central Methodist College (now University) opened at Fayette in 1857. The Disciples of Christ opened Columbia College in 1851. One of Missouri's most famous universities, Washington University in St. Louis, was founded in 1853 as Eliot Seminary by Unitarian minister William Eliot. Many other religious schools and colleges have opened and closed over the decades, and it seems no denomination came to Missouri without founding at least one educational institution.

While colleges generally hired only male professors, primary and secondary schools hired many unmarried young women, giving them one of their only opportunities for professional work. Sometimes the teachers were no older than some of their students. In 1858, a young woman named Josephine Marr wrote to her cousin in Canada about her and her friend Lizzie's experiences in their first year teaching at a school in Carondelet.

> I am, as I suppose you know, chief "school marm". . . . I have got a reputation around here, of being very a dignified, smart young lady, and of course I try as much as I can to keep up my name. I feel like a decided "young lady" now, I can tell you. The change was so sudden, you know in Milton, I was regarded as a little girl but as soon as I came out here, I had to step into the shoes of a young woman, no escape there was for me. Of course I did my hair up in a knot, and looked as dignified, and sedate as possible. I succeeded in making people think I was a young female of twenty, but Lizzie did not care about enacting the part of old maid, so she let the cat out of the bag, by informing every one, that I was only fifteen, and she but eighteen.[3]

The large black community in St. Louis was eager to establish an educational system for themselves, despite a city ordinance forbidding them to do so. The first recorded school was started in the 1820s by John Berry Meachum, a black minister and former slave ordained by Reverend John Peck, in the basement of his church. This was followed by other schools that had varying luck circumventing the law. Many of the schools ran by subscription, costing about one dollar per month or more. This was prohibitively expensive for many, and the added burden of illegality meant that most children were denied an education. When, in 1847, the General Assembly passed a law banning black education statewide, the schools faced an even greater challenge.

Meachum did not let the law stop him. He opened up a "Freedom School" on a boat out on the Mississippi. Since the river fell under federal, not state, jurisdiction, the authorities could do nothing. Meachum died in 1854, but his widow, Mary, continued his work. In 1855 she was arrested trying to help runaway slaves flee to Illinois. The site where she was caught was designated The Mary Meachum Freedom Crossing in 2001 and is the first site in the state to be accepted into the National Park Services Underground Railroad Network.

---

3. Document 3803 from the Western Historical Manuscript Collection, Columbia, Missouri. Used with permission.

$100 REWARD:

RAN AWAY from the subscriber, living in Boone county, Mo. on Friday the 13th June,

THREE NEGROES,

viz DAVE, and JUDY his wife; and JOHN, their son. Dave is about 32 years of age, light color for a full blooded negro—is a good boot and shoe maker by trade : is also a good farm hand. He is about 5 feet 10 or 11 inches high, stout made, and quite an artful, sensible fellow. Had on when he went away, coat and pantaloons of brown woollen jeans, shirt of home made flax linen, and a pair of welted shoes. Judy is rather slender made, ab. ut 28 years old, has a very light complexion for a negro ; had on a dress made of flax linen, striped with copperas and blue ; is a first rate house servant and seamstress, and a good spinner, and is very full of affectation when spoken to. John is 9 years old, very likely and well grown ; is remarkably light colored for a negro, and is cross-eyed. Had on a pair of brown jeans pantaloons, bleached flax linen shirt, and red flannel one under it, and a new straw hat.

I will give the above reward and all reasonable expenses, if secured any where out of the State, so that I can get them again, or $50 if taken within the Staie—$30 for Dave alone, and $20 for Judy and John, and the same in proportion out of the state, The above mentioned clothing was all they took with them from home, but it is supposed he had $30 or $40 in cash with him, so that he may buy and exchange their clothing.

WILLIAM LIENTZ.

Boone county, Mo. June 17, 1834:   52-2

Advertisement in the Columbia Missouri Intelligencer *on June 21, 1834, offering a $100 reward for the capture of a slave family who ran away from William Lientz. Running away was the most common form of rebellion against slavery, but slaves sometimes murdered their masters, despite the certainty of execution if caught.* USED BY PERMISSION, STATE HISTORICAL SOCIETY OF MISSOURI.

Meachum was part of the small black elite in the city that had become rich through business. This upper crust of black society was recorded in 1858 in a curious registry titled *The Colored Aristocracy of St. Louis*, by Cyprian Clamorgan. Like many of those listed in his book, Clamorgan was a barber. In those days barbers did far more than offer a shave and a haircut; they also sold perfumes, did styling, and ran bathhouses, all important services in the age before interior plumbing and regular bathing. Shaving gentlemen was a good way for black barbers to get ahead and, as Clamorgan notes, "they take white men by the nose without giving offense."[4]

His book gives a very detailed account of the leading blacks in the city and their net worth. He even notes important possessions such as pianos, or the fact that a certain merchant sent his children to be educated in Europe. But aristocracy necessitates a certain amount of snobbery, and apparently the black community was not immune. As Clamorgan notes in the section about ship steward London Berry, his wife Virginia (who "will be worth fifty thousand dollars at her mother's death") "was guilty of a faux pas last winter, which for the present has thrown her out of society. The colored people of the second class gave a ball which she attended, and was consequently not invited to a subsequent ball of the first class. Her husband became indignant at the slight, and tried to create a disturbance, but made nothing by the attempt. They are both no doubt sorry for their conduct, and will be again received next winter and their indiscretion forgiven."[5]

Clamorgan notes some businesswomen in his registry. Women of the poorer classes usually worked on their husband's farm or business or might be independently employed as maids, teachers, or washerwomen. Few of these jobs held any hope of wealth, but some industrious women, both black and white, managed to get ahead by working as nurses, owning their own businesses, or running boardinghouses.

Libraries began to appear as townspeople had more time for leisure. Franklin had a subscription library as early as 1820, and Fayette had one by 1826. Mark Twain's father served as president of the Hannibal Library Institute, formed in 1844. The 1850 census listed nine counties that had one or more libraries. While only the larger towns had such facilities, early Missourians did not lack reading material. Newspapers

---

4. Clamorgan, p. 52.
5. Clamorgan, pp. 60–61.

cropped up in every town, and even small villages often had competing papers. They got much of their material from larger papers back east, while the editor wrote local news and opinion.

Another staple of the frontier was the almanac. These annual publications were directed toward farmers and featured advice on cultivation, essays on various subjects, details on the motions of the planets, phases of the moon, times for sunrise and sunset, and predictions of the weather for the following year.

The Christian Almanac for Illinois and Missouri was unusual in that it did not give weather predictions. "The predictions respecting the weather we continue to omit," the editor proudly stated, "for the obvious reason that man is not a prophet." It did give advice to farmers, however. The 1827 issue recommended:

> "Keep no more cows than you can keep well. One cow well fed will give as much milk as two treated indifferently, and produce more butter."
>
> "Do not drink ardent spirits unless prescribed by a physician. Instead of it drink beer, milk, cider, water-gruel, sweetened water."
>
> "Use an onion on wasp stings."

As cities and towns grew, they offered a wider variety of entertainment. Public speakers drew large crowds for talks on politics, religion, travel, and science. People also went to hear debates at the courts and government assemblies. A speaker with a pleasant voice and quick wit always earned respect. People also enjoyed the theater but generally had to satisfy themselves with amateur productions since professional actors in the early decades of statehood rarely ventured beyond St. Louis. Later there were traveling theater troupes who hit the road with circuses and vaudeville acts to vie for audiences in the smaller towns. Horse and steamboat races were also popular.

Circuses became a big draw throughout the United States in the middle of the nineteenth century, and Missouri was no exception. Before the spread of the railroad, they had to travel by wagon or boat and only reached the larger towns. Circus boats were especially profitable since they would go up the Mississippi or Missouri and stop at every landing, sometimes doing shows at two or three towns in a single day. Circuses at the time were smaller-scale versions of the ones today, with menageries, clowns, horse acts, parades, lion tamers, high-wire

THE CIRCUS PARADE

Small towns couldn't always attract a traveling circus, so the people of Reed's Spring, in Stone County, made their own. Note the "elephant" in the center. Photo c. 1920. COURTESY MISSOURI STATE ARCHIVES.

acts, and trained elephants. New technology could also be a draw; in 1858, North's Circus advertised that they had a steam-powered calliope that cost ten thousand dollars. The newly invented device was drawn by a team of fifty horses and could blare out music that could be heard (their advertisement claimed) ten miles away.

Most areas, however, lacked regular entertainment. Newspaper editorials often lambasted the morality of their towns, complaining that drunkenness and card playing were rife and threatened to corrupt the youth. There was a call for more "proper" entertainment that advanced the mind and cultivated the personality. Many newspapers actively promoted any new endeavor that promised to bring the higher aspects of civilization, urging their readers to attend local plays or debate clubs rather than the tavern. While any form of diversion usually brought a big turnout, the taverns did not seem to suffer from the competition. In Columbia, for example, a Thespian Society put on its first performance in 1832. This was an impressive accomplishment in a town that did not even exist twelve years before and still had fewer than seven hundred people, but there were already two taverns and four grog shops in operation.

Another major reason to gather was for worship. Catholicism had been the predominant religion in Spanish and French times, but now Baptist and Methodist churches took precedence. The Methodists, and later other denominations, served the rural flock with circuit riders, traveling preachers who rode around a set route in the hinterland, relying on little more than rural hospitality and faith to sustain them. Methodists and Baptist preachers often rode together for company and safety. Their camp meetings became important events where people's spiritual and social needs could be met. The days of the circuit rider were short, however, as communities built churches as soon as they were able to afford them.

Neosho was a typical example. In its earliest days, people gathered in cabins or outdoors to worship. A Methodist circuit rider passed through the area as early as 1836, and the town had irregular visits after that. A Presbyterian congregation met on a nearby campground, but the town did not get a church until 1847, when the First Baptist congregation built one. It is interesting that at least three congregations were in operation in a town that, according to the 1850 census, had only 210 people. Farmers from more outlying areas doubtless came in for these services, and many members of one congregation probably attended the services of the others out of a desire to socialize and hear

A circuit rider. These traveling preachers had an established route that took them to dozens of villages over a large area. For rural Missourians, circuit riders were not only religious teachers, but important sources of news and contact with the outside world. USED BY PERMISSION, STATE HISTORICAL SOCIETY OF MISSOURI.

some extra preaching. Cooperation between denominations was strong. In Columbia, the Methodists and Baptists erected a church in 1836 that they shared until 1844. While the early Missourians lacked a strong church infrastructure, they had no shortage of faith.

Missouri's rural nature meant that medical care was rare for most people, but it was easy enough to obtain in any town of decent size. While early-nineteenth-century medicine was crude, it was no worse in Missouri than anywhere else. The state even had its innovators. St. Louis researcher Dr. William Beaumont was the first to make a scientific study of the digestive system by opening up the abdomen of a French Canadian *voyaguer* and watching him eat. Dr. John Sappington from Arrow Rock rebelled against the primitive practices of his day and looked for more effective cures than old favorites such as bleeding, in which the patient's veins were cut open "to let the sickness out." He developed "Dr. Sappington's Anti-Fever Pills" out of quinine to make the first effective treatment for malaria, a common disease in Missouri at the time. He patented his cure and made a fortune.

Dentists were even harder to find in the early years. People could always use Sherman's Orris Tooth Paste ("recommended by chemists, physicians and clergy") or wait until they needed Doctor Silver and Butler's "Incorruptible Porcelain Teeth," made in St. Louis. The city had a dentist as early as 1809, but citizens of Kansas City could put off seeing one until 1855.

By the 1850s, Missouri had become a thriving and diverse state, but it remained deeply divided over slavery. The following years would see that division increase, culminating in the worst years of its eventful history.

CHAPTER 5

A STATE TORN ASUNDER

(1854–1865)

Thomas Jefferson once said "maintaining slavery is like holding a wolf by the ears, you did not like it much, but you dare not let it go."[1] While his greatest document, the Declaration of Independence, guaranteed broad and unprecedented rights to some citizens of the new United States of America, it left unanswered what would become of the large population of slaves who ran much of the economy.

The question remained unresolved thirty years later when Jefferson bought the Louisiana Territory from the French. A slave owner himself, Jefferson knew slavery's spread to the West was a contentious issue and deliberately avoided it. He neither proclaimed Louisiana a slave territory nor liberated the slaves already there. When Missouri came up for statehood, the controversy was only resolved after much political wrangling.

Missouri congressional elections in the 1850s hinged on the question of slavery in the new territories opening up in the West. It was the issue that finally led to Benton's downfall from the Senate and Senator David Rice Atchison's rise to political dominance.

In 1854, Senator Atchison teamed up with other proslavery senators to pass the Kansas-Nebraska Act. The bill created the two territories and allowed settlers to vote on slavery in a referendum, effectively repealing the Missouri Compromise. The justification provided by the two senators depended on their audience. When speaking with Southerners, they said this "popular sovereignty" was more democratic than the Missouri Compromise and gave slavery a chance to spread to the Pacific. To Northerners, they pointed out that in a free market, merchant capital would eventually overpower the antiquated institution, so the bill was at most a temporary concession. Thomas Hart Benton was

---

1. DuBois, p. 2.

the only Missouri member of Congress to come out against the bill, but his popularity had long been on the wane and most Missourians supported popular sovereignty.

What no one predicted was the sudden influx of immigrants of both political persuasions into Kansas, the territory seen as most likely to come up next for statehood. If there was going to be a vote on slavery, these immigrants decided, they wanted their voice heard.

Proslavery men founded the town of Leavenworth next to the frontier fort of the same name, while abolitionists sent by the Massachusetts Emigrant Aid Society founded Lawrence. The latter group brought with them a printing press and promptly began issuing copies of the *Herald of Freedom*. Other Emigrant Aid members founded several towns, such as Manhattan and Topeka.

When Kansas held an election in November to choose its territorial delegate to Congress, the flood of immigrants became a torrent. Armed bands of Missourians poled barges across the river to "settle" in Kansas for the day and vote for the proslavery candidate, who easily won.

The same thing happened when Kansas held elections for the territorial legislature in March of 1855. Led by Claiborne Jackson, who took time out from running for Congress to make his politics known in Kansas, a thousand Missourians converged on Lawrence. Senator Atchison also came to show his support. The Missourians armed themselves with revolvers, rifles, shotguns, and, in case they were not taken seriously enough, several cannon. Although they only stayed overnight, their ballots were initially accepted, since the law was not clear on exactly what constituted a resident.

Not surprisingly, the election was a resounding proslavery victory. The moderate Kansas governor Andrew Reeder, who had been appointed by President Franklin Pierce, threw out the returns in six districts that he considered the most rigged and made them hold new elections. He let fraudulent results in other districts stand for fear of retaliation; there had already been threats on his life. Abolitionists won in the areas that held second elections, but they were not enough to tip the balance in the Kansas legislature. Fearing the Missourians' return, the abolitionists in Lawrence built a fort, while wealthy members of the Emigrant Aid Society sent them Sharps rifles, the best guns money could buy.

Kansas now had about fifteen thousand people, not counting visitors from Missouri. The legislature opened in July of 1855 in Pawnee,

Going to vote in Kansas. Thousands of proslavery Missourians crossed the Missouri River to "settle" in Kansas during its territorial elections. USED BY PERMISSION, STATE HISTORICAL SOCIETY OF MISSOURI.

a tiny settlement near Fort Riley, which was commanded by Captain Nathaniel Lyon, a hot-tempered professional soldier who quickly tired of the lawlessness of the proslavery men. The first day the legislature met, the abolitionists who had won in the second elections left in disgust when they saw their defeated rivals take their seats as if the results of the first elections were still valid. The proslavery faction's next move was to get the president to replace Governor Reeder with Wilson Shannon, a Democrat who had voted for the Kansas-Nebraska Act.

The legislature did not stop there. It restricted the abolitionist press and barred abolitionists from serving on jury duty. It also stipulated that voters in territorial elections need not prove any prior residence in Kansas. Being there on Election Day was residence enough.

The governor of Missouri at this time was Sterling Price, who served from 1853 to 1857. His tobacco farm near Keytesville in Chariton County was one of the largest in Little Dixie and was worked by dozens of slaves. Price was obviously a strong supporter of slavery, and he earned his office after his faction of the Democratic party defeated the more moderate Benton faction. During his tenure he did little to stop the proslavery "border ruffians," as the Northern press liked to call them.

The "Free-Staters," meanwhile, were being fired up by newcomer Jim Lane, a former Indiana politician known for his ranting speeches on the evils of slavery and Southerners. In January of 1856, they founded a rival government in Topeka, sparking bloodshed on both sides. The Topeka legislature applied to the federal government for admission of Kansas as a free state, but the request was rejected.

Meanwhile, Southerners formed their own emigrant aid societies and started sending settlers to the territory. The legislature charged free-state leaders with treason, but many were saved from arrest by sympathetic mobs. By May, all free-state leaders had either fled or been arrested. Lane went east to whip up support. On May 21, 1856, a proslavery army marched into Lawrence to make arrests and seize the Sharps rifles. They ransacked the *Herald of Freedom* and the *Kansas Free State* offices and threw their presses into the river. They also looted the town and burned the Free State Hotel, a popular meeting place.

In retaliation, John Brown, a fierce abolitionist who had settled with his sons in the territory to defend it against slavery, joined with some of his followers and hacked five proslavery men to death with swords. The incident became known as the Pottawatomie Massacre and caused indignation throughout the South.

On June 17, the fledgling Republican Party held its first national convention in Philadelphia. It was made up of abolitionist Democrats and disaffected Whigs who saw slavery as the burning issue of the day. They wanted to stop the spread of slavery in order to give free labor a chance to thrive. Most of the delegates were Northerners who were not necessarily all true abolitionists, but they saw that the country's future belonged to Northern industrialism rather than the Southern plantation economy that relied on bonded labor. The convention nominated John Frémont as the presidential candidate on an antislavery ticket. Thus the Republican Party was born, as a liberal alternative to the Democrats.

Lane returned to Kansas leading an "Army of the North." With these reinforcements, the Free-Staters defeated their rivals in a series of skirmishes. A bloody preamble to the Civil War had erupted in the territory. Governor Shannon resigned in despair, not knowing that a letter from the president was already on its way to remove him. The openly proslavery Daniel Woodson became acting governor as the violence continued, with free-state guerillas called "jayhawkers" raiding into Missouri, while proslavery "bushwhackers" did the same in Kansas.

President Pierce quickly replaced Woodson with John Geary, a more neutral figure. Geary was more of a man of action than his predecessors. He twice averted a Missourian attack on Lawrence. While supporting the proslavery government, he made an earnest attempt to stamp out lawlessness on both sides. This earned him the gratitude of the many moderates who were terrified at the territory's spiral into chaos.

In the presidential election of 1856, Democratic candidate James Buchanan won on the platform that the federal government should not interfere with slavery in the territories. The day Buchanan came into office, Geary resigned, another political casualty of Kansas politics. President Buchanan made Robert Walker the new governor. The following year Walker called for elections and threatened to use the army to crush anyone causing trouble. This cowed the Missouri "border ruffians" and "bushwhackers," without whose interference the Free-Staters, their numbers buoyed by new immigrants from the North, won the election. The old legislature, nearing the end of its term, drafted a proslavery constitution without the people's approval, but Congress sent it back to Kansas for a referendum and it was easily defeated. Kansas would be a free state.

While the issue of slavery in Kansas was decided with both the gun and the ballot box, another fight was going on in the nation's courts.

In 1846, a slave in St. Louis named Dred Scott sued his owner, Irene Emerson, claiming he was not a slave because his master, Irene's late husband, Dr. John Emerson, had resided with him in Illinois and the Wisconsin Territory, both free areas. Numerous courts had ruled that a slave who lived for any significant time in a free area would then be free. Scott also claimed that his wife, Harriet, was free as well because she had lived in the Wisconsin Territory, and their two daughters, being born to free parents, were also free.

His suit was funded by the sons of a previous master, who had fond childhood memories of their favorite slave and wanted to help him. After delays caused by technicalities, the case was heard by a St. Louis court, which ruled that Scott was, indeed, free. Emerson appealed to the state supreme court, which ruled against Scott. The grounds for this reversal were more political than legal. Chief Justice William Scott ruled that times had changed since previous rulings on cases of this kind, and that "not only individuals but States have been possessed with a dark and fell spirit in relation to slavery, whose gratification is sought in the pursuit of measures, whose inevitable consequence must be the over-throw and destruction of our Government. Under such circumstances, it does not behoove the State of Missouri to show the least countenance to any measure which might gratify this spirit."[2]

While the chief justice proved to be remarkably prescient, such a ruling did nothing to calm matters. Abolitionists railed against the ruling. Scott had no intention of giving up and appealed to the federal court. Emerson moved away and remarried, so now the struggle was with her brother, John Sanford. The case of *Dred Scott v. Sandford* (a clerk misspelled Sanford's name) would become one of the most bitterly divisive court cases in the nation's history. In 1854, the federal court upheld the previous ruling, so Dred Scott was forced to take his case to the U.S. Supreme Court, where it finally came to trial in 1856.

Scott did not have a very sympathetic audience. Of the nine Supreme Court justices, three owned slaves and two more had relatives who did; nor were the others particularly abolitionist. The chief justice, Roger Taney, came from a family that had made its fortune from a huge tobacco plantation manned by slaves. The court ruled 7–2 against Scott, and the ruling Taney wrote for the case became the object of anger and scorn throughout the North. He wrote that blacks were not actually

---

2. *Scott v. Emerson*, 15 Mo. 576 (1852), 586.

citizens of the United States, despite being state citizens, and were "so far inferior . . . that they had no rights which the white man was bound to respect."[3]

Taney went on to rule that the federal government could not legislate on slavery in the territories, despite the fact that the Constitution explicitly gave Congress that power. Through rather shaky logic, he maintained that the Constitution referred only to territories belonging to the United States when the document was written, not later ones. He went on to say that banning slavery, or freeing slaves who went to a free territory, deprived people of their property and so was in violation of the Fifth Amendment. Even a popular vote could not get rid of slavery, because that too would deprive people of their property. The idea of "popular sovereignty" that had made Kansas a free state was declared unconstitutional.

Just as with the Missouri court ruling, it was clear to everyone that this decision was a political one. Many Northerners, especially Republicans, were outraged. Abraham Lincoln claimed Taney and the Court were conspiring with President James Buchanan and other Democrats to spread slavery throughout the United States. If it were unconstitutional to ban slavery in the territories, they reasoned, would not the courts eventually rule that it was unconstitutional to ban it anywhere?

Such fears buoyed up the Republican cause and helped the party win the 1860 election, prompting the Southern states to secede. Thus, the Dred Scott decision on one end of Missouri and Bleeding Kansas on the other end of the state were two major stepping stones to the Civil War.

After the ruling, the Blow family bought Dred Scott and his family and freed them. Scott lived only nine months in freedom before he passed away and was never to see the upheaval his tenacious fight for freedom helped bring about.

Others fought against slavery in more violent ways. On October 16, 1859, John Brown, the instigator of the Pottawatomie Massacre, led a band of heavily armed followers to Harper's Ferry, Virginia, where they took over the Federal armory. Brown hoped to use the hundred thousand guns kept there to arm a slave insurrection. He and his men were quickly surrounded, however, and two days later a group of soldiers led by Lieutenant Colonel Robert E. Lee retook the armory. Many

---

3. Dred Scott, 19 How. 407.

of Brown's men were killed, but Brown was only wounded and stood trial for treason. A court sentenced him to hang. His last words were, "I, John Brown, am now quite certain that the crimes of this guilty land will never be purged away but with blood. I had, as I now think, vainly flattered myself that without very much bloodshed it might be done."[4] These words proved to be prophetic.

While Missouri was profoundly affected by the situation in Kansas, it profited from the opening up of the territory and the mass movement of people westward. The period just before the war was a boom time for St. Joseph. In 1858, a prospector found a small amount of gold on Pike's Peak, Colorado. The following year saw a gold rush as people from all over the country hurried to stake a claim. Like the forty-niners who went to California, the fifty-niners were mostly inexperienced and ill-equipped for a transcontinental voyage and the hardships waiting for them at the end. Many Easterners and Southerners suffering from gold fever passed through St. Louis, took a boat to Hannibal, and boarded the Hannibal–St. Joseph railway line that had just opened that year. Charles Krone, a traveling actor who made the journey to perform in a local theater, described the chaotic scene:

> The hardware stores were busy selling staves, pans and knives, and the groceries and meat shops were reaping a golden harvest; while from the saloons, billiard rooms and bowling alleys resounded the rattle and roll of balls far into the night. Around the old market house and the square a motley crew of peddlers and Peter Funk auctioneers were selling bogus jewelry and watches, and clowns offering pot-metal knives and pepper-box revolvers for sale . . . Indians and half-breeds, some dressed in their native garb, offered bronchos from the distant prairies.[5]

Krone's account is interesting not just for its colorful descriptions but also for its mention of Indians. Since their expulsion a couple of decades before, they were not supposed to enter the state, but apparently that ban was waived in St. Joseph at least, probably because the Indians could provide excellent and much-needed horses. In the frontier atmosphere, laws were things of convenience rather than necessity.

4. DuBois, p.170.
5. Krone, p. 281.

Another account of early St. Joseph could apply to most frontier towns. In the February 23, 1940, edition of the *St. Joseph Union-Observer*, elderly resident J.B. Moss recalled:

> When I was a boy there was a saloon on almost every corner, and two in between, with gambling rooms upstairs over all of them. There were several variety theatres, a chicken fighting main where they fought roosters and dogs, and where rat dogs killed rats for sport.
>
> There were all kinds of lotteries and every skin game imaginable for relieving the sucker of his money. Fist fights and fights with pistols were in evidence everywhere. The marshal had a man's job, for this was the hottest little town in the Central West.

Whether St. Joseph was indeed the "hottest little town in the Central West" is debatable, since along the frontier, settlements usually arrived before the law did, but St. Joseph certainly got hotter when the prospectors returned empty-handed from Pike's Peak. It turned out there was little gold in the area, and the prospectors accused St. Joseph merchants of spreading rumors of gold to turn a profit. Angry prospectors threatened to burn the town in retaliation, and the militia was called out to patrol the area until the situation calmed down.

St. Joseph became even more famous the following year, when the freight company of Russell, Majors & Waddell founded an innovative mail service to California. Previously the mail had been sent via stagecoaches run by the Butterfield Overland Mail Company, a trip of twenty-five days. The new system, called the Pony Express, used riders on fast horses working on a relay system. Russell, Majors & Waddell set up 190 stables at twenty-five-mile intervals, outfitted with five hundred horses purchased specifically for their speed. The first delivery left St. Joseph on April 3, 1860, and made it to Sacramento, a distance of nearly two thousand miles, in just ten days. Despite this impressive feat and the fact that they never lost a delivery, the Pony Express went out of business after only eighteen months, the victim of a new telegraph line, but it captured the state's imagination and became a source of pride for later generations of Missourians. In the short term, however, they had more serious affairs on their minds.

The postmark of the Pony Express service. This service more than halved the time it took for letters to get to California. Courtesy Patee House Museum.

In a tense political atmosphere the Republican Party held its convention in Chicago to pick a presidential candidate for the 1860 elections. Missouri Germans wanted Edward Bates, a prominent St. Louis Republican and successful lawyer. Abraham Lincoln won the nomination instead but placated Missourians by promising that if he won, Bates would become attorney general and another prominent lawyer, Montgomery Blair, would become postmaster general. The up-and-coming party recognized Missouri as a major player in national politics.

This represented a fundamental shift in Missouri culture. While many Missourians, especially in rural areas, still identified with their Southern heritage, large numbers of newcomers from the North and from Europe changed the political landscape. The economy was becoming increasingly based on manufacturing, and many leading Missourians saw their economic future tied to the industrial North, not the agricultural South.

Despite the state's power in Republican politics, Lincoln got only 10 percent of the vote and carried just two German-dominated counties, St. Louis and Gasconade. He won the national vote, however, and made good his promise of patronage to the two Missouri lawyers, Bates and Blair. Claiborne Jackson won as Missouri governor and Thomas Reynolds as lieutenant governor. Both were conservative, proslavery

Democrats; Jackson was famous in the state as the author of the Jackson Resolutions and leader of efforts to defeat Thomas Hart Benton, one of Missouri's greatest politicians. Jackson had barely won the election, having to play to the middle to an increasingly worried electorate who were frightened by the factionalism of America's elite. His true sympathies, however, were never in doubt to those who knew him best and would become apparent to all soon enough. The new lieutenant governor, Reynolds, had been born in South Carolina and hated the North even more than Jackson did.

Lincoln's election set off a wave of secession across the South. Although the Republicans insisted they wanted to limit slavery, not abolish it, slave owners knew their agrarian economy needed to expand to survive competition from Northern mercantile capitalism. Without new territory, the slaveholding economy was doomed.

In his inaugural address as governor, Jackson railed against the election of a "Black Republican" to the White House and advocated standing by the seceding states, but he did not explicitly call for the secession of Missouri. In St. Louis, Germans and other abolitionists joined military companies called Wide Awake Clubs. Many Germans had already organized militias through their gymnasiums after the Know-Nothing riots. Congressman Frank Blair, Montgomery Blair's younger brother, started organizing these militias into Home Guard units, some of the best forces in the Union army in the upcoming war. Secessionists created their own militias, including one called the Minute Men, named after the fighters in the War of Independence.

On March 4, 1861, Lincoln took the oath of office after sneaking into the capital to avoid assassination. Seven states had already formed the Confederate States of America, electing Jefferson Davis as their president, and other states were considering seceding as well. A state convention in St. Louis called by the General Assembly voted against secession, despite the fact that someone had raised a Confederate flag over the nearby Berthold mansion, a meeting place for the Minute Men. Kansas had already entered the Union as a free state on January 29, 1861, with Jim Lane as its senator. Lane, concerned with an assault on Washington, organized a Frontier Guard to watch over the White House. They camped in one of the finely carpeted rooms, performing their drills under crystal chandeliers.

News came that Rebel batteries had fired on Fort Sumter on April 12. Rival militias started drilling openly in the streets of St. Louis and

👉 NOTICE! 👈

The **REPUBLICANS** of Macon City are requested by an assemblage of Southern citizens, to settle their business as soon as possible, and

WITHDRAW FROM THE CONFINES OF THE

HONORABLE STATE OF MISSOURI,

and travel to parts better suited to their Abolition views, on or before the

4th OF MARCH, 1861.

👉 We are determined and resolved to rid ourselves of Black Republicanism.

👉 BEWARE, THE TIME IS CLOSE AT HAND!

TRUE SOUTHERNERS.

A notice calling on all "Black Republicans" to leave Macon City, in Macon County. Persecution went both ways in Civil War Missouri. Unionists were often robbed or killed by bushwhackers, while secessionists were persecuted by Union soldiers or Kansas Jayhawks. USED BY PERMISSION, STATE HISTORICAL SOCIETY OF MISSOURI.

other towns. When Lincoln called for seventy-five thousand volunteers from the states to put down the rebellion, including four thousand from Missouri, Governor Jackson refused to send a single man. He told the president, "Your requisition, in my judgment, is illegal, unconstitutional, and revolutionary in its objects, inhuman and diabolical, and cannot be complied with."[6] He mobilized the state militia and asked Confederate president Jefferson Davis for artillery.

On April 19, Jackson wrote to David Walker, leader of the Arkansas State Convention, which was then debating secession: "I have been, from the beginning, in favor of decided and prompt action on the part of the southern states, but a majority of the people of Missouri up to the present time, have differed with us. What their future action may be, no man, with certainty, can predict or foretell, but my present impression is—judging from the indications hourly occurring—that Mo. will be ready for secession in less than thirty days; and will secede."[7]

Jackson was only half right. Secessionists stormed the arsenal at Liberty and out in the countryside would-be Rebels began to organize. Captain Lyon, back from Kansas and now helping Frank Blair consolidate Union support in St. Louis, wanted to protect the federal arsenal in town, which housed forty thousand guns and a huge store of gunpowder, enough for an entire army. Lyon hailed from New England and was an ardent Unionist. The lawlessness he had witnessed while stationed in Kansas strengthened his convictions. He did not trust the state government to give these munitions to the right side, and he suspected his commander, General Harney, of having Southern sympathies. Taking advantage of Harney's temporary absence, Lyon shipped most of the weapons to Illinois and took the Home Guards and other loyalist units into service.

As the Missouri legislature debated the issue of secession, Brigadier General D. M. Frost, commander of the St. Louis area state militia, encamped with a proslavery force at Lindell Grove in St. Louis for their regularly scheduled drill. He named his encampment Camp Jackson in honor of the governor. There is a story that Lyon, suspicious of Frost's intentions, scouted out the camp disguised as a blind woman, but this is unlikely considering he had a bright red beard. In any case, the hotheaded Captain Lyon would not have needed to see the camp's street

---

6. Rhodes, p. 26.
7. Document number C1786 from the Western Historical Manuscript Collection, Columbia, Missouri. Used with permission.

signs, with names such as Jeff Davis Avenue, to be convinced that the camp was a nest of Rebels that needed to be rooted out.

On May 7, Lyon assembled his officers and told them Frost intended on taking the arsenal and then St. Louis. "We must take Camp Jackson and we must take it at once," he announced.[8] If his men were not convinced of the seriousness of the situation (their forces numbered ten thousand to Frost's seven hundred) they changed their minds when several crates at the St. Louis docks labeled "marble" turned out to contain mortars and siege guns sent by Jefferson Davis.

On May 10, Lyon set out with a battalion of regulars and four regiments of mostly German volunteers. A huge crowd followed them. Among the curious throng were Ulysses S. Grant, an officer from Illinois on vacation, and William Tecumseh Sherman, who was president of a local street railway company. Both would become famous Union generals in the war to come. The soldiers surrounded the camp and sent a message to Frost demanding his surrender. Frost had no choice but to comply. Flush with easy victory, Lyon dismounted, only to get kicked in the stomach by his aide's horse. Lyon recovered his poise quickly enough, and soon he and his troops marched back into town with their prisoners. Southern sympathizers lined the streets, cheering for Jefferson Davis and hurling insults and rocks at the soldiers. A man was knocked down in the confusion, got up, and fired a pistol on the troops. The Germans responded with a volley of musket fire. Soon there was chaos in the streets as some people fled and others attacked the Germans, who kept firing into the crowd. The troops made it back to their barracks with their prisoners, leaving twenty-eight civilians dead in their wake. Two soldiers had also been killed, and a few more wounded.

When the legislature heard about the capture of the camp and its bloody aftermath, they gave the governor complete military power and the right to raise money to fight against the Union. Jackson named Sterling Price a major general, authorizing him to raise an army called the Missouri State Guard to defend Jefferson City, where a thousand volunteers had already gathered to fight for the Confederacy. The ex-governor had fought in the Mexican War and was popular throughout the state, so Jackson hoped this would help with the recruiting.

Harney returned to St. Louis the next day. Lyon's suspicions of him seem to have been exaggerated. He approved of the seizure of Camp

8. Monaghan, p. 130.

Rebel shooting a Union picket. Much of the fighting in Civil War Missouri was sniping and small skirmishes. USED BY PERMISSION, STATE HISTORICAL SOCIETY OF MISSOURI.

Jackson and sent troops to protect the Iron Mountain Railroad running from St. Louis to the Arcadia Valley, as the iron and lead there would be useful in the upcoming fight. Harney also forged a truce with Price in the hope that war could still be averted. When the uncompromising Congressman Frank Blair heard of it, he persuaded President Lincoln to relieve Harney of his command and make Lyon a brigadier general to take Harneys' place.

With the battle lines drawn, Governor Jackson asked for and received a conference with Lyon. They met on June 11 at the Planters House in St. Louis. Blair came, as did Price and Jackson's secretary, Snead. They talked for several hours, going around in circles and resolving nothing. The impetuous Lyon, able to stand it no longer, stood up and pointed at each man in turn, declaring, "Rather than concede to the State of Missouri for one single instant the right to dictate to my government in any manner however unimportant, I will see you, and you, and you, and you, and every man, woman and child in the state, dead and buried. This means war. In one hour my officers will call for you and conduct you out of my lines."[9] Lyon then turned his back on the astonished meeting and strode out of the room.

On that note, Jackson's group headed by train back to Jefferson City, cutting the telegraph wires behind them. The next day Jackson called for fifty thousand volunteers for the Confederacy. Price ordered the bridges over the Osage and Gasconade rivers burned to slow any Federal advance. Back in St. Louis, Lyon organized two thousand of his men for a trip up the Missouri River after the rebellious government. His troops almost forced a riverboat pilot named Samuel Clemens to man one of the transports, but he slipped away and joined the Rail County Rangers, a Southern militia. He saw no action and soon deserted to join his brother in the Territory of Nevada, where he got work as a newspaper reporter and started using the pen name Mark Twain.

Lyon and his men got to Jefferson City on June 15 and found the government had fled to Boonville, fifty miles up the Missouri River in the heart of Little Dixie. He left some men to hold the capital and followed with 1,700 troops. On June 17, they disembarked a few miles from Boonville and followed the river road until it passed over a low rise. There they found several hundred members of the State Guard waiting for them on a ridge. Commanding them was Colonel John Sappington Marmaduke,

9. Snead, pp. 197–200.

Governor Jackson's nephew. Many of his troops would see much more fighting before the war was over. The Union force lined up, unlimbered their artillery, and scattered the Rebel force, mostly untrained volunteers, with a few well-placed shots. The Rebels re-formed at the crest of another hill. The Union troops advanced in neat lines as if on parade. Sensing a superior foe, the inexperienced State Guard retreated. They turned to make another stand near their camp, but cannon fire from a steamboat, combined with the resolute Union advance, sent them running for the final time. The first battle of the Civil War in Missouri was over in twenty minutes. The Rebels had fled so quickly that both sides dubbed the skirmish the "Boonville Races."

Lyon's men helped themselves to the Rebel's uneaten breakfast but did not get their main prize—the secessionist government. Lyon set out in rapid pursuit, pushing his men hard as they struggled along muddy roads in a pouring rain. On the way, he got word of the creation of the Department of the West, a military region under the command of John Frémont. Another bit of important news came from Colonel Franz Sigel, an excitable and energetic German artillery expert nicknamed "The Flying Dutchman." He was in southwest Missouri with about a thousand German volunteers and had learned that several groups of Rebels had joined up with Jackson nearby. Although outnumbered more than five to one, Sigel knew his Germans were better trained than most of the men they would face, so he decided to hit the Rebels before their army could get any bigger. If he could hold them for a time, Lyon could arrive from the north and the Missouri rebellion could be crushed between their two forces.

Sigel and Jackson's armies met on an open prairie north of the town of Carthage on July 5. The Rebels were tired from a long march, already defeated once, and about a third were unarmed, but riding with them came Jo Shelby and his cavalry, experienced fighters from the Kansas campaigns. Shelby owned a hemp plantation at Waverly and stood to lose his livelihood if slavery became illegal. At the time, the colors blue and gray were not yet symbolic of the two armies; this distinction came only later. Sigel's Union Home Guard troops wore gray, but Jackson's Rebel State Guard did not wear uniforms; its officers distinguished themselves by tying a strip of red flannel around their arm.

Sigel's Germans advanced their artillery batteries with military precision. At seven hundred yards they stopped and fired grapeshot, cutting great holes in the Rebel lines. The infantry joined in and both sides, unmoving, traded fire for half an hour. Then the Rebel cavalry moved out on both flanks. Most had no guns, but Sigel did not know that, and, fearing encirclement, the Union commander withdrew his men into the woods. The Rebels followed, but Sigel's cannon expertly covered his retreat, two batteries firing while the third one withdrew, before switching roles and allowing another to withdraw. Jackson chased Sigel in a running battle nine miles south and right through Carthage, which had recently opened its first hotel in the hope of attracting visitors. Nightfall allowed the Union army to finally escape. The Battle of Carthage was the first major engagement of the Civil War, coming more than two weeks before the Battle of Bull Run. While it was a Confederate victory, the Germans had shown their mettle. They had only thirteen dead and thirty-one wounded. The Rebels lost about two hundred killed, wounded, or captured. While casualty figures for the Civil War are not always reliable, and commanders from both sides were not above occasionally minimizing their own losses while exaggerating the enemy's, it is clear that the Rebels suffered the most in the battle.

Sigel joined Lyon at Springfield. After calling for help from all surrounding states, Lyon had been reinforced by the First Iowa Volunteers. Union troops from Kansas, Iowa, and Illinois converged on Missouri and occupied several towns and railway lines. This must have seemed like a nightmare come true to secessionist Missourians.

Jackson's army went to Cowskin Prairie, now Southwest City, in the far southwest of the state to meet up with Price and his force. Faced with a mixture of about eight thousand soldiers and raw recruits, Price set about turning them into a trained and efficient army. He treated his soldiers well and they affectionately called the aging veteran "Old Pap."

He had a lot of work to do if he were going to take the state for the Confederacy. All the major cities were in the hands of the Union, as were the Missouri River and the railroads. Even Little Dixie was occupied. Lyon's quick move up the Missouri River led to an imbalance that the Missouri Confederates would never correct. But they did not know that at that time and hoped that their wild enthusiasm would eventually help them prevail.

Camped at Springfield, Lyon mulled over his next move. Almost half of his six thousand men were volunteers whose enlistment time had expired and were beginning to leave. Even worse, Frémont had not sent him the supplies and reinforcements he promised because he feared a Rebel incursion into southeast Missouri might threaten St. Louis. Lyon realized he needed to act before his army melted away. He got word that Price was on the move, accompanied by Brigadier General Ben McCulloch, a famous frontiersman and Texas Ranger who had once traveled with Davy Crockett and now commanded volunteers from Arkansas, Louisiana, and Texas. A group of Arkansas volunteers under Brigadier General N. Bart Pearce was with him. The total force was about thirteen thousand, outnumbering Lyon by two to one, but Lyon headed south to engage them anyway. The odds would only get worse if he waited.

The vanguards of the two armies skirmished not far from Springfield on August 2, 1861. Lyon continued his advance until he became worried about being encircled by the larger army and withdrew. By August 5, he was back in Springfield, where there were still no supplies from Frémont. They finally arrived on August 8, along with a letter from the commander urging him to withdraw. With more men reaching the end of their enlistment period, Sigel and Lyon decided on a bold plan. They would divide their smaller force in two, perhaps thinking the less-experienced Rebels would panic if hit from two sides at once. The two groups set out for Wilson's Creek, ten miles southwest of Springfield, where the combined forces of Price and McCulloch were camped and foraging for young corn amid the oak-covered hills. After a march through a rainy night, they attacked on August 10.

Lyon came to the Rebel camp at dawn. Approaching from the northwest, he smashed an outlying encampment of Missouri volunteers and camp followers. The Rebels had failed to put out sentries during the foul weather of the night before, and Lyon's men got to within a mile before they were noticed. As soldiers, volunteers, and various camp followers fled in disorganized panic to the main camp, Lyon headed for a thickly wooded bluff that had a commanding view of the area. At the same time, Sigel attacked from the south. The Rebels scrambled out of their tents and hurried to form up.

Lyon arrived at the bluff to find a hastily assembled group of Rebels had made it there first. The high ground would be the key to the battle. The feature would soon be dubbed "Bloody Hill."

Down at the creek, Price organized his troops while the Union artillery kept the camp under steady bombardment, setting wagons on fire and flinging deadly shrapnel among the sleepy men. Stray shots hit a Confederate dressing station, killing a doctor as he treated the growing number of wounded. The men on the bluff needed to hold off Lyon long enough to get the rest of the camp organized.

Both sides slugged it out on Bloody Hill. Lyon got hit twice and had his horse shot from underneath him, but he refused to leave the field. Price's men reeled back down the other side of the bluff in the face of the fierce gunfire. Twice they tried to retake the position, but both times they fell back with heavy losses. Price himself was wounded in the side, and the hefty 250-pound Rebel general joked that had he been as thin as Lyon, he would not have been hit at all.

Sigel did not do so well. As he approached the camp, he saw a large body of men dressed in gray. At first he mistook them for the First Iowa, a Union regiment that dressed in gray. In actuality, they were McCulloch's 3rd Louisiana force. He learned his mistake too late, and his troops were scattered and destroyed. Sigel fled the field and, accompanied by only one private, rode to Springfield without bothering to rally his men or even report to Lyon.

With Sigel out of the fight, the Rebels massed their entire army for another assault on Bloody Hill. They advanced, and the two sides poured fire into one another's ranks. Lyon was shot through the heart and killed. Major Samuel Sturgis took command, and after another hour of fighting the Rebels withdrew again. Sturgis, seeing his men exhausted and low on ammunition, decided not to risk holding off another advance. He took advantage of the lull in the fighting and ordered a retreat.

In all, more than 1,300 Union men were killed, wounded, or reported missing, more than a quarter of the Union army involved in the battle and the highest percentage of any major battle in the Civil War. Confederate losses were about 1,200. Surveying the carnage in and around his camp, Colonel John Hughes of the Missouri State Guard wrote, "I have never before witnessed such a heart-rendering scene. State, Federal and Confederate troops in one red ruin, blent on the field—enemies in life, in death friends, relieving each other's sufferings. . . . President Lincoln ought to suffer death for this awful ruin, brought upon a once happy country."[10]

The Union troops retreated to Rolla, while District Commander Frémont worked at creating a replacement army. He fortified St. Louis, now the de facto state capital, and sent troops to fight Rebel bushwhackers who were causing trouble and gathering recruits in northern Missouri.

---

10. "Further from the Battle of Oak Hill," by Colonel John Hughes. In *Little Rock Arkansas True Democrat*, 5 September 1861.

The death of General Lyon at the Battle of Wilson's Creek. Lyon was the first Union general to be killed in the Civil War and became an instant celebrity in the North. USED BY PERMISSION, STATE HISTORICAL SOCIETY OF MISSOURI.

Meanwhile the state convention that had declared loyalty to the Union reconvened and named Hamilton Gamble as governor, calling for elections in November. Having lost many of their members to the Rebel legislature, it did not actually have a quorum, so its rulings were in fact illegal. But given the chaotic times, the federal government was not about to complain. Gamble was a moderate who wanted to limit the war in Missouri to the extent possible, and his first official statement was that slavery in the state would be protected. He hoped this would keep those who had not chosen sides from becoming Rebels.

On August 30, Frémont decided to put a stop to rampant Confederate recruitment by placing the state under martial law. Anyone found with a gun without permission would be shot, and slaves of Southern sympathizers, essentially all slaves, would be set free. Gamble and Lincoln, fearing the loss of the border states to the Confederacy, requested that he delete these clauses. When Frémont refused, Lincoln used his presidential authority to override him. Slavery would remain legal in Missouri throughout the war.

Flush with victory, Rebel generals Pearce and McCulloch returned to Arkansas. General Price and Governor Jackson led their victorious men to the center of the state, gathering recruits as they went. After taking Springfield on August 12, they marched on Lexington, an important town along the Missouri River, where Colonel James Mulligan was dug in with 3,500 Union soldiers around the Masonic College on a low hill. Price arrived on September 13 and quickly surrounded them. Frémont sent reinforcements, but they shied away from the fight. Over the course of the next week the Rebels kept up a steady fire on Mulligan's hilltop position and cut off his water supply. Then they hit upon the idea of making a moveable wall of hemp bales behind which they could take cover as they advanced up the hill. It was slow going, but it worked. The bales proved to be bulletproof; even cannonballs merely shook them.

The thirsty Union soldiers, hemmed in and with little remaining ammunition, had to surrender. Governor Jackson treated them to an impassioned speech on states rights and let them go after they swore never to take up arms against the Confederacy again. Mulligan, a proud Irishman, refused to take the oath and remained a prisoner in Price's army for some time. He and his nineteen-year-old wife rode in Price's carriage and were often seen dining with him. Such acts of chivalry would become increasingly rare as the war dragged on and became more brutal. Price led his men back south to Springfield, then further south to Neosho. His army had again struck a major blow, but he was too exposed in Lexington to risk staying.

Back in St. Louis, the blame game had begun. Congressman Blair and Governor Gamble, who were in a power struggle with Frémont, took advantage of the twin defeats to claim that the district commander was incompetent. They pointed to the wastefulness and cliquishness of Frémont's staff and accused him of corruption. While his staff spent extravagant sums on flashy uniforms and large numbers of unnecessary retainers, Frémont could hardly be blamed for the defeats at Wilson's Creek and Lexington. He had advised against the first battle and tried to send reinforcements to the second. The disorder prevailing in the Department of the West was partially the result of a lack of federal or state funding. While Frémont could have done better, he had little to work with.

On October 28 the General Assembly, made up of those members who had fled Jefferson City with Governor Jackson, met in the Masonic hall in Neosho and voted to secede from the Union on the thirtieth. Like the Unionist assembly, this meeting probably lacked a quorum and legality. Nevertheless, Jackson signed the bill the next day. It was now official. Missouri was part of two countries, holding two loyalties, on two sides of the war.

Frémont realized he needed a victory to keep his job. He headed out with an army and entered Springfield on October 27 with little resistance. But before he got any further, a letter arrived from Washington on November 2 relieving him of duty and ordering the army to return to central Missouri. They would have been just as exposed at Springfield as the Confederates had been at Lexington. It was now early November and getting snowy. Neither side would conquer the state this year.

Lincoln named General Henry Halleck as the new district commander. Halleck was an able administrator who had earned the nickname "Old Brains" for his scholarly writings; he had even translated a French book about Napoleon. Halleck reorganized the Western Department after the chaos under Frémont and put an extra tax on rich Southern sympathizers to support the flood of refugees pouring into the city. In some cases he kicked proslavery families out of their homes and gave them to refugees.

Among the refugees were large numbers of escaped slaves and free blacks. Several charitable institutions, both white and black, helped provide food, lodging, and work. Despite laws forbidding education to blacks, several schools opened up for them at this time. As local leaders turned more and more against slavery, the political climate improved and the schools soon enjoyed a semi-official status, although they would not be fully legal until the state law forbidding black education was taken off the books in 1865.

Halleck sent Brigadier General Samuel Curtis, a West Point graduate and Mexican War veteran, on a winter campaign with 10,500 men. Riding with him as one of his scouts was Wild Bill Hickok, who would become a famous gunfighter after the war. Price's army, weakened by disease and desertion, had to withdraw to Arkansas. Curtis took Springfield without a fight on February 13, 1862, and it remained a Federal stronghold for the rest of the war. Benjamin McCulloch, commanding his own Confederate army, also fled before the Union advance. Neither Rebel commander wanted to be under the orders of the other—Price thought McCulloch stubborn and arrogant, McCulloch thought Price incompetent—yet neither had the strength to defeat Curtis alone. They retreated all the way to Arkansas before Jefferson Davis solved their bickering by placing Major General Earl Van Dorn above them.

Van Dorn was a West Point graduate and experienced soldier. Quick to assert his authority over two generals, he unified the two armies and turned them around. With sixteen thousand soldiers, including eight hundred mostly Cherokee volunteers from the Indian Territory, they headed north to fight Curtis. Hickok and his fellow Union scouts saw them coming and warned the Union general, who chose to make a stand in the area of Pea Ridge and dug in behind a long line of log and earth fortifications on either side of Telegraph Road, where he thought the Rebels would arrive.

The battle began on March 7, after a night of snowfall. The Confederates came at the Union lines from the north, advancing around both sides of Pea Ridge. Van Dorn sent Price and part of the army to attack Curtis on his right (east) flank where the terrain was flatter and more open and the fortifications ended. At that spot stood a lone house called Elkhorn Tavern, the site of the first telegraph office south of Springfield. Here the Union force fought off three attacks from a foe twice its size. Sunset spared them from having to fight off a fourth. They withdrew and the Confederates took over the immediate area.

Another contingent under McCulloch struck at the more fortified part of Curtis's line on the Union left (west) flank. This did not work as well, as McCulloch was felled by a sharpshooter's bullet and the Confederates retreated, but not before some of the Indian volunteers scalped some of the Union dead.

Colonel Henry Little, in command of a brigade of Missouri Confederate volunteers, recounted later that "Our men, exhausted by the exertions of the day, after a fast of thirty-six hours, were now released by the descent of night, and, under favor of the obscurity, rested upon their arms on the field whence they had driven an obstinate and stubborn foe."[11]

The next day Curtis took the initiative. The Confederates now held Pea Ridge and the tavern. Sigel opened up his expert artillery on the Confederates positioned at the base of the ridge and inflicted heavy losses, one cannonball decapitating Churchill Clark, grandson of the

---

11. Evans, Volume 10, Chapter 4.

Confederate General Sterling Price, mounted with his arm in a sling, leading his men at the Battle of Pea Ridge. Price was wounded in the abdomen and right arm but did not leave the field. USED BY PERMISSION, STATE HISTORICAL SOCIETY OF MISSOURI.

famous explorer. The Flying Dutchman's cannon then cleared off the Indians and artillery stationed on the ridge. The infantry moved in, slowly pushing the Rebels back. No longer supported by their artillery or the Indians, and short on ammunition, the Rebels retreated.

Casualty figures vary, but the Confederates probably suffered about a thousand men killed or wounded and several hundred captured or missing. Curtis was more precise with his figures, reporting 1,384 Union men killed, wounded, or missing.

The defeated Confederate army split up as the state legislature, thinking Little Rock would fall, prepared to flee. Most of the Indians went home, while Van Dorn's men crossed the Mississippi to fight in the campaigns against Grant's huge army in the East. Price and some of the Missourians went with them, swearing to return someday to retake their state. Van Dorn also went east. His replacement was Major General Thomas Hindman, who stood only five feet, one inch tall, dressed in the latest fashions, and was the proud author of a novel. He was also a determined fighter who had once killed a man in a duel.

As a reward for providing the Union with a much-needed victory, Curtis received the district command and a promotion to major general, but he still had serious problems on his hands. His army had suffered in the fight and his supply lines had become greatly extended. On the western border, bushwhackers like Charles Quantrill and Bloody Bill Anderson were raiding at will, even winning small battles at Independence and Lone Jack in Jackson County.

Frustrated that much of the state was under Union control, many Missourians chose to join guerrilla bands rather than try to make the long journey to the Confederate territory. These groups numbered from a few to several hundred men who ranged through the land burning bridges, cutting telegraph wires, and attacking isolated outposts. They also took their revenge on Union civilians, looting their property and sometimes killing them. This led to reprisals against people with Southern sympathies, and the cycle of violence made life a misery.

Union Brigadier General James Blunt, commanding eight thousand troops, faced Colonel Marmaduke at Cane Hill in northwestern Arkansas on November 28 and pushed him back, but just as he thought Marmaduke had left for the winter, the Rebel commander returned with a larger force of eleven thousand under Hindman. Blunt called for reinforcements from the Union troops stationed at Wilson's Creek. The men there hastened to join him, marching 125 miles through snow

As Missouri became ever more divided, atrocities began to mount on both sides. The epitaph on this tombstone tells an all-too-common tale. USED BY PERMISSION, STATE HISTORICAL SOCIETY OF MISSOURI.

and freezing rain in four days. Hindman heard they were coming and decided to go after this weary relief force first, then strike at Blunt.

On December 7, the Rebels surprised the advance guard of the strung-out relief column and captured many wagons and prisoners, but they did not press their advantage fast enough. The Union troops reorganized and advanced in good order, attacking the Rebel lines on Prairie Grove Ridge. Blunt, eight miles south and distracted by feints from a small Confederate force, remained unaware he was missing the real battle until he heard Hindman's artillery booming faintly to the north. He hurried his troops up to the fight, and soon Hindman was caught between two foes.

Night fell before Hindman could be crushed. With no food and little ammunition, he abandoned the ridge under cover of darkness. Each side in the Battle of Prairie Grove lost about 1,300 men. Hindman was replaced by West Point graduate Lieutenant General Kirby Smith as the Confederate commander of the Trans-Mississippi Department. The now-unified Union army pushed farther into Arkansas, and the Little Rock legislature prepared once again to escape, but now Blunt's lines had become seriously extended and he withdrew to Fayetteville. Northwestern Arkansas, however, would remain under nominal Union control for the rest of the war.

While the battle raged at Prairie Grove, Confederate governor Claiborne Jackson lay on his deathbed with pneumonia. Weakened by cancer, the strong-willed governor could not fight off his illness and passed away on December 6. Lieutenant Governor Reynolds now became governor, but he would never rule in Missouri.

Frustrated by their losses, Marmaduke, Shelby, and Quantrill's men (their leader was away meeting with the Confederate government, trying to get a higher commission) decided to go on a winter raid, looting as they went. With their army twice defeated and many of the men deserting, Rebel leaders in Arkansas and Missouri hoped bushwhacking might prove more successful. The opportunity became all the more enticing as Union soldiers got siphoned off to the East for Grant's ambitious campaign, leaving the countryside undermanned. The year 1863 became a year of bloody raids across the state.

While the Union governor Gamble had been avoiding the issue of slavery as much as possible to placate the populace, Lincoln's Emancipation Proclamation went into effect on January 1, 1863, right in the middle of the state's wartime election campaign. The proclamation only freed slaves in states then in rebellion, so it did not actually include

Missouri, but it did force Gamble to take a stand. Radical abolitionists called for immediate abolition, while Gamble chose a more moderate course. Abolition was now inevitable, he felt, but he wanted it to be gradual. He called for a state convention, which declared that slavery would be abolished in Missouri on July 4, 1870. Hardcore abolitionists responded by holding a massive rally in Jefferson City to found the Radical Union Party and call for immediate emancipation.

East of the Mississippi, Grant's campaign was a success. The Confederate stronghold at Vicksburg fell on July 4, 1863, and the Mississippi became a Union river, leaving the Confederate West alone and isolated. Also in July, General Robert E. Lee suffered a major defeat at Gettysburg that seriously weakened the South's ability to continue the war.

But this did not stop the Rebel bushwhackers. Quantrill rode with about four hundred men to that old hotbed of abolitionism, Lawrence, Kansas. Enraged by the death of some of their female relatives when the Union prison where they were being kept collapsed, the bushwhackers hungered for revenge.

They rode at night, kidnapping farmers as guides and executing them once they traveled beyond their local area. The killing did not stop there. Quantrill took Lawrence completely by surprise on August 21 and slaughtered 200 men and boys, all civilians. Curiously, no women were harmed. Quantrill's raiders could be brutal, but they had a strict code regarding the female sex. This was the general rule among bushwhackers, but sadly it only applied to white women. There are numerous reports of black women suffering at the hands of Rebels and occasionally Union troops.

Jim Lane was in town that day, taking some time off from his raids against pro-Southern civilians in western Missouri. He escaped by hiding in a ravine as the bushwhackers torched his home. As soon as Quantrill was gone Lane organized townsmen to go after him, but the raiders disappeared into the Missouri woodland.

The raid prompted Brigadier General Thomas Ewing, commander of the District of the Border, which included parts of western Missouri, to clear the border of bushwhackers once and for all. The area was rife with Confederate irregulars, and the town of Nevada, in Vernon County, was such a popular base of operations that it earned the nickname "Bushwhacker Capital." Ewing issued Order Number 11 on August 25, ordering everyone in Jackson, Cass, Bates, and the northern part of Vernon County who did not live near Union garrisons to leave their homes. They would be fed in Kansas City and Independence, but their houses, farms, and businesses were left unattended in a war zone. After the war, many returned to find their property stolen or destroyed. Thousands became destitute. For many years afterward the area was known as the "Burnt District."

At this time Missouri took the first steps to recruit black soldiers. Kansas had already done so. The First Kansas Colored Volunteers had fought a successful skirmish against bushwhackers at Island Mound, Bates County, becoming the first black unit in U.S. history to see action. The men received national press, and their victory, while of little strategic importance, helped change the minds of many whites who had doubted blacks could make good soldiers. Eventually some 8,400 Missouri blacks served in the Union army. Like the First Kansas, they were underpaid and underappreciated, but they proved their worth on the battlefield.

A Union army finally captured Little Rock on September 10, 1863, taking away the main Confederate base of operations and opening up the rich Arkansas valley to Union occupation. Governor Reynolds fled with his government and ended up in Marshall, Texas, which would serve as the seat of the Confederate Missouri government for the rest of the war.

Shelby followed Quantrill's lead with an epic 1,500-mile campaign that fall, getting as far as Boonville. He and his six hundred men killed Union sympathizers and looted their homes, fighting several skirmishes with Union troops as well. The exploit earned him the rank of general. On October 6, Quantrill ambushed a small contingent of soldiers escorting Blunt to Fort Smith near Baxter Springs, Kansas, and slaughtered most of the Union soldiers accompanying him, including an unarmed military band. Blunt barely escaped with his life.

While the exploits of men like Quantrill are legends in Missouri, the Union had its own bushwhackers. One of the most colorful was Jacob Terman, who went by several aliases, his favorite being Harry Truman. He worked as a scout and spy for Union forces and claimed to have infiltrated Quantrill's band, even doing his share of the fighting and looting to protect his cover. He led bushwhacking raids against Rebel sympathizers in northern Missouri that equaled the worst depredations of Quantrill in viciousness, if not in magnitude. Local Rebels responded with raids of their own. Union officers did not know what to think of him. He occasionally gave good intelligence on Rebel activities,

During the war large numbers of escaped slaves followed the Union army. After Emancipation, as this contemporary engraving from Harper's Weekly *shows, the roads were filled with black migrants looking for a better life.* COURTESY MISSOURI STATE ARCHIVES.

but he was usually drunk and completely immune to orders. While he had been sent to reduce Rebel activity, his attacks actually encouraged it. He was even arrested by his own superiors and sentenced to death, but he got out of prison in a matter of months. In those lawless days, bold men were able to make their own rules.

John Schofield was now the Union district commander, Curtis having transferred to the command of the Department of Kansas. The Radicals, as members of the Radical Union Party were called, criticized Schofield for allowing Rebel deserters and known sympathizers into local militias, and they also complained that he was not stopping the bushwhackers. Frustrated by these constant complaints, Schofield applied for a transfer out of the state and was replaced by William Rosecrans in January of 1864. Although Rosecrans had seen a great deal of action in the large campaigns east of the Mississippi, he was considered a lackluster general, and his transfer to Missouri was essentially a demotion. He arrived with a burning desire to redeem himself. On the last day of that month, Gamble died of pneumonia, like his rival Governor Jackson had before him. Lieutenant Governor Willard Hall took over until the elections in November.

The bushwhacker raids were followed by a more organized invasion by Price in early September. His force numbered only about twelve thousand, a third of them unarmed, but most were well mounted and included Marmaduke and Shelby's experienced troops. Governor Reynolds came with them. Their goal was nothing less than to take St. Louis. They crossed the border on September 19 and headed to Pilot Knob, a railway terminus in the mining region of the Arcadia Valley, guarded by about nine hundred men at Fort Davidson, commanded by Brigadier General Ewing. Shelby advised a quick thrust toward St. Louis, but the fort was small, basically an earthen rampart topped with sandbags and surrounded by a ditch, and it had a magazine holding weapons and gunpowder that Price desperately needed. He attacked on September 27.

Price's men charged in wave after wave against the earthworks, getting cut down in droves by deadly rifle fire and swathes of grapeshot from the fort's several cannon. By the end of the day, the fort still stood, and nearly a thousand Rebels lay around the earthen walls. But sharpshooters and Confederate cannon in the surrounding hills had done damage as well, killing or wounding a quarter of Ewing's force. The Union commander decided that the next day would bring him defeat and probably execution, so he marched his men out of the fort under cover of darkness, passing right by the Confederate sentries, who mistook them for fellow Rebels. As the Union force hurried away, a slow-burning fuse lit the powder kegs in the fort's magazine and the valley rocked with an immense explosion. Price had gained nothing. He pursued the fleeing Federals but was not able to destroy them. The five days he had lost in his advance may also have cost him his campaign. Union reinforcements were already converging on St. Louis, so Price decided to take Jefferson City instead.

Rebel bushwhackers raided all across the state to support Price's campaign. The same day armies clashed at Pilot Knob, Bloody Bill Anderson appeared in Centralia. Two young Rebels named Frank and Jesse James were among his men. The brothers had already earned a name for themselves as guerillas. On that day, Frank stayed in the camp while Jesse, Anderson, and about eighty men, some dressed as Union soldiers, headed into town. They took it without a fight and proceeded to loot a store for some much-needed boots. Some of the men found some whiskey barrels, and the boots quickly became drinking cups. Then the drunken bushwhackers heard the whistle of the 11:30 train arriving into town. They held it up and slaughtered twenty-five furloughed Union soldiers who were aboard, sparing only their sergeant. Returning to camp, they were intercepted by a small Union force and easily defeated them, cutting off their scalps as trophies along with, according to one account, their ears and noses.

Price arrived at Jefferson City to find it defended by about seven thousand men hastily assembled from the surrounding countryside. They sat behind the parapets of five forts. Price remembered what happened the last time he tried to take a fortification, so he left without entering the capital. He headed to the pro-Southern town of Boonville before continuing west, gathering recruits as he marched through Little Dixie. Anderson met up with him there, but the old general, disgusted with the guerrillas' grisly trophies, refused to see him. When Anderson ordered his men to throw away the body parts, Price consented to a meeting and, not wanting such a man riding with him, sent Anderson off to destroy the North Missouri Railroad.

Blunt, leading two thousand hurriedly assembled Kansans, met Price's advance guard at Lexington. They were too few to stop him and so they retreated west, skirmishing all the way. They were reinforced just east of Independence at the Little Blue River and made a stand there, but Price pushed them into town and fought a bitter house-to-house battle until the Federals retreated.

Curtis arrived with a larger force and tried to stop Price at the Big Blue River, west of town, but he got pushed back all the way to Westport, near Kansas City. Another Union force approached Price from behind. On October 23, the Union armies tried to close the noose. To avoid getting surrounded with his back against the river, Price ordered a retreat back to Arkansas. The Battle of Westport was the largest and last major engagement of the war in Missouri.

Price moved south, with Union troops harrying him all the way. He suffered a defeat at the Marias des Cygnes River in Kansas in which Marmaduke was captured, but once again Old Pap got away with his army intact. At Newtonia, Shelby's rearguard fought a Union force to a standstill, allowing the bulk of the Confederate force to escape into Indian Territory and then into Arkansas.

Anderson would not survive the campaign. On October 26, a Union militia ambushed him near Albany, and the notorious "Bloody Bill" fell from the saddle with two bullets in his head. The militia was overjoyed with their prize and took a photo of Anderson's corpse before cutting his head off and sticking it on a telegraph pole.

Price arrived back in Arkansas with only a fragment of his army, starved, sick, and exhausted from its long ordeal. Some idea of the condition of these men can be determined by the description of Confederate prisoners in the November 7, 1864, edition of the *St. Louis Democrat*. While these men were prisoners of war from the campaign, they were perhaps better off than their compatriots, who trudged all the way back to Arkansas.

At 3 o'clock yesterday evening two trains of cars on the Pacific Railroad arrived at the 14th Street Depot with 620 of the Rebel prisoners captured by General Pleasonton in the running fight on Prairie Creek near Mound City, Kansas. . . .

The Rebels were the toughest looking set of men we ever saw. There was hardly a man among them in healthy looking condition. Their faces were lean, haggard and cadaverous, their cheeks sunken, their forms bowed, and the whole appearance wretched in the extreme.

Among them [were] quite a number of boys from 14 to 16 years of age and a few old men over 50. They were clad in rags, some without shoes, some without hats, some with greasy blankets or ragged strips of carpeting thrown over their shoulders. The prevailing style was butter-nut, two or three of the officers only being clad in what had once been regular Rebel uniforms. Not a few of them were sick and scarcely able to walk.

The same could be said for much of the Confederate army throughout the South. Now resigned to defeat, General Robert E. Lee surrendered the Army of Northern Virginia to Ulysses S. Grant at Appomattox on April 9, 1865.

Quantrill set off with some men in Union uniforms to Washington in a bid to assassinate the president. John Wilkes Booth killed him first, on April 14, and the veteran bushwhacker fell in a skirmish in Kentucky.

After Lee's surrender, army after army gave up their guns and went home. In Shreveport, Louisiana, on June 2, Price formally disbanded the Missouri forces. By that time, many Missourians had already left the service by simply walking away from their units and heading home. Others, like the James brothers, continued to fight on as bushwhackers. Now that the war was over, they were renamed "outlaws." Confederate leaders Shelby, Price, Kirby Smith, Reynolds, and several hundred men and their families refused to surrender and settled in Mexico. After a few years, when it became apparent that they would not be tried for treason, most returned to the United States.

CHAPTER 6

RECONSTRUCTION AND EXPANSION

(1865–1900)

The war left much of Missouri in ruins. The armies that had marched back and forth across the land for four years left vast destruction in their wake. Farmhouses were burned, bridges destroyed, fields left untended, and railroads torn up. As Missourians began to put their lives back together, they faced the even more difficult task of learning to live in peace. Bitter guerilla warfare and heavy-handed tactics by Union soldiers left animosities that would not die down for many years.

The end of the war saw a new political reality in Missouri. In November of 1864, Missourians had gone to the ballot box. The devastation of the past few years and the scare of Price's campaign had changed the outlook of many in the state. The fact that an oath of loyalty to the Union was required in order to vote also affected the results. The Radical Union Party, which had been strongly abolitionist during the war and wanted severe punishment of the Rebels, won a majority in both houses of the General Assembly and got Colonel Thomas Fletcher elected governor. It called for a state convention that on January 11, 1865, abolished slavery in Missouri once and for all.

Other points in the new constitution included giving the General Assembly more authority in stimulating economic growth and funding a public school system for both whites and blacks. It also gave blacks all the rights of whites, except for the rights to vote and hold public office.

The constitutional convention that abolished slavery also ruled on how to deal with those Missourians who had allied themselves with the Confederacy. Radical Unionist leader Charles Drake included in the new constitution what he called an "iron-clad oath" that every Missourian must take in order to vote, sit on a jury, practice law, hold public office, teach, or preach. Voters had to swear they had not fought or supported, or ever publicly shown sympathy for, the Rebel cause. The convention also declared 842 law enforcement posts vacant, from Supreme Court justices down to local sheriffs. Since all of these posts were appointed by the governor, this amounted to a purge of Democrats from the legal system. Such strident measures brought resistance from moderates, especially from clergy, lawyers, and the influential German population. Even Governor Fletcher, elected as a Radical, expressed his reservations. The constitution was put to a popular vote on June 6 and won by a very narrow margin. After many complaints and lawsuits, the requirement of the oath for lawyers and ministers was declared unconstitutional by the U.S. Supreme Court in 1867. The requirement for voting still held, so the Radicals did well in the 1866 state elections, and the General Assembly made Drake a senator.

The black community, freed from the burden of slavery, lost no time in pushing for full equality. As early as 1865, prominent blacks from St. Louis and soldiers in the 56th Colored Infantry asked the Radical leadership to include black suffrage in the constitution. Drake turned them down at the time, fearing a constitution that included black suffrage would fail in the referendum, but the black community kept up the pressure.

They quickly organized, especially in large towns. Churches operated schools, a black bank opened in St. Louis, and a lawsuit brought by black passengers desegregated the St. Louis streetcars. The state provided public schools, but many blacks, if they could afford it, sent their children to private school because the funding and quality of education were better.

Higher education got attention too. Men from the 62nd and 64th Colored Infantry and their white officers pooled their money to found the Lincoln Institute in Jefferson City, now known as Lincoln University. It opened in the fall of 1866 with only two students, but by the next semester the student body numbered about seventy and continued to climb.

One of the most successful former slaves made his name outside the state. George Washington Carver was born in Diamond Grove, Newton County. During the Civil War, Carver, then an infant, was kidnapped along with his mother by Confederate raiders who hoped to make some money selling them. Carver was eventually retrieved, but not before he contracted a serious respiratory illness that permanently weakened him. Unable to work in the fields, he spent much of his childhood studying the wild plants around the plantation and became known as the "plant doctor" for his ability to make sick plants thrive. At the age of twelve, and now free, he set out to get an education. He got a high school diploma in Kansas and a university education in Iowa, where he studied scientific agriculture. At the Tuskegee Institute in Alabama, he became famous for his pioneering research. Carver advocated rotating cotton crops with peanuts and other legumes to restore nitrogen in the soil. He also invented several hundred products from peanuts and other plants, everything from hand lotion to glue.

Many freemen, however, lived lives not much better than before. There was little work in the cities, so most continued to work as hired hands or sharecroppers on farms, sometimes at the same ones where they had been slaves. They had their freedom, but it would be a long fight to get more than that.

The university at Columbia, reserved for whites, had fallen on hard times during the war, when funding and students almost disappeared. James Rollins, state representative for Boone County and a co-founder of the university, managed to get a law passed reserving 1.75 percent of state revenues for the institution. This money put the university on the firm footing as the leading public university in the state that it still enjoys today. An agricultural school, along with more funding, came in 1870.

After so much war and destruction, Missourians wanted to enjoy life. The years after the war saw a great expansion in traveling entertainers such as vaudeville, theater troupes, and circus acts. The *Jasper County Democrat* ran an ad on September 7, 1899, for Carthage's Second Annual Market Fair, promising "a solid day's amusement" and declaring that

> The Diving Horses—Powder Face and Cupid, the same horses that made the thrilling dive last year at our Fair, from a tower 32 feet high into the water, will be with us this year. The tower will be raised to 42 feet, and Powder Face will be ridden off this high tower by a man. Think how high 42 feet is. These animals don't jump. They dive. Ask any one of the 45,000 people who saw it last year and they will tell you all about it . . . four magnificent Elk weighing 800 pound each make the same daring dive as the horses. They enjoy it.

The fair also featured "the champion rifle shot of the world" and a bicyclist who dove off the tower after the horses and elk.

For those with stronger stomachs, boxing became big business in the 1860s. At that time there were no gloves and virtually no rules. The sport was so bloody that Missouri followed the lead of many states and banned it in 1872. The old territorial entertainments of cockfighting and ram fighting remained popular and stayed legal for many years because no human suffering was involved.

A more civilized sport was baseball, which came into prominence during the Civil War and soon became the national pastime. Towns and counties across the state started teams, as did unions, schools, and companies. Bush leagues sprang up across the state. Early games could get rough, especially in the Ozarks, where umpires sometimes backed up their decisions by carrying pistols. Apparently, the umpire at the Lebanon vs. Marshfield match in 1902 left his guns at home, for when he called a Lebanon player out, the crowd rushed onto the field. The *Marshfield Chronicle*, perhaps not the most objective source in this instance, said of the Lebanon fans that "for half an hour they indulged in the most violent, abusive language to the umpire and the visiting team and so great was their rage that for the space of nearly half an hour there was imminent danger of a riot."[1]

Just as with the close of the War of 1812, the cessation of hostilities after the Civil War led to a large influx of immigrants who helped lift Missouri out of its wartime doldrums. With cheap public land, lots of room, and a growing infrastructure, it became one of the most attractive parts of the country for those looking to start a new life. The 1870 census counted 1.7 million people in the state, up more than half a million from 1860. St. Louis doubled in size to more than three hundred thousand and became the fourth largest city in the United States.

The number three city was Chicago, and St. Louis tried to rival it to be the leading economic center of the middle part of the country. Chicago had the twin advantages of better railroad connections and having been untouched by the war. The Mississippi river trade was not as efficient as the railroad and had begun to wane. The situation improved somewhat in 1871, when St. Louis was made a port of entry, hastening the processing of shipments and lowering costs to importers, but the municipal government made a serious mistake in 1876 when it seceded from St. Louis County to become an independent city. Urban voters did not want to spend their tax money on the rural and underdeveloped county, but a

---

1. *Marshfield Chronicle*, August 4, 1902.

century later it would be the county, not the city, that would be more populous and have a larger tax base. In modern times, the city struggles with funding, while the county is the richest in the state. At the time, however, no one saw that the glory days of the steamboat, which Mark Twain immortalized in his *Two Views of the Mississippi*, were actually its final period. The nation's railway system was growing at a furious pace. Train travel became cheaper and had the advantage of not having to rely on the natural course of waterways.

The rapid expansion of Missouri's railroads was the state's most important economic development in the decades following the Civil War. Before and during the war, there had only been a few main lines and a surplus of failed projects, but once freed of the uncertainty of war, railways expanded quickly. The destroyed track was rapidly replaced, and a new line was completed between Kansas City and St. Louis only a few months after the end of the hostilities. A southern line got to Belmont in 1869 and reached the Arkansas border in 1872. Another route connected Iowa to the Kansas City–St. Joseph line by 1869. Springfield got a railroad in 1870. Now the state was connected on all sides except the east, where the Mississippi blocked train travel until the skillful engineering of James Eads put a bridge over it in 1874. Eads used an innovative design that incorporated steel trusses instead of the usual iron, a first for the country. Secondary lines developed to serve more remote areas, so that by 1870, there were two thousand miles of track, up from eight hundred in 1860. By 1880, there were almost four thousand miles of track. By the turn of the century, the figure stood at eight thousand.

The effect of a railroad coming through town was enormous. In 1857, the Pacific Railroad was building a line through Pettis County. George Rappeen Smith bought land along the right of way and laid out a new town named Sedalia, after his daughter Sarah's nickname, "Sed." Smith started selling the lots in 1860 and found no shortage of takers, as everyone knew the railway would mean good business. By the time the line was completed a year later, Sedalia had become a town of three hundred people. Even the Civil War could not stop its growth. By 1866, the population had increased fivefold, and by 1868, it was up to six thousand people. By then it had its own steam-powered fire engine, two banks, and a thriving downtown business area. Gas lighting came to town the following year.

Neosho, briefly the Confederate capital of Missouri, got train service in 1870 as part of the southwestern branch of the Atlantic and

Pacific Railroad. This sparked a period of rapid expansion and modernization to fit its new cosmopolitan image. The town had 875 people when the railroad arrived and more than doubled in size in twenty years to become a regional center. It boasted plank sidewalks, a fire station, a black school, and a library and shortly thereafter got its first telephone lines. The two trains a day to St. Louis opened up a whole new market for the area's agricultural produce, lead, and tobacco and brought in immigrants from the big city.

Train travel shrank distances, making it easier to visit family and friends and look for work in other regions. It also brought an influx of consumer goods at cheap prices. Stores became larger and more numerous. The trains also expanded markets for Missouri goods. Farmers, soon helped by the increased availability of innovative farm equipment, were able to cultivate more land and make bigger shipments. On the other hand, the increased mechanization cost some farm laborers their jobs. Many found work with the railroad companies that had been the indirect cause of their unemployment. Others added their numbers to the burgeoning populations of the cities and towns. Increased access to the outside world also led to more competition, so farmers had to become more adaptable. They struggled with the railroads' high fees and monopolies.

Oddly, the ability for small Missouri towns to communicate with the outside world had probably its greatest impact across the Atlantic in France. In the 1870s and 1880s an infestation of root louse all but wiped out the country's vineyards, but a Swiss immigrant named Herman Jaeger heard about the problem and decided to help. He pruned some of his prized vines from the Ozark hills around Neosho and sent seventeen carloads of them to the coast, where they were shipped to France. The vines thrived and, in gratitude, France awarded Jaeger with the Legion of Honor in 1889.

New industries appeared alongside traditional ones. Zinc started being used for the galvanization of metals and creation of alloys. What had originally been tossed aside as a worthless byproduct of lead mining became a whole new industry. The June 7, 1890, issue of *Frank Leslie's Illustrated Newspaper* reported "four-fifths of all the zinc used in the United States is supplied from Jasper County, and this section can supply the entire world." While this proved to be overly optimistic, Missouri remains a major zinc producer.

Threshing crew near Corder, Lafaytte County, Missouri, 1893. Steam threshers saved a great deal of manual labor but were so expensive for the average farmer that they were often bought by a group of several farmers or the local chapter of the Grange. COURTESY MISSOURI STATE ARCHIVES.

Fredericktown, in Madison County, had been a lead mining center since before statehood, but in the 1870s it became even more prosperous when someone discovered silver a few miles west of town. In the early 1900s, it got another unexpected windfall when barely a mile from town, miners struck a rich vein of lead that also contained copper, nickel, cobalt, and iron.

When the Missouri, Kansas and Texas Railroad (MKT) got to Bates County in 1880, it led to a jump in population and a boom in coal mining. The work was dangerous, and the meager pay was often in scrip that could only be used at the overpriced company store. This tough life made the coal miners organize some of the most radical unions in the state. Long and sometimes violent strikes became part of the miner's life.

Southwest Missouri was also opening up for mining. A mine opened at Granby, Newton County, in 1850 after a local resident discovered ore while sinking a well, but isolation and the Civil War kept the industry from booming until the end of hostilities, when the Granby Lead and Zinc Company restarted operations and opened mines throughout the area. This led to the creation of many new towns, one of them being Minersville (later Oronogo), where the company hosted a competition to see who could bring the most ore from a single shaft in a four-month period. E. R. Moffett and J. B. Sergeant won and used their prize money to buy ten acres from John Cox in the Joplin Creek Valley, where they hoped to strike a big vein of ore. At first they found nothing, and their funds had nearly run out when they hit a major vein. John Cox, realizing he had just sold away a rich mine for a low price, decided to make his fortune a different way. He platted a town just to the east of the diggings and called it Joplin, which, like the creek, was named for a much-loved Methodist Episcopal preacher who had served the area thirty years before. The town of Joplin would become the center of the southwest Missouri mining boom.

Webb City is another town that owes its existence to mining, but it served the even more important function of transport hub. Alfred Rogers had been running a mule-powered trolley in the town when he managed to raise enough capital to start the Southwest Missouri Electric Railway Company in 1889. Based in Webb City, this light railway eventually served the whole mining region, transporting miners and their families to and from work and from outlying areas to bigger towns where they could find shopping and entertainment. For a time it was the largest intercity system west of the Mississippi.

Workers at one of the lead and zinc mines in Joplin, Jaspar and Newton Counties, c.1910. The man second from left is Herbert C. Fateley. The sixth man from the left is Ebonezer "Ebb" Wilson and to his right with arms folded is his brother Dote. The others are possibly Noah Calton, James Thomas, Charles Cornett, Charles Galgar, and John Waldney. Courtesy Shirley Gentry Humble.

The rise in industrialization led to an increase in organized labor. Workers campaigned for higher wages, better and safer conditions, and an eight-hour day. The St. Louis chapter of the Eight Hour League fought a long battle for this cause, but their dream would not be realized for many years.

Rural workers organized, too. The Missouri branch of the Patrons of Husbandry, popularly known as the National Grange, was founded in 1870. This organization unified farmers to better fight for their interests, especially against the unfair price structuring of the railroad companies that shipped their goods. Within five years there were two thousand chapters in Missouri, more than in any other state. The Grange organized collectives to give farmers more bargaining power and opened collectively owned stores to supply farmers at reasonable prices. Interestingly, the Grange gave equal status to women right from the start, a rarity at that time. Like the earlier barn raising and roadwork "bees," Grangers mixed business with pleasure, so meetings became popular for their social aspects while making progress in securing farmers' rights throughout the state.

Now that the Radicals were in firm control of the government, they began to fight among themselves. Senator Drake pushed for black suffrage, something many Radicals could not accept. Drake's domineering manner did not help his popularity. The Democrats played on the dissatisfaction of many outstate (rural) Missourians and began winning seats in local contests. They argued that the Radicals were more concerned with the rights of blacks than they were with those of whites and played on racial fears of what would happen if blacks got full equality. They also sharply criticized the biased test oath. Fearful that the Democrats might make gains in the statewide elections, the Radicals created officers to oversee voter registration. These men were appointed by the Radical governor, and so were generally biased against any supporter of the opposition.

It would be some time before the Democratic opposition could have any real effect. The 1868 election was as sweeping a victory for the Radicals as the one in 1866. Even when Democrats won, as they did in two congressional races in 1866, their victories were declared invalid by the Radical-dominated election commission, which claimed voter fraud and refused to recognize votes from Democratic districts.

The debate over black suffrage led to the beginnings of another movement—women's suffrage. The Women's Suffrage Association of

Missouri was founded in 1867. Encouraged by some Radical leaders who said all Americans should be able to vote, they began to lobby the General Assembly. They received some support—Governor McClurg even signed one of their petitions—but the idea of women voting was still too new and would not become law for another two generations.

With the passage of the Fifteenth Amendment to the U.S. Constitution in 1870, guaranteeing black men the right to vote, some Radicals felt they could afford to let the people decide on re-enfranchisement of former rebels. This brought about a split in the Radical Union Party during the 1870 elections. Those advocating re-enfranchisement of former rebels, higher tariffs, lower taxes, and other issues broke off to create the Liberal Republican Party of Missouri. The Radicals had always been a coalition of convenience, and now that the urgency of the post-war situation had worn off, their differences on other issues began to show.

The Radicals responded by purging state employees who would not donate 5 percent of their salary to the Radical campaign fund. These heavy-handed tactics, typical of the Radicals, did more harm than good. Liberal Republicans and Democrats alike claimed the Radicals had become a dictatorial organization. Many voters were inclined to agree.

Election Day in 1870 was a historic date for the black community. Twenty thousand turned out in St. Louis, and significant numbers registered in other towns as well. Black leaders went on the campaign trail with their white counterparts. This important new voting bloc was split between Radical and Liberal Republicans, although the majority supported the former. Given their stance on black suffrage, it is not surprising that the Democrats got few of their votes.

The Democrats knew they could not win, so they put their support behind the Liberal Republicans and helped them put Benjamin Gratz Brown into the governor's mansion. Brown had originally been a Radical but was appalled by the Drake Constitution and campaigned on a platform of "Universal Suffrage and Universal Amnesty."[2] The Democrats won four congressional seats and a majority of the lower house of the General Assembly. The Liberals also fared well, gaining numerous seats. Combined with the Democrats, they easily outnumbered the Radicals in both houses of the General Assembly. Their job of smashing the

2. Reprinted from *A History of Missouri, Volume IV: 1875–1919* by Lawrence O. Christensen and Gary R. Kremer, p. 123, by permission of the University of Missouri Press. Copyright © 1997 by the Curators of the University of Missouri.

The year 1870 marked the first time blacks were allowed to vote in Missouri. Tens of thousands voted across the state, and in many of the larger towns they held parades to celebrate. Their support became an important factor in elections. USED BY PERMISSION, STATE HISTORICAL SOCIETY OF MISSOURI.

Radicals complete, the Liberal Republicans soon disappeared into the ranks of the other parties. The "iron-clad oath" and other restrictions on former rebels were done away with. Drake, sensing his defeat, left the Senate for a federal job in Washington, D.C., and never returned to Missouri politics.

While no blacks got a post in Missouri government at this early period, one black Missourian did get a federal job. President Grant named James Milton Turner, a freed slave who had risen to become an important Radical campaigner, as counsel to Liberia. This former student of John Berry Meachum's illegal school became the second black American to work in the diplomatic corps.

The Democrats called a constitutional convention in 1875 to replace Drake's constitution. Of the sixty-eight delegates, only eight were Republican, and many of the Democrats had served in the Confederate army or government. In just ten years, Republican power had been swept away. The governor's term was extended to four years and he was given more power, while the General Assembly, to curb the abuses of the Radical years, was given less. The governor also got a line-item veto on appropriations bills, while the number of votes needed for the General Assembly to override a veto was raised from half plus one to two-thirds. As a concession to the Grangers, the constitution included some regulation and price controls of the railroads. The constitution also limited the power of the government to create test oaths, convict someone for treason, raise taxes, or borrow money. The public, tired of the excesses of the Radical years, passed it by a large majority.

The governorship stayed in Democratic hands for the rest of the century, but the Democrats did little with their power because they generally stood for laissez-faire government, despite the serious problems that the state experienced. The James gang and other outlaws robbed banks and trains with impunity, and farmers complained of being robbed by outlaws of a different sort—greedy railroad monopolies. A strike among railroad workers and several other trade unions nearly stopped commerce in St. Louis in 1877. Voters were frustrated by Democratic inaction, but they were not yet ready to return to a Republican government.

Blacks had an especially hard time after the national election of 1876. The Republican presidential candidate, Rutherford B. Hayes, lost the popular vote by a quarter of a million votes but promised the

Southern delegates in the U.S. electoral college that if they voted for him he would pull the federal troops out of the South. The delegates swung their support to Hayes. It was one of the few times a candidate lost the popular vote and got elected anyway. The deal Hayes made, known as the Compromise of 1877, effectively ended Reconstruction. Blacks were barred from the polls and many had their land stolen by vigilantes. Tens of thousands became "Exodusters," heading north in search of a better life.

During this time Missouri's two major cities underwent major expansion. Kansas City became the destination for cowboys bringing cattle to the slaughterhouses and meatpacking factories. The city became a major meat-processing center and shipping point. In 1890, Kansas City processed 581,520 cattle, 2,348,073 hogs, and 199,000 sheep. Like St. Louis, it also had a large number of flour mills and supplied the surrounding area with baked goods.

Over in St. Louis, Anheuser-Busch was sending beer down to Texas. The company had become a major regional brewery after the innovative German immigrant Adolphus Busch had married Lilly Anheuser, daughter of brewery owner Eberhard Anheuser. Busch soon became president and began shipping beer south in refrigerated railroad cars. In 1876, he introduced Budweiser, a pasteurized beer. The company changed its name to the Anheuser-Busch Brewing Association in 1879, and then to Anheuser-Bush, Inc., in 1919. They became famous for their innovative marketing, including such promotions as giving bar owners giant paintings of "Custer's Last Fight" with the company logo emblazoned on it. Why the sight of the 7th Cavalry getting wiped out by Indians led people to drink Budweiser is a bit of a mystery, but the campaign worked and Anheuser-Busch became the largest brewery in the country.

St. Louis was also a major producer of shoes, with the Brown Shoe Company operating the largest shoe factory in the world. Clothing was another big industry, and the city still made fur coats and engaged in the fur trade, although on a much smaller scale than during the early years. One entrepreneur took advantage of the city's position as a regional agricultural center to develop one of Missouri's most successful companies. In 1894, William Danforth started the Ralston Purina Company to supply farm feed. Its product line soon expanded to pet food and food for humans as well, including breakfast cereal and soda crackers. The company eventually sold off the food division to General Mills, and Purina was acquired by Nestlé in 2001.

The Exodusters, as black migrants arriving in St. Louis, Missouri, from the Deep South were called, often arrived with little or no money. They were helped by both white and black citizens, and many moved on to Kansas or Oklahoma. Used by permission, State Historical Society of Missouri.

Men cutting blocks of ice from a frozen pond in Renick, Randolph County. In the days before refrigeration, ice was stored in insulated icehouses, although by the end of Missouri's long, hot summers, it could be in short supply. Courtesy Missouri State Archives.

Local boosters were proud of their city and constantly tried to improve it. They even pushed to have St. Louis named the nation's capital, and while this plan went nowhere, optimism helped the city progress. By 1890, it had the world's largest electrical grid, with public and private lighting and electric streetcars.

Despite this rise in railroad building and industry, many areas, especially in the Ozarks, had no easy access to trains. With the generally poor state of Missouri's roads, these regions kept their traditional economies more or less intact, while more connected areas moved toward industrialization.

Contact with the outside world became easier in 1896 with Rural Free Delivery. This made it much cheaper to keep in touch with distant friends and buy from mail order catalogs, which offered everything from guns to prefabricated houses. Local merchants objected to this out-of-town competition, and the question "Is patronizing mail order houses detrimental to the best interests of the country?" became a common one in debating clubs.

Easier transportation, the attraction of Missouri's two big cities, and the exodus of blacks from the South led to a rapid rise in population. In 1880, Missouri's population stood at 2.2 million, but it increased nearly 50 percent to 3.1 million by the end of the century. There was also a movement from rural areas to the towns. Regional centers grew throughout the state. St. Joseph in the northwest and Joplin in the southwest doubled their populations in the last decades of the century. St. Joseph prospered as a regional marketplace and major clothing producer. Joplin owed its wealth to lead and zinc mining. Lead had been discovered in southwest Missouri in the 1850s, but operations were disrupted during the Civil War. After stability came back to the region and railroads connected it to the outside world, the mining industry became as important as the older mining region of southeast Missouri.

The 1880 election saw Democrat Thomas Crittenden elected governor, and he wasted no time getting to work on the unresolved problems of the earlier administration. He forced the Hannibal–St. Joseph Railroad to pay back more than $3.5 million owed to the government and offered a bounty for Frank and Jesse James. Quantrill's former guerillas had become infamous for robbing banks, trains, stagecoaches, and stores in Missouri and other states. Working with Cole Younger, another Quantrill veteran, as well as other outlaws, they are credited with the first daylight bank robbery in peacetime and the first train robbery in Missouri.

The Noce family grocery store in Burfordville, Cape Girardeau County, 1901 or 1902. In small communities, the town store often doubled as a post office and social center. COURTESY MISSOURI STATE ARCHIVES.

Frank and Jesse James had been tutored in the ways of guerilla warfare during the Civil War. Frank rode with a few different bushwhacker
bands and fought under General Sterling Price at Wilson's Creek. He
learned the tactics of hit-and-run warfare, which would prove so useful
to his career as a criminal, from experts such as William Quantrill
and "Bloody Bill" Anderson. A reserved and educated man who liked
to quote Shakespeare, Frank was nevertheless a respected fighter. His
younger brother Jesse was very different, having been immersed in fun-
damentalist Baptist religion and being of a louder, showier nature. He
did not join his brother as a bushwhacker until late in the war. The story
goes that some Union soldiers came to the James farm near Kearney,
Clay County. The family was well-known for its secessionist views, and
the troops whipped Jesse and put a noose around his stepfather's neck,
hauling him up a tree and letting him drop, before hauling him back up
again. While we have only Jesse James's word for this story, similar out-
rages by Union troops were all too common. Jesse certainly did harbor a
deep resentment to the Union and became one of the most feared members of the most fearsome bushwhacker bands in the state.

After the war, the brothers could not adjust to peacetime life. On
February 13, 1866, less than a year after the end of hostilities, they and
some accomplices robbed the bank at Liberty in broad daylight, making
away with more than sixty thousand dollars. They went on to commit
several other daring robberies, including a bank at Gallatin in 1869,
and the holdup of a train at Gads Hill in 1874, the state's first peacetime train robbery. Their most daring heist was at the box office of the
Kansas City Fair in 1872, which they cleared out amidst a crowd of several thousand people.

Despite committing numerous crimes in Missouri and several
other states, and leaving a trail of dead lawmen, Pinkerton detectives,
and innocent bystanders, the James boys earned the reputation of being
Robin Hoods, taking from the rich and giving to the poor. They were
certainly generous with their money. It was normal at that time for travelers to lodge at farmhouses as they rode across the countryside and pay
for their lodging and board, and the James brothers generally paid far
more than was necessary. Just before the Gads Hill job, local legend says
the James gang ate at the farm of a poor widow named Sarah Hamil.
When the five men left, each placed a five-dollar gold coin under his
plate. The James brothers enjoyed their reputation and encouraged it.
Jesse would compare himself to famous old English outlaws in letters

Postcard of Frank James in front of the James Farm, already turned into a tourist attraction by the early twentieth century. Frank James lived long enough to see he and his brother Jesse become legends. Courtesy Missouri State Archives.

to the press, while Frank quoted Shakespeare to his victims. In postwar Missouri, where anger at the federal government ran high and many thought the wrong side had won the war, the exploits of these daring ex-bushwhackers earned them widespread respect.

Even some of the people they robbed could not help liking the two and gave excited and flattering interviews to the press about their brush with Missouri's most famous men. These accounts stressed how polite the robbers were and how they avoided robbing women and working men. While this was not always true (a woman was robbed of five hundred dollars on the Gads Hill train), the James boys had become legends in their own lifetime.

In 1881, Governor Crittenden offered a five thousand dollar reward for the capture of either of them, and double that amount if they were convicted. This did not stop the James brothers. In fact, they were never caught. The following year, Jesse was shot in the back by a supposed friend while straightening a picture in his home in St. Joseph. Crittenden, satisfied that the notorious outlaw had at least been stopped, pardoned his murderer. Frank gave himself up the following year and after being tried for several crimes was acquitted of all charges against him. The veteran of the Wilson's Creek battle and the raid on Lawrence lived a quiet life until his death in 1915. Cole Younger, who reformed himself after a long prison term, died a year later.

In 1884, Democrat John Sappington Marmaduke was elected governor despite his having been a former Confederate general. He had to deal with further railroad strikes as workers protested pay cuts. Marmaduke responded by getting the legislature to ban railroad monopolies and their rate discrimination against the short-haul loads mostly used by farmers. This move was widely popular in a state becoming increasingly reliant on trains. Marmaduke also passed a local option law in 1887 allowing counties to ban liquor. Alcohol was blamed for a variety of social ills, and a significant percentage of people did not drink. Many church and secular groups called for an end to drinking. The Prohibitionist Party had run a candidate in the 1884 elections, and there were advocates for banning alcohol in every other party as well. Within two years of the passage of Marmaduke's local option law, fifty counties had banned drinking.

Democrat David Francis won the governorship in 1888, but by then the power of the Democratic Party was slipping. The Republicans made a strong showing, and the new Union Labor Party—which called for public ownership of communication and transportation, abolition of prison labor on the grounds that it was unfair competition, and other pro–working class reforms—won several seats in the General Assembly, including eleven of the fourteen representing St. Louis. The Prohibitionist Party also ran, but the Democrats had stolen some of its thunder by allowing the local option law.

Like his predecessor, Francis had to deal with the legacy of hatred left over from the Civil War. Taney County, in the Ozarks on the southern edge of the state, still suffered from the years of bloodshed. The courthouse had been burned during the war, and the county was too deep in debt to rebuild or even really govern. Murders and lawlessness were rife, in great part due to a lingering feud between former Union and Confederate supporters. Confederates who left Taney County during the war came home to find their lands confiscated for failure to pay taxes. Having few opportunities, they either drifted away or turned to crime, especially targeting the Union men who had taken over their land. In 1885, an imposing Union veteran named Nat Kinney, who stood six feet seven inches tall and always carried his pistols—"Short Tom" and "Long Tom"—organized a group of men one night atop a bare hill. They formed a vigilante group that came to be known as the "Bald Knobbers" after their meeting place. This soon developed into a secret society with its own rituals and secret handshakes. The Bald Knobbers wreaked a terrible vengeance upon the lawless element of the region.

As with all vigilante groups, their methods went beyond the law. Personal hatred, rather than fighting crime, often motivated their punishments. Other Bald Knobber and anti–Bald Knobber groups sprang up in the region, and soon the fighting was as bad as it had been during the war. Kinney himself was gunned down in 1888, and Governor Francis hanged three Bald Knobbers for murder and forced the organization to disband.

The Bald Knobbers were the last gasp of the Civil War in Missouri. By 1898 the *Taney County Republican* could report that a Civil War reunion attended by veterans of both sides had "no ill feeling manifested whatever. The Yank and Johnney buried the hatchet a thousand fathoms deep, never to be resurrected. All are now Americans and comrades in Taney County."[3]

The state's increased prosperity led to advances in social services. Schools went through a great expansion in the 1880s and 1890s, helped by an 1887 law that raised funds for state schools from one-fourth to one-third of the budget. Despite this, many schools were still primitive one-room schoolhouses serving farm children, open as few as four months a year. While more remote areas would not see much change for several decades, schools in towns expanded and bought better equipment. Larger cities experimented with opening kindergartens and high schools, but these were slow to evolve as most people saw little need for them, and those wealthy enough to spare their children's labor in their teenage years sent their children to private schools anyway.

Educational opportunities increased for women; they broke into the male-dominated university system, and the first woman to attend the University of Missouri enrolled in 1868. But those who gained an education found they had few opportunities. Mary O'Neill, a twenty-three-year-old farmer's daughter who lived near Osborn, DeKalb County,

3. *Taney County Republican*, Sept. 1, 1898.

read voraciously and sprinkled her diary with quotes from the classics, including several in Latin, yet she worked on the family farm. Her diary records her daily grind, broken occasionally by simple pleasures. The entry for January 6, 1899, reads:

> Busy. Arose before 6. Milked six cows, breakfast, washed dishes, swept three rooms, dusted, filled lamps, did chamber work, wrapped up mother's gown, cooked dinner, put bread in tins, clean papers on kitchen shelves, washed good share of kitchen woodwork, mopped floor, blacked range and cleaned out oven. Read part of Tennyson's "Princess," heated calf milk, milked six cows, cleared supper table, read newspapers and want to go skating tomorrow.[4]

As before the war, a variety of educational opportunities existed outside the framework of formal schooling. In Jefferson City, whites came to hear visiting lectures at the Lincoln Institute, the black college, while blacks were often denied the same right at white colleges. Although the Lincoln Institute was the premier seat of higher learning for black Missourians, it was not the only one. The George R. Smith College, a teacher training school, opened in Sedalia in 1894. Besides training teachers, it offered a complete range of education from elementary school to college preparatory and Bible study. It was named after Sedalia's founder, whose daughters donated the land. Another college, the Bartlett Agricultural and Industrial School, opened in 1907 in Dalton, Chariton County.

Schools were important social centers, especially in rural areas. Teachers were expected to organize entertainments at the end of the school year to show off the students' ability. Boys and girls read essays, answered questions, gave speeches, and put on plays before the assembled parents. While these were primarily for fun, they had a serious side. Parents judged the teacher by the quality of the show, and since most of the hiring and firing was done on the local level, students must have been under some serious pressure to do well.

People also took time out for simple pleasures. Mary O'Neill's diary records almost daily visits from friends and neighbors. Often they would

---

4. Document C3945 from the Western Historical Manuscript Collection, Columbia, Missouri. Used with permission.

go out for walks or Mary's favorite pastime, skating. After her hard day on January 6, she got her wish and went skating with two friends on the seventh.

> Skating forenoon and afternoon. William's first experience on skates this forenoon. Brown's this afternoon. William as enthusiastic as I am. Brown afraid. William covered with black and blue spots but wants to get up at twelve tonight when it is moon light and go again. Got Ruth's old skates all muddy, took a pail of hot water and scrubbed them in great shape. . . .Wish Ruth might have been here.[5]

O'Neill made frequent reference to reading newspapers. The end of the century was a golden age for Missouri papers. There were 530 daily or weekly periodicals in the state in 1880, with a circulation of almost one million at a time when Missouri's population was only 2.2 million. Since papers were often read aloud and passed around, it seems virtually everyone paid attention to the news. Mary O'Neill read the newspaper most days and often read it to her sick grandmother. Papers not only offered readers current events, but they also serialized novels, essays, and poetry. Many of these included religious themes. In 1899, the *Jasper County Democrat* started running a serial of Charles Sheldon's popular novel *In His Steps: What Would Jesus Do?*

Missouri papers were read far beyond state lines. Especially influential in the region was the *St. Louis Post-Dispatch*, owned by Joseph Pulitzer, a Hungarian immigrant who started his career at the German-language *Westliche Post* and became famous for his harsh attacks on corruption and wealth. He soon owned several papers in Missouri and New York, but the *Post-Dispatch* had the widest reach, gaining readers throughout the Midwest. His style of going after the rich, exposing their slightest foibles to the harsh light of scrutiny, made him many enemies, but more readers. Common people liked his "muckraking," because it made them feel that something was being done about the rampant political corruption and social inequalities of the day. Pulitzer endowed the famous Pulitzer Prize, which rewards journalists who have exposed important stories. The Pulitzer Prize also has categories for photojournalism, writing, drama, and music.

---

5. Document C3945 from the Western Historical Manuscript Collection, Columbia, Missouri. Used with permission.

The baptism of Lou Mickels by Rev. David Lyons in March, 1897, in Medicine Creek just below Collier Mill dam. The creek was frozen over, so the congregation cut a path through the ice. Used by permission, State Historical Society of Missouri.

Church socials were another way for neighbors to get together. Preachers had revivals under the shade of brush arbors, roofs of leafy branches. Families would come from miles around to camp for days or even weeks to get the chance to meet people and hear a series of preachers. Like in frontier days, these were generally interdenominational affairs where Baptists, Methodists, and members of other faiths would all listen to each others' preachers. Doctrinal differences were put aside as the speakers concentrated on preaching from the Bible. In the Ozarks, brush arbor meetings lasted until recent times.

Christmas became a time for the community to get together for both worship and fun. While the holiday was primarily a religious one, people took time out to enjoy themselves. The December 20, 1895, issue of the West Plains paper, *Howell County News*, listed the Christmas activities of all seven churches in town. West Plains had little more than two thousand people at the time, so the number of churches shows how seriously Missourians took religion. The same paper had a regular column called "Sunday School," which recounted Bible stories. West Plains residents could expect a good show and happy children at the church events:

> At the Washington Avenue M.E. church they will have a chimney built of boxes of candy and a live Santa Claus will come down it and distribute the candy to the children, after they have treated the audience to a short but well-directed program.
>
> A Christmas concert will be given by the children at the Christian church, after which presents will be distributed from a tree for the Sunday School. The public are also invited to use the tree as a medium for distributing their gifts.

All the churches had Christmas trees except for the Cumberland Presbyterian, which had a "decorated cross, from which to distribute their treat to the Sunday School." Most churches seemed to have offered entertainment, usually provided by the children of the congregation.

Missourians were also being brought closer together by the development of the telephone. Hannibal opened the first telephone exchange in the state in 1878. St. Louis started phone service a few months later, and Kansas City followed suit the following year. By 1885, the two major cities were linked, and other lines started connecting smaller towns.

More remote areas had to wait for phone service, but they were eager to have it when it came. Sheldon, in Vernon County, granted the Kinloch Telephone Company the rights to put in a line in 1904. On September 30 of that year, the *Sheldon Enterprise* reported that "Mart McClenagan and a crew of hands are putting up a telephone line from Sheldon to Bellamy where it will connect with Dr. Popplewell's line to Montevallo. We will soon be saying 'hello' to all south Vernon County." The paper eagerly followed the line's development, although it made the wry comment on March 4 that the poles on every street made it look like "a forest of dead trees."

The growth of the middle class, which had time and money to spare, led many women to join literary and debating societies in which they discussed artistic and philosophical issues. One such society was the "Wednesday Club," founded in 1890 by writers Kate Chopin and Charlotte Eliot, poet and mother of T. S. Eliot. Another form of entertainment was the lyceum, which brought in famous speakers and sponsored debates ranging from the political to the scholarly. The town of Osborn had one, and Mary O'Neill and her relatives often attended.

The most famous of Missouri's many great writers, Samuel Langhorne Clemens, rose to international prominence in the late nineteenth century. Clemens was born in 1835 in Florida, Monroe County, but his family soon moved to Hannibal, a bustling Mississippi riverboat town in Marion County. Growing up along the river had a profound effect on him. In 1859, he got his license as a riverboat pilot and later recalled his time navigating the river as the best years of his life. The Civil War induced him to move to the Territory of Nevada, where he gained a reputation for his humorous essays and stories under the pen name Mark Twain. Soon he was on the lecture circuit, proving to be just as witty in person as he was on paper. He toured the country, and eventually the world, giving readings from his books and humorous lectures on whatever took his fancy. His running monologues often lasted all night and kept audiences in stitches wherever he went. He would occasionally play tricks on his audience, such as walking onstage and just standing there. The crowd's anticipation at hearing Twain's famous wit would grow and grow until they burst into laughter while Twain kept silent, a slow smile spreading across his lips. While the lecture circuit exhausted him, Twain had large financial obligations and kept it up until his death in 1910. When the author of this book was a boy, he met an old man who had attended one of Twain's later appearances. Despite the passing of eighty years, the man still laughed at the memory.

Mark Twain's tales of Tom Sawyer and Huckleberry Finn are his most enduring works and have become icons of small-town life in the United States. They represent, however, only a small fraction of a voluminous body of writings ranging from travel narratives to indictments of imperialism. He lived most of his life outside Missouri, but his love for its people and its rivers come out in much of his work.

While Samuel Clemens was busy creating the persona of Mark Twain, another Missourian reached the height of his fame. George Caleb Bingham grew up in Franklin and developed a local reputation as a portrait painter in the 1830s. National fame eluded him until the 1850s, when his richly colored paintings of Missouri life, such as *The County Election* and *The Jolly Flatboatmen at Port*, earned him a place among the greatest painters of the nation. Eastern buyers were intrigued by the Missouri frontier, which they considered exciting and exotic, but they also appreciated Bingham's accessible style, which smoothed over the rougher aspects of frontier living. He did occasionally paint to make a point, and his *Order No. 11*, showing the upheaval that military order caused, remains his most enduring work within the state.

Literature and painting were not the only forms of cultural expression. During the 1890s, a new style of music emerged from the black communities in Sedalia and St. Louis. A fusion of gospel and spiritual singing, and the marching songs of fraternal orders such as the Masons, it was called ragtime. Ragtime featured a syncopated beat on the piano, with the bass notes making the beat and the melodic notes both on and off the beat, allowing for a lot of creativity and energy. This "ragged time" may be the origin of the style's name, but this is not certain. Soon ragtime entertained audiences as far away as New Orleans and Chicago. One of the earliest ragtime composers was Tom Turpin, who played in clubs in Sedalia and St. Louis and wrote a number of pieces including the "St. Louis Rag" and the "Harlem Rag." He eventually opened his own saloon in St. Louis, where his performances packed the house. Besides being a successful businessman, he became deputy constable and a political leader of the city's black community. Turpin's music reflected his mastery of the piano; most other players had trouble playing his music and had to be content buying a piano roll to put into their player piano.

Another successful composer was Scott Joplin, a black man who lived in both Sedalia and St. Louis playing in "gentlemen's clubs," a term for disreputable bars where female companionship was available for a price. He composed such enduring tunes as "The Entertainer." Joplin's death in 1917, along with the decline of live piano in favor of recorded music and jazz, was the beginning of the end of ragtime, although it enjoys occasional revivals.

Perhaps the best known musician in Missouri, John William "Blind" Boone had a long career in music before he started playing ragtime. Born during the Civil War to an escaped slave, he had his eyes removed as a child to cure him of "brain fever." Boone showed a talent for music from an early age and studied at the Missouri School for the Blind. While he loved the music room, he showed little interest in school and spent much of his time hanging out in cheap dives in the city's "tenderloin" district. He picked up an ability to play any composition on the piano after hearing it only once. Boone dropped out of school and made his living as a traveling musician, playing classical and spiritual pieces and amazing crowds with his imitations of other instruments on the piano. When ragtime came along he composed his two most enduring pieces, "Strains from the Alleys," perhaps in honor of his time in St. Louis backstreet saloons, and "Strains from the Flat Branch," a tribute to the stream that runs through his longtime home of Columbia.

While blacks made gains in education and culture, a growing number of women joined the suffrage movement to demand the right to vote. The suffrage movement was closely tied to the temperance movement. The women's movement pointed out the connection between drunkenness and domestic abuse. Missouri got its first chapter of the Women's Christian Temperance Union in 1882, joining a growing national movement to prohibit the sale of alcohol. Its most radical leader was Carrie Nation, who divided her time between Kansas and Missouri, bursting into saloons and smashing everything in sight with a hatchet while her entourage sang hymns. She called herself "a bulldog running along at the feet of Jesus, barking at what he doesn't like."

Temperance was only one of many reform movements at the end of the century. People were increasingly troubled by the hard conditions in factories, unhealthy slums, and other byproducts of ungoverned capitalism. Workers joined groups such as the Knights of Labor, who called for an eight-hour day, the end of child labor, the elimination of private banks, and equal pay for blacks and women. By 1886, the Knights of Labor had a national membership of more than seven hundred thousand. In 1892, the Missouri Farmers Alliance joined the national Populist Party, also known as the People's Party, and held their first convention in Sedalia. They called for an eight-hour day, more public roads, an end to convict and child labor, and other reforms. Some workers even resorted to socialist or anarchist labor unions, but the majority of Missourians wanted social reform, rather than the overthrow of the established order. An emerging Populist movement called for government ownership of public utilities, an end to trusts, and a host of other reforms. The middle and upper classes, always the most powerful political groups, saw little need for change. Governor David Francis thought all social problems would eventually be solved by bringing more industry to the state, and that the government should not interfere with society too much. The wealth, he claimed, would benefit all Missourians. Using this line of reasoning, Francis cut taxes and spending on public institutions, although he was a generous supporter of the University of Missouri, which he saw as a good investment, and lowered the cost of school books to reduce the burden on poor families.

The economy was not as stable as the Democrats had hoped. The nationwide Panic of 1893 and the recession that followed it dampened spirits for a time. As credit and banking foundered, speculative ventures such as mining suffered. Many farmers lost their land to creditors. Others lost their land to the government because they had spent all their money servicing loans and did not have any left for taxes.

The long recession of the 1890s hastened calls for reform. Governor Francis got the legislature to pass an antitrust bill in 1889, requiring corporations to sign an affidavit swearing they were not engaged in any trusts, price fixing, or other attempts to control the market. About two hundred companies refused to sign, and the Missouri Supreme Court eventually ruled the law was an unfair restriction on business. Another antitrust law passed in 1891, but only a few companies suffered small fines. The Panic of 1893 led to a stronger law, but corporate lobbyists made sure it was limited to outstate Missouri, where few large corporations were based.

Things finally began to change under the administration of Lawrence "Lon" Stephens, elected governor in 1896. With his attorney general, Edward Crow, the government sued the powerful insurance company trust for price gouging. The exception for companies in Kansas City and St. Louis was abolished in 1899. Soon the government was trying to break up trusts all over the state. Stephens tried to create a corporate tax to get companies to pay their share of the cost of government, but this divided the Democratic Party and the measure was defeated. Crow also went after the meat trust, accusing them of price fixing and peddling rotten meat, but the company got off with a small fine. Even when the government made a serious effort to stamp out corporate corruption, they often found the task too big to handle.

At the end of the nineteenth century, Missouri was undergoing rapid change. The outstate region was opening up, and the main cities became centers of industry. Despite a troubled economy and corporate underhandedness, Missouri experienced rapid modernization and an increase in wealth and productivity. All of these trends would continue and increase in the beginning of the next century.

Chapter 7

Missouri on the World Stage
(1900–1941)

Missouri entered the twentieth century in a state of rapid transformation. In the previous twenty years its population increased by almost 50 percent to 3.1 million, with most of the increase taking place in the expanding industrial centers of major cities and larger towns.

The dawn of the twentieth century saw acceleration in technology. Probably the most popular innovation was the motion picture. The films of that time were black and white and generally only ran a few minutes. They had no sound and so a pianist or even an entire orchestra accompanied them, playing music suited to the mood of the scene. Movies were still a novelty and were usually accompanied by a lecture or vaudeville act, but the crowds packing local opera houses and theaters to see the new "moving pictures" were a sign of things to come.

On December 24, 1899, the *Moberly Evening Democrat* carried a review from the *Cincinnati Telegraph* of a Christmas movie that was coming to town:

An Impressive Spectacle: The famous "Passion Play" was produced by means of the Cinematograph, accompanied by a lecture and several vocal solos by Mr. Walter Kilrain. The success, which attended the production of the play was very great, and deservedly so. The pictures are life like and very realistic portraying with great exactitude the various scenes of the greatest drama and producing upon the beholder a deep religious impression. We see the important happenings in the life of the Savior from his birth until his Ascension to Heaven, the figures moving before us so vividly and naturally, that we bridge over centuries of the past, and place ourselves among the people of that age. A sermon is no more impressive and can carry no deeper feelings of religious awe and reverence, than this splendid presentation produces upon the beholders.

The film, which must have been one of the very first in the town, cost twenty-five or thirty-five cents, depending on the seats. Unlike modern movies, there was no discount for the matinee.

One of the innovators of the new medium grew up on a small farm near Marceline, straddling the borders of Chariton and Linn counties. Walt Disney moved there as a boy from Chicago in 1906. Farming proved difficult for the Disney family, however, and they relocated to Kansas City in 1910. This proved to be a fortunate move, because Disney was able to take classes at the Kansas City Art Institute. After serving briefly as an ambulance driver in World War I, he got a job making short cartoons that ran before the main movie. He tried to found his own animation company but struggled financially, and in 1923 he moved to Hollywood. There he found a much better market for his work and soon had enough money to start the Disney Brothers Cartoon Studio, which later became the Walt Disney Company. His fortune was made with the production of *Steamboat Willie* in 1928, the first sound cartoon and first appearance of Mickey Mouse. It was followed by a host of other characters who became icons of American culture. His retellings of folk tales such as *Cinderella* and *Snow White* kept these old stories alive, although in greatly altered forms. Many of Disney's films remain classics of animation and cinema.

In the field of music, ragtime remained popular for the first two decades of the twentieth century, and a more vocally based style called blues appeared shortly after ragtime, although it did not replace it. Blues took its inspiration from ragtime and folk music, but it was more melancholy. Like ragtime, it developed in the bars and social clubs of the Mississippi River valley. Traveling black musician William Christopher Handy made St. Louis a center of blues early on through his runaway hit "St. Louis Blues" in 1914. The song was based on his experiences as a poor musician having to sleep on the levee. Handy wrote the song to "combine ragtime syncopation with a real melody in the spiritual tradition."[1] Although not the first blues artist, Handy became instrumental in publishing and popularizing blues music and is often called "The

---

1. Christensen and Kremer, p. 185.

Father of the Blues." Blues remained an enduring style and has inspired modern musicians as diverse as Jimi Hendrix and Tom Waits.

The black community created a third style of music with jazz, which became popular in the 1920s and had Missouri as one of its homes. Jazz takes its name from a slang sexual term and its inspiration from earlier forms of black music, especially blues. It features experimentation with a small number of musicians or full orchestras. Jazz not only inherited many elements of blues music, it also inherited some of its best composers. Both Scott Joplin and W. C. Handy became accomplished jazz composers, as did the musicians in many bands working out of Kansas City. The style became wildly popular during the Prohibition era, when it was associated with speakeasies, the illegal bars that became social centers for people who didn't want to give up alcohol. Jazz lost its illicit flavor after Prohibition, but it remains popular to this day.

Despite new innovations and an expansion of industry, Missouri leaders felt their state was not getting its fair share of the nation's progress. Boosters in St. Louis managed to raise $5 million to hold a World's Fair in 1904, the centenary of the Louisiana Purchase. Voters approved a special tax so the city could raise $5 million more. Congress approved another $5 million, bringing the total to $15 million, the exact amount Jefferson paid for the Louisiana Territory.

The World's Fair was the largest exhibition seen in the state, both before and to the present day. The fairgrounds stretched across 1,272 acres. The centerpiece was the Palace of Agriculture, a massive structure with ten thousand exhibits of Missouri produce and that of other regions. On a slope in front of the north entrance was a 112-foot clock face made out of thirteen thousand flowering plants. It was the largest clock in the world at the time, with a minute hand that was seventy-five feet long and weighed 2,700 pounds; the hour hand was fifty feet long. In front of the elaborate Festival Hall stretched the Cascades, a series of waterfalls, fountains, and a large lake where the public took boat rides. It was truly a World's Fair, with forty-three countries and forty-five states and territories represented.

According to St. Louis attorney Edward Schneiderhahn:

The multiplicity of beautiful views was astonishing. On account of the manner in which the Fair was laid out, focusing toward Festival Hall, the avenues were not all straight. In consequence the eye sweeping down an avenue, would meet an inspiring

Horse-powered ferry near New Haven, Franklin County. These primitive ferries survived in parts of Missouri well into the twentieth century. Courtesy Missouri State Archives.

view caused by Exposition palaces that flanked the avenues. . . . It was a pleasure to ramble among the walks. The flower ornamentation had been most lavish. The shrubbery was profusely scattered. Everything looked fresh. There was a touch of green that enlivened the whole picture. . . . The pen cannot describe the beauty of the Illumination. Words fail. Magic picture. A flood of light and how harmonious the arrangement? One was lost in wonder. And how the beautiful Grecian columns stood out? And the Festival Hall with its changing illumination of white, red and green. Wonderful! Wonderful. Never expect to see anything so grand again.[2]

---

2. Clevenger, pp. 57, 70–71.

The Fair brought the attention of the world to Missouri and represented what the state aspired to be. Ambitious improvements to the city's roads, infrastructure, and waterways helped make it look its best for the almost 20 million visitors who came over the course of the Fair's 184 days.

Like many people, Schneiderhahn went to the Fair on a regular basis and sorely missed this part of his routine when it came to a close. On the final night, after he had joined a great throng to get a final look at this wonderland, he penned in his diary, "The night was wonderfully mild. Shortly before twelve, midnight, the scene was illuminated by beautiful fireworks, but the German House bells tolled a wonderfully solemn farewell. It was most affecting. . . . The flood of light grew fainter and fainter and of a sudden all was darkness. The Cascades were silent. The scene was dead. The World's Fair no more. Passed into history forever. . . . It is a hard task to become reconciled to the end of the World's Fair. But everything human will have an end. Sic transit gloria mundi."[3]

The World's Fair wasn't the only big event in St. Louis that year. The city also hosted the first Olympic Games ever to be held in the United States, and only the third held in modern times. The games were smaller then, with athletes from eleven different countries and four continents competing in fifteen different events on the grounds of Washington University. Women were only allowed to participate in archery, but African-Americans were allowed to play for the first time, and two of them won medals. One event that grabbed the headlines was the marathon. The competition took place on a hot August afternoon with the temperature in the nineties. The competitors ran over dirt roads, choking on dust raised by Olympic officials riding ahead of the runners in their automobiles. Of the thirty-two competitors, eighteen of them dropped out from heat prostration, but some athletes had other problems. Len Tau, a Tsuana tribesman from South Africa, got chased nearly a mile off course by a dog, but he still managed to come in ninth. Cuban runner Felix Carbajal, who had to walk and hitchhike to St. Louis after losing all his money his money in a dice game in New Orleans, spent some of the race chatting with spectators and stealing peaches from an official. Observers noted that if he had taken the race more seriously he may have come in first instead of fourth. Thomas

---

3. Clevenger, p. 50.

At night the Palace of Electricity, which showcased advances in electrical technology, was the most impressive sight at the 1904 St. Louis World's Fair. From *The Cosmopolitan*, restored by Jim Crawford.

Pool Hall and Barber Shop, Blue Springs, Jackson County, 1907. Barbershops had long been social centers, and the pool tables gave an added excuse to hang around. Courtesy Missouri State Archives.

Hicks of Chicago almost did not survive the run. A little more than halfway through, he became exhausted and asked officials if he could lie down. Instead they gave him egg whites, brandy, and a shot of strychnine and told him to keep moving. It is rather doubtful that these "stimulants" actually helped him, but Hicks made it to the end and won first place.

While the World's Fair and Olympics showcased the bright side of the modern era, Missouri also became acquainted with the problems of the modern world. Much of the state's industry lay in the hands of a few men who quashed union organizing, fixed prices, and bought politicians. There had been complaints about this for some time, but little was accomplished until the formidable Democrat Joseph Folk became St. Louis circuit attorney in 1900.

He had first come into the public eye as a mediator during a prolonged streetcar strike in St. Louis, when he managed to forge a settlement that both sides could agree on.

Folk was part of the political machine of Boss Ed Butler, who stuffed ballot boxes to get his candidates elected. Word of the fraud got out and Congress refused to recognize the victory of Butler's son to the U.S. House of Representatives. Folk called for an investigation of the election, a curious thing considering how he got elected, and the outcome indicted both Republicans and Democrats.

From then on, Folk was his own man. He uncovered bribes to local officials to approve a streetcar company merger and convicted thirteen of them for corruption. He could not fight the battle alone, however, and the state supreme court overturned the convictions. He went after city contractors, too, uncovering corruption in the lighting and garbage services. This led him back to his old boss, since Ed Butler held a large number of shares in the St. Louis Sanitary Company. Butler tried to bribe the Board of Health to give a contract to the company, and Folk got him sentenced to three years in prison. Once again, the state supreme court overturned his conviction. He brought Butler to trial twice more, and, while he failed both times, he succeeded in ruining Butler's reputation and influence. His greatest victory as circuit attorney came in 1903, when he revealed that Democrat lieutenant governor John Adams Lee had taken and given bribes for the Royal Baking Company to ensure its monopoly in the state. Lee had no choice but to resign.

Folk won the governorship in 1904 on a wave of support for Progressivism, a political philosophy that advocated government as a force to improve all aspects of life. He promised to eliminate tax shelters for corporations, shift control of utilities from private companies to local governments, and many other reforms. His platform of an honest government as the watchdog against special interests became known as the "Missouri Idea." This was a sharp departure from the traditional Missouri belief in limited government and showed that the people were increasingly worried about market forces and the abuses of powerful capitalists.

Folk found the post of governor a difficult one. As circuit attorney he had been able to run a one-man crusade, but now he had to rely on goodwill and compromise, something not suited to his nature or forthcoming from the many politicians of both parties who felt threatened by him. He used his patronage to appoint supporters of the Missouri Idea to various offices and won passage of a number of reforms, including a ceiling on railroad freight fees (a boon to farmers), increased regulation for industry, banning additives in food and drugs, antitrust legislation, child labor laws, and much more.

The Folk administration gained national fame through the efforts of his Republican attorney general Herbert Hadley. Hadley charged Standard Oil of New Jersey, owned by John D. Rockefeller, with operating an illegal monopoly in Missouri. He called Rockefeller to testify, but the famous millionaire fled the country in disguise. Other states joined the fight and broke Standard Oil's monopoly.

This success led Hadley to gain the governor's seat in the 1908 election. With the help of Progressives in the General Assembly, he passed laws to create bipartisan election boards to fight corruption and set up the office of dairy commissioner, food and drug commissioner, and game and fish commissioner. He also reformed the state's primitive prisons, installing showers, serving better food, and teaching job skills.

The prisoners got a chance to repay him in 1911, when lightning struck the capitol building and set it on fire. Hadley and members of the General Assembly fought the flames alongside firemen and a hastily assembled crew of convicts. They managed to save most of the records, but the building burned to the ground.

Hadley's successor, Democrat Elliot Major, was another Progressive. Besides overseeing the construction of a new statehouse, completed in 1917, and approving the design for the state flag, he increased government scrutiny of state contracts, created the highway department, banned prison labor, and secured compensation for injured workers and the blind.

Young women and girls, and a lone boy, working in a shoe factory in 1905. Increasing industrialization offered opportunities for women outside the home, but hours were long, pay was minimal, and harassment common. USED BY PERMISSION, STATE HISTORICAL SOCIETY OF MISSOURI.

The Missouri State Capitol was completely gutted by fire on February 5, 1911, and only a heroic effort by government employees, firemen, local residents, and a team of prisoners saved the state records. COURTESY MISSOURI STATE ARCHIVES.

While Major was trying to reform Missouri, events in Europe threatened to embroil the state in a world war. The assassination of Archduke Franz Ferdinand, heir to the Austro-Hungarian throne, by a Bosnian Serb nationalist in Sarajevo set off a string of events that plunged all of Europe's major powers into war.

In Missouri the general feeling was in support of the Allied Powers (England, France, Belgium, and their allies) against the Central Powers (Germany, the Austro-Hungarian Empire, the Ottoman Empire, and Bulgaria), but most wanted to stay out of the war. Missouri's German settlers felt torn. Many had fled oppression in Germany, but they did not like to see their countrymen die on the battlefield. They pushed for complete neutrality as the best solution; many non-Germans agreed.

But this was not to be. England's powerful navy blockaded German ports, and the German U-boats responded by attacking British shipping. On May 7, 1915, a U-boat sank the *Lusitania*, a British ocean liner carrying war materiel from the United States. Many of the civilian passengers drowned, including more than a hundred Americans. The American public was enraged, and President Woodrow Wilson and Congress doubled the size of the army and vastly expanded the navy. Germany agreed to restrict its use of submarines to sinking warships, but increasing economic hardship brought on by the British blockade forced them once again into unrestricted submarine warfare. Then British intelligence intercepted the Zimmermann telegram, in which the German foreign secretary unsuccessfully tried to get Mexico to declare war on the United States. Wilson asked Congress to declare war on Germany, which they did on April 6, 1917.

There were patriotic displays throughout the country. Government officials and the Red Cross launched bond sales, recycling drives, and food conservation programs. Tens of thousands of Missourians volunteered their time, and many more participated in "Wheatless Mondays and Wednesdays" to save bread for the soldiers. Women signed up to be nurses and spearheaded food conservation drives. Girl Scouts collected peach stones to be converted into charcoal for gas masks.

Missouri Germans generally supported the war once it got underway, but they faced considerable backlash at home, including harassment in the streets and discrimination at work. German theaters closed, and many German schools were forced to teach in English only. Sauerkraut became "liberty cabbage," and frankfurters became hot dogs.

Perhaps Missouri's greatest contribution to the war effort was General John J. "Black Jack" Pershing of Linn County, who got his nickname for advocating the use of black troops. Pershing became supreme commander of the American Expeditionary Force and faced the monumental task of taking an undersized, inexperienced army and a mass of draftees and turning them into a viable military force. At the beginning of the war, the army numbered 127,000 men and was ranked seventeenth in the world in size, just below Portugal. By the end of the war, Pershing commanded more than two million well-trained soldiers. As part of the trend to expunge German names in Missouri, the town of Pottsdam in Gasconade County changed its name to Pershing.

Missouri troops found themselves in some of the heaviest fighting the American Expeditionary Force encountered. The 35th Division, made up of Missouri and Kansas volunteers and including an artillery battery commanded by a young officer from Independence named Harry S. Truman, was in reserve for the AEF's first offensive at St. Mihiel in northeast France. A couple of weeks later, the 35th led the attack in the Meuse-Argonne offensive. The objective was a German rail line that supplied much of their front line. On September 26 at 5:30 a.m., with Truman's battery and other batteries firing explosive and poison gas shells, the entrenched Missouri and Kansas soldiers went over the top and into a hail of German machine-gun fire. The troops advanced seven miles in two days, a significant breakthrough in a conflict infamous for static trench warfare.

Three days later, the Americans' luck began to change. The Germans brought in six fresh divisions and launched a major counterattack, forcing the Americans to fall back with heavy losses. The 140th regiment, made up of volunteers from the National Guard, started the battle with more than three thousand men; by September 29, they had one thousand. The soldiers withdrew to a ridge and held it against fierce German attacks until they were relieved. More than seven thousand Missouri and Kansas men had been killed or wounded in a few days.

Back home, politicians roundly criticized the Meuse-Argonne offensive. Congressional hearings revealed the men had been worn out from a long march just before the battle and had not been provided with winter clothing. Truman's superior officer, General Lucien Berry, did not believe in using airplanes to direct artillery fire. Poor communications and inadequate medical facilities exacerbated the situation. The United States had learned its first hard lessons in modern warfare.

Battery C, 130th Field Artillery in September 1918, Varennes, France. Future U.S. president Harry Truman served as an artillery officer in France during World War I. COURTESY LIBERTY MEMORIAL MUSEUM.

An automatic rifle team, from Co. B, 137th Infantry in Alsace, Germany, August 1918. Trench life was cramped, unhealthy, and did not guarantee protection from artillery and infantry attacks. COURTESY LIBERTY MEMORIAL MUSEUM.

Private firing his rifle, from Co. F, 139th Infantry, at Verdun, October 1918. After four years of artillery barrages, much of the Front in World War I resembled a moonscape. Courtesy Liberty Memorial Museum.

Despite this, the United States played a major role in ending the First World War. Germany was near exhaustion from three years of bloody conflict, and despite initial setbacks, the Meuse-Argonne offensive continued, draining away more German lives until peace was declared on November 11, 1918. After stalling in its advance into France at the beginning of the war, and facing dogged resistance from the Allied Powers for three years, the prospect of fighting another large army broke Germany's will to continue.

Even the famous Missouri mule did its part. Trucks could not make it through the mud to the front lines, so soldiers had to rely on horses and mules to transport supplies. The Missouri mule soon became the troops' favorite because of its strength and ability to go without food for long periods of time. The firm of Guyton & Harrington of Lathrop, Clinton County, sold about 350,000 horses and mules to the U.S. Army and its allies during the war, earning Lathrop the title, "Mule Capital of the World."

Mule train bringing ore out of a mineshaft at Pilot Knob, Iron County, in 1919. Standing in the ore car is Herman Amelung, who owned a saloon in town but had to close it during Prohibition and return to work in the mine. COURTESY MARCINE (AMELUNG) LOHMAN.

The government honored Pershing with the title of General of the Armies, a rank shared only by George Washington. In St. Louis, Berlin Avenue (where, at number 4664, a young William S. Burroughs was dreaming up his first stories) was renamed Pershing Avenue in his honor. Pershing went on to write a Pulitzer Prize–winning memoir, while Burroughs grew up to shock the nation with experimental novels about heroin addiction and homosexuality.

A total of 156,232 Missourians served in the armed forces in World War I, 2,801 of whom died. In 1926, the University of Missouri at Columbia honored its fallen students with the completion of Memorial Union. The neo-Gothic tower rises above an arched passageway bearing the names of the 117 student soldiers who died. It is a tradition for men to tip their hats and speak in a whisper while passing through the arch, a sign of respect now all but forgotten in a careless age.

Veterans of the war founded the American Legion in 1919 in St. Louis as an organization to foster patriotism and community service among veterans. Truman helped form a chapter in Independence. The organization now numbers nearly three million.

The people of Kansas City decided to honor the soldiers by erecting the Liberty Memorial, raising $2.5 million in less than two weeks. The memorial, dominated by a 217-foot-tall tower with statues symbolizing Courage, Honor, Patriotism, and Sacrifice, opened in 1926 and is the largest World War I memorial in the United States. In 2004, Congress named it the country's National World War I Memorial and a new, state-of-the-art museum opened in 2006.

World War I did not create a flood of immigration like earlier conflicts. New laws in the 1920s established quotas on the number of people coming into the country. The quota allowed very few immigrants from Central and Southern Europe and barred people from East Asia and India altogether. Latin Americans and Western and Northern Europeans had a better chance of gaining entry.

Furthermore, Missouri had long ceased being a frontier and few Americans moved there. Southern blacks, who left states such as Mississippi and Arkansas to seek better opportunities in the factories of St. Louis and Kansas City, were the one exception. Others went to the Bootheel region of southeastern Missouri to work in cotton fields created to replace the newly drained swamps. While life was better than in the Deep South, blacks still suffered segregation and occasional lynchings. The latter was usually prompted by accusations of sexual assault on

The Liberty Memorial in Kansas City, built in 1926. In 2004, Congress declared it the country's national memorial to World War I. The National World War I Museum opened on site in 2006. Courtesy Mike McMullen.

white women. A young white girl was attacked in Columbia in 1923, and her alleged attacker, a black man, was carried away by a lynch mob. The victim's father tried to intervene, but the mob threatened to lynch him, too. Missouri soldiers returned from France to a sluggish economy. Manufacturing in the two main cities failed to expand as quickly as in other states. The timber of the Ozarks was being depleted, and most zinc mining had moved to Oklahoma and Kansas. Agriculture remained the main employer, with corn as the number one crop. Farms consolidated, as small farmers found it hard to compete and sold out to larger farmers, a process that continued throughout the twentieth century. Missouri's farm population had peaked at the turn of the century. At that time, two million people lived on 284,886 farms. By 1930, the number of people engaged in agriculture was declining, while the number working in the manufacturing and service sectors grew. As farms consolidated, farm size increased. Thanks to increased mechanization and scientific principles taught by the University of Missouri's Agricultural Extension Program, productivity increased, too. Unfortunately, crop prices fell as Europe regained its stability and reduced imports and the federal government stopped placing huge orders to feed the troops.

St. Louis specialized in several industries, including clothing, shoes, meat processing, and, until Prohibition, brewing. This diversity helped it weather the postwar slump better than some other cities. Kansas City thrived as a major regional meatpacking center and had important mills, bakeries, and other processing centers for agricultural products. It was also a major agricultural market, where buyers from across the nation came to make their orders. Other Missouri cities and towns had their own specialties and made money as retail centers for area farmers.

Kansas City grew quickly at this time, and one of the main benefactors was the Pendergast family. Jim Pendergast moved to Kansas City in 1876 and worked as a laborer. Winning big at the racetrack, he used his money to buy a hotel and saloon and from there worked his way up the political ladder as a Democrat with a combination of patronage, dirty tricks, and sheer willpower. "Big Jim" was well loved by the people in his old working-class neighborhood of the West Bottoms. He believed in returning favors, so when these people voted for him (often more than once), he improved their neighborhood and passed legislation to help workers. He spent many years as an alderman, but his influence reached far beyond his post. His political machine made sure elections

Edgar Muench and his sister Adele (later Adele Kasel) swimming with their friends in the "Big Muddy" in 1919 near Washington, Franklin County. COURTESY LESLIE GRANGER.

Inside the Amelung Saloon at Pilot Knob, Iron County, a popular hangout in the early twentieth century. Herman Amelung is tending bar. According to Amelung family tradition, there was a secret window so that the owner could see what was going on in the saloon from upstairs. COURTESY MARCINE (AMELUNG) LOHMAN.

would be won by Pendergast candidates, who in return disbursed lucrative city contracts to Pendergast and his friends.

His younger brother, Thomas, took over the machine upon Jim's death in 1911. By then the Pendergast fortune included a large number of saloons, stores, and the Ready-Mixed Concrete Company. Tom continued the practice of buying votes from the poor by offering jobs, patronage, and support for the black, immigrant, and poor white communities. His free turkey dinners at Christmas were famous for feeding thousands. His election rigging and corruption were equally famous (on Election Day the turkey dinners were replaced with free beer), but many people in Kansas City, cynical of government corruption, put their support behind Pendergast because at least he was sympathetic to their needs.

Not everyone appreciated Tom's free booze. The temperance movement had been gaining momentum for several decades, and by the twentieth century an increasing number of Missouri counties became dry. Despite protests from those who wanted to keep Missouri "wet," there were four referendums from 1910 to 1919 to ban drinking in the entire state. During the 1916 referendum, the Women's Christian Temperance Union organized a march with Sunday school children singing, "We can't vote / neither can Ma / If Missouri goes wet / shame on Pa."[4] The struggle was part of a national trend that culminated in the passage of the Eighteenth Amendment to the Constitution in 1919, which made the consumption of alcohol illegal in the entire country.

Prohibition was a serious blow to the Missouri economy. Brewing was the fifth largest industry in the state. Anheuser-Busch employed thousands. The company managed to convert its breweries to the manufacture of truck bodies and refrigerator cabinets, and still sold a rather unsuccessful alcohol-free beer, but many smaller breweries closed. The German community was especially hard hit. The Stone Hill Winery in Hermann resorted to growing mushrooms in its wine cellar, while the neighboring Hermanhof Winery converted into an apartment complex. All across the state, small business owners suffered financial setbacks when they had to turn their liquor stores and bars into other, usually less profitable, businesses.

This did not stop drinking, of course. Speakeasies flourished in this era, especially in Kansas City. Out in the countryside, people set up stills to make moonshine (in the Ozarks they called it "mountain dew")

---

4. Renner, p. 385.

Established in 1847 by German immigrants, the Stone Hill Winery in Hermann, Gasconade County, became one of the leading wineries in the state. Employees are showing off the various vintages in this photo from c. 1890. COURTESY STONE HILL WINERY.

During Prohibition, Missouri's breweries and vineyards had to take up other trades. The Stone Hill Winery in Hermann, Gasconade County, turned its wine cellar into a mushroom farm. COURTESY STONE HILL WINERY.

Prohibition bust, Kahoka, Clark County, c. 1920. While the Ozarks were home to the most famous moonshiners, they operated all over Missouri. Note the hammer in the sheriff's hand, used to ensure that this particular still would never operate again. COURTESY MIS-SOURI STATE ARCHIVES.

and made good money selling what was now a controlled substance. The prices for alcohol rose and the quality fell, but with a little effort anyone could find a drink.

Politics changed too. The Democrats became divided over Prohibition and U.S. involvement in the League of Nations, the precursor to the United Nations. City voters tended to be against Prohibition and for the League, while the reverse held true for the important rural vote. Democrats also suffered from being the dominant party during the postwar downturn and took the blame for it. The Republicans won a sweeping victory in 1920, gaining control of the state legislature, fourteen of Missouri's sixteen seats in the U.S. House of Representatives, and got Arthur Hyde, a Prohibitionist who vowed to break the Pendergast machine, elected governor. They were helped by blacks who did not like outstate Democrats' segregationist attitudes. Hyde rewarded the black community in St. Louis by hiring black police officers and placing blacks on Republican committees, but he was unable to hurt the entrenched boss of Kansas City.

Another issue Hyde pushed forward was road improvements. There were about three hundred thousand automobiles in Missouri when he took office, but almost no paved roads. Rural roads were especially bad. Drivers who ventured into the countryside could expect flat tires, jarring stops in cavernous potholes, and getting mired in mud slicks. Counties still controlled road building as they had a century before, but President Warren G. Harding had signed the Federal Highway Act in 1921, offering matching funds to state governments that centralized their building operations and linked their roads with those of neighboring states. A state highway department came into being in 1917, but it was not until Hyde's administration that the state was able to secure for it sufficient funding through a $60 million bond. The government spent well over $100 million in the 1920s on their campaign to "Lift Missouri out of the Mud." Main roads and smaller county roads got nearly equal funding and helped connect Missouri to itself and the rest of the nation. This led to an expansion of tourism and the roadside businesses that catered to it.

One of the regions that changed the most from tourism was the Ozarks. Recreational hunters and fishermen had been coming for some time, and a few health-conscious vacationers were already "taking the waters" at the region's springs, but the real influx of tourists came after the publication of Harold Bell Wright's *The Shepherd of the Hills*, a religious tale of a city man who finds peace tending sheep and souls in the backwoods. The book was a runaway bestseller in 1907, and people flocked to the Ozarks to see the place for themselves. Hotels and resorts opened up, while other tourists decided to rough it by camping or staying in "genuine" log cabins. Wright set three other books in the Ozarks, but none matched the sales of *The Shepherd of the Hills*. Its contrast of big-city corruption and weakness to backwoods honesty and strength struck a chord in an increasingly urbanized and disillusioned country.

The book was set in Taney County, where Wright resided while writing it, and included many real places and characters based on real people. Coincidentally, the Frisco Railroad had laid their White River line through Taney and Stone counties the previous year, and now the line began to serve tourists as well as locals. Visitors from smoke-clogged cities were fascinated by the life in the backwoods, where people still lived in log cabins, played old ballads on the fiddle, and hunted wild animals for food, not sport. "Hillbilly" culture became a mainstay of the entertainment world, with backwoods families doing their acts on radio and the vaudeville circuit. Visitors to Branson in the 1920s could be driven around by Pearl "Sparkie" Spurlock in her Shepherd of the Hills taxi. Sparkie, like other Ozark guides of her day, entertained visitors with local tales and backwoods humor.

With the tourists came facilities to serve them. Local booster organizations put ads in big-city newspapers urging people to visit. The Ozarks Playground Association, based in Joplin, called the Ozarks "The Land of a Million Smiles." Roads improved, especially in the 1930s, and locals set up shops and offered float trips, while those with more capital set up hotels and resorts. Some wealthy St. Louis sportsmen bought the building from the State of Maine's exhibit from the 1904 World's Fair and shipped it down to the Ozarks. The Maine Club, as it was called, lasted less than ten years and was sold to the School of the Ozarks, now known as the College of the Ozarks, a leading liberal arts institution.

A more successful venture followed when a hydroelectric dam on the White River twenty-five miles downstream from Branson created Lake Taneycomo in 1912. The lake proved to be good for fishing, and in the teens and twenties the Rockaway Beach Resort on its shores became popular because of its combination of natural beauty and modern facilities. Visitors could stroll along backwoods trails or take a motor tour, watch the sunset, or have their hair done, all from one convenient location. It

Many traditional crafts like basket making survive in the Ozarks and became alternative sources of income for local residents when tourism grew in the twentieth century.
COURTESY LELAND PAYTON, USED WITH PERMISSION.

epitomized the ideal of the American vacation, which Missouri author William Least Heat Moon summed up in his book *Blue Highways* as "getting away from it all while taking it all with you."

The increase of visitors, whom local people called "furners," began to change Ozark culture, making it more cosmopolitan and economically savvy. People wanted to experience traditional Ozark crafts and hear traditional music, but they came with preconceptions of what those were. Like other traditional cultures today, tourism affected how the local people lived. Academics began to study the culture in case it vanished. The preeminent Ozarks scholar of the time, Vance Randolph, lived for many years in the area and wrote a small library of books on Ozark culture and music. His body of work is a priceless museum of a vanishing lifestyle.

The rise of the automobile and the improvement of rural roads led to a consolidation of schools. Many farmers' children attended tiny classes in one-room schoolhouses. While integral parts of the community, they were expensive to maintain and offered only limited educational opportunities. A new school bus system brought students from outlying areas to more central locations.

During the twenties, Missouri followed national trends, with a decline in the number of farmers as people moved from the countryside and small towns to find jobs in new industries in the big cities. Kansas City experienced a construction boom as its population swelled. Springfield grew nearly 50 percent in that decade and became a major center for butter and poultry production, while St. Francis County became the world's biggest lead-producing region. St. Louis, using quality clays from the riverbed, became a leader in brick making.

Farm prices remained low compared with the wartime years, and farmers had to work together to push for better deals. The Missouri Farm Bureau Federation organized at the beginning of the decade and founded farmers' cooperatives while lobbying for increased rural development. The Missouri Farmers Association, formed in Columbia in 1914, helped create a whole cooperative infrastructure for agriculture, including everything from grain elevators to marketing associations. They even had their own oil company. Within ten years the MFA had a membership of more than forty thousand. The cooperatives were a natural extension of Missouri farm culture. Farmers had always banded together to get big jobs done, and with the changing market they unified to increase their prosperity.

Sawmill operation, Ozark County near Howards Ridge, 1930. Timber has been an important industry in the Ozarks for more than 150 years. Courtesy Missouri State Archives.

Industrial workers organized, too. The Missouri Federation of Labor had a fluctuating membership because of union-busting tactics by big companies, but their numbers stayed between fifty and sixty thousand throughout the 1920s and into the 1930s. This represented about half of all union members in the state. Unions managed to raise wages, install safety measures, and reduce hours, but they were not always successful. Many strikes failed when companies brought in workers from outside the state or intimidated labor leaders with beatings and shootings.

After being smashed in the 1920 election, the Democrats worked to regain control of the state. They got support from labor unions, who thought the Republicans were not doing enough for workers. Large numbers of blacks became attracted to the party because they were dissatisfied with the lack of Republican action against lynching and the Ku Klux Klan. The Democratic party, however, suffered from divisions over whether to support the Klan, which many outstate Democrats did, and fighting political machines, which greatly benefited Democrats in Kansas City and Jackson County but embarrassed those elsewhere.

Another political change came at the beginning of the decade with the ratification in 1920 of the Nineteenth Amendment to the Constitution, granting women the right to vote. But it would be a long time before women flexed their political muscle; traditional attitudes still prevailed and leaders such as Emily Blair, born in Joplin and one of the founders of the League of Women Voters, complained a decade later that women voted mostly the way their husbands did, and there were few women in positions of influence.

This was not for lack of trying. In 1922, four Missouri women ran for Congress. One of them, Luella St. Clair Moss, won the Democratic primary in the 8th District. St. Clair Moss had been president of the Women's Suffrage Association, later to become the League of Women Voters, and president of Christian College, now known as Columbia College. She ran a vigorous campaign against Republican incumbent Sid Roach. Newspapers across the state covered the race. The *St. Louis Post-Dispatch* quipped, "Any good housekeeper ought to be able to get rid of Roaches."[5] The *Moniteau County Herald*, while endorsing Roach, called her a "distinguished Missourian . . . well balanced, capable and sincere . . ."[6] In her campaign she visited nearly forty towns, driving a thousand miles around

---

5. *St. Louis Post-Dispatch*, August 13, 1922.
6. *Moniteau County Herald*, July 18, 1922.

central Missouri. Her driver was a young law student named John Dalton, who would be elected governor in 1960. Dalton said he learned a great deal about campaigning from watching his boss. Despite earning widespread respect, St. Clair Moss lost the election. Missouri would not have a U.S. Congresswoman until 1952, when Leonor Sullivan was elected for the first of her twelve terms in office.

Women made similar efforts to get ahead in employment and education. The number of female college graduates increased throughout the decade, and many women worked in factories, although usually at lower wages than men. More than a quarter of these working women were married. The two-income family, while more common today, is not a modern development. Rural women, of course, helped out on the farm as they always had, supporting the family but earning no income.

The 1920s saw the spread of three forms of entertainment: movies, radio, and football. With the addition of sound, movies became more popular than ever before. Even small, rural towns had a picture house, giving hardworking families a window on a world of glamor and fantasy.

Experimental radio stations had been operating for several years, but the first licensed commercial station in Missouri was WOQ in Kansas City, which began broadcasting in 1922. Within a year, a couple dozen stations sprouted up across the state, mostly run by newspapers or radio supply stores. Inexpensive crystal sets, which did not require electricity to operate, were within the means of most people. One popular early program was the "Nighthawks Frolic," on WDAF, the station for the *Kansas City Star*. Sometimes titled "The Enemy of Sleep," the show featured music every midnight except Sundays. The show often broadcast direct from the city's famous nightclubs.

Universities sponsored their own football teams. The University of Missouri Tigers was the most popular and successful. In 1926, the university opened Memorial Stadium, with a capacity of twenty-five thousand, at a time when the university had fewer than six thousand students. In 1924, local radio station WOS broadcast a football game live by stringing a telephone wire from an announcer in the stadium to Neff Hall where the equipment was set up.

On the professional level, baseball was still king. The game was segregated, so black players formed the National Negro Baseball League in Kansas City in 1920. There were two Negro League teams in Missouri, the Kansas City Monarchs and the St. Louis Giants (which became the St. Louis Stars in 1922). In 1922, the Monarchs played an exhibition series with the Kansas City Blues, a minor league white team, and beat them five games out of six. The *Kansas City Star* noted that "it isn't lack of ability that keeps the Negro ball players off the big time—it's color." The Blues redeemed themselves by winning the Little World Series the next year, but they never dared to play the Monarchs again.

Missouri baseball swept to national prominence with the St. Louis Cardinals under the creative leadership of Branch Rickey, who created the farm system to bring in talent from minor league teams. The method worked, and the Cardinals won the 1926 World Series against the Yankees. Rickey was also instrumental in developing and introducing batting helmets. The team went on to win the World Series again in 1931, 1934, 1942, and 1944. The period after World War II saw further victories. In 1942, Rickey moved to New York to manage the Brooklyn Dodgers, and five years later he broke the race barrier in the major leagues by hiring Jackie Robinson.

But the main event that brought Missouri to international attention in the 1920s was a daring nonstop, solo flight from New York to Paris in 1927. The flight, the first of its kind, was achieved by Charles Lindbergh, a member of the Missouri Air National Guard and a pilot on the St. Louis to Chicago airmail route. Most of his funding came from St. Louis citizens, and he named his plane "Spirit of St. Louis" in gratitude.

Lindbergh's feat spurred the growth of aviation in Missouri and throughout the nation. St. Louis turned Lambert Field, an old military balloon base, into the municipal airport. Lambert served only a little more than twenty-four thousand passengers that year. In 2004 it served more than 13 million. Lindbergh presided over the opening of Kansas City Municipal Airport in 1927, a Pendergast project using concrete from his Ready-Mixed Concrete Company. It was replaced by Kansas City International in 1972.

The post-war era of slow economic growth and rapid social change was completely transformed in 1929 with the onset of the Great Depression. Unlike the regular downturns that any capitalist system undergoes, the Depression was worldwide in scale and saw bank closures, a sharp rise in unemployment, and a massive slump in production that lasted a decade. Missouri was no exception. Value added by manufacturing dropped by more than half from 1929 to 1933, the Depression's worst year. Farm prices fell as well, exacerbated by a series of droughts that caused the Dust Bowl in neighboring Oklahoma. The price of corn dipped so low that in some counties farmers burned it for fuel. Farmers who could not pay their mounting debts faced foreclosure. Some switched to earlier patterns of subsistence farming so at least they could eat, and many farm boys who had optimistically moved to the big city to seek their fortune trudged back home to the only job left open to them. Urban workers struggled to survive in the cities. In St. Louis many ended up in the "Hooverville," a shantytown next to the Mississippi, named like hundreds of similar slums across the country after the president. Most state employees managed to keep their jobs but had to deal with pay cuts and lack of funding for projects. State and private charities provided some relief, but there was never enough to go around.

In Sedalia, twenty bankers held a press conference on October 21, 1931, to reassure the public that all was well, but less than three weeks later the Citizens National Bank, considered one of the most respectable and stable banks in central Missouri, had to close. It turned out to be buried in debt. The same day, the Sedalia Clearing House Association announced that members could only withdraw twenty-five dollars per day. Long lines of people snaked through the streets, hoping to salvage as much of their savings as they could before this bank, too, went under. Other banks also limited withdrawals, as banks did all over the country. Many simply closed. Depositors were lucky if they recovered even a fraction of their accounts.

Henry Thompson, chronicler of mining history in southeast Missouri, wrote vividly of the struggle he and his fellow workers at the St. Joseph Lead Company (which owned mines across the state) experienced. At first all was well; the demand for lead remained high and everyone kept their jobs, but on March 31, 1931, employee wages were cut by 20 percent. Six months later, each worker only worked three weeks out of five so that the company would not have to lay anyone off. In April of 1932, operations were cut by half, and the workers had to take another 10-percent pay cut. In 1933, neighboring plants began to close, and "St. Joe" reduced output to 25 percent. The company allowed workers to plant gardens on company land to feed their families, and local stores extended credit, with wholesalers extending credit to the stores. The hope was that the Depression would soon pass and the debts would be repaid, but as time wore on, many businesses could no longer afford to extend credit and had to close.

Luckily, 1933 was the lowest point for the region. The company started operating one-third of the time, then half, and by summer restored the 10-percent pay cut. Between 1934 and 1939, the situation fluctuated, with no one knowing how much they would work the following week and how much they would get paid. Thompson notes that despite this, the miners felt relieved because at least they had some work, unlike friends and family in St. Louis.

In Kansas City, Pendergast continued fuelling the construction boom that employed thousands and, conveniently, used concrete from his own company, in his typical style of doing well while doing good. Roads and public buildings were repaired or expanded, while new ones sprang up. Another bright spot was the choice by Transcontinental Air Transport (later TWA) to base its operations in Kansas City and use it as the hub for airmail. In many ways, the Depression was the golden era for Kansas City. It fared better than many other cities and underwent a cultural renaissance. Pendergast saw the financial attractions of jazz and got his friends on the police force to turn the other way as speakeasies, jazz clubs, and casinos raked in money for the local economy.

An unexpected benefit for Kansas City came when William Rockhill Nelson, publisher of the *Kansas City Star*, bequeathed his entire estate for the establishment of an art museum. The will did not include funding for a building, however, as Nelson assumed the city would build one. It was not forthcoming, and the museum seemed to be doomed until a reclusive schoolteacher named Mary Atkins left $300,000 for the project in her will. Various other donations came in, and construction began in 1930. The Depression hit the art market especially hard, and art dealers were desperate to sell at almost any price. Since the Nelson-Atkins Museum of Art was one of the only museums with the money to buy at the time, it brought together an impressive collection of European, American, and Asian art. The Asian collection is especially fine and is considered one of the best in the nation.

For those who found the speakeasies of Kansas City too wild, there was always radio and the movies. By 1930, more than a third of Missouri homes had a radio, and movies were more popular than ever. Theatergoers could collect ticket stubs to redeem for dishes and other household items while enjoying a few hours in a warm, dry theater, forgetting their troubles. Movies at the time started with a cartoon, a serial, and a newsreel, and often a second "B" movie after the main feature, making for an entire afternoon's entertainment.

In the 1928 election a Republican, Henry Caulfield, became governor. Both governor and legislature were cautious on spending, although they expanded the roads program to create jobs. Federal funds helped with this, as well as with relief for the poorest in the state and an old-age pension plan.

Change at the national level came in 1932, when Franklin Delano Roosevelt, a Democrat, was elected president on the promise of a "New Deal." Roosevelt advocated increased government regulation of the economy as the only way to fix capitalism's inherent instability. He declared a "banking holiday" for four days so he could push through the Emergency Banking Act, which offered federal assistance for troubled financial institutions. This was a major relief to many Americans, but it came too late for those who had already lost their savings to failed banks. He also created the Federal Deposit Insurance Corporation (FDIC) to insure accounts. Missourians who had been hoarding their cash under mattresses and in tin cans returned it to their banks, bringing a much-needed influx of money into the system.

Roosevelt also established a host of organizations to employ people in building projects. Many Missourians found work with the Civilian Conservation Corps, which created work camps for young men throughout the state, providing jobs by day and education by night. In the Ozarks they planted trees and built cabins that were then rented out to tourists. The Civil Works Administration employed more than a hundred thousand Missourians, building roads and public facilities. Other agencies, especially the Army Corps of Engineers, worked to control flooding and improve navigation on the state's major rivers.

While everyday people were the main beneficiaries of the work programs, even famous painters got extra work. Thomas Hart Benton, great-nephew of the influential senator, traveled the country painting murals for various public buildings. His energetic and colorful style, which did not flinch from portraying gangsters and Klansmen alongside more respectable citizens, made him famous and controversial, even putting him on the cover of *Time* magazine, a first for an American artist. In 1937, he created his masterpiece, a mural for the capitol building in Jefferson City. This vibrant mural, called *A Social History of Missouri*, contains hundreds of figures, from hardworking frontiersmen to leading politicians. His depictions of blacks being lynched, Tom Pendergast having a drink with two trustees of the Nelson-Atkins Museum of Art, and various other embarrassing scenes from Missouri history led to calls for its removal, but popular acclaim kept it in place.

Another big employer was Bagnell Dam, a private hydroelectric dam on the Osage River. Construction began just a few months before the Wall Street crash, but the Union Electric Light and Power Company continued to fund the project, designed to bring more power to urban areas and the region's mining industry. More than twenty thousand men worked on the dam, and when it was completed in 1931, it filled up several valleys and created the Lake of the Ozarks. The meandering lake has more than 1,300 miles of shoreline. Fishing spots and locally run resorts soon sprang up along the shore, but it was not until after the interruptions of the Depression and World War II were over that it became a major tourist attraction.

The Depression hit blacks especially hard. They were usually the first to be fired and the last to be hired. There was discrimination in the handing out of federal aid, and the labor unions, which got most of the construction contracts, generally did not accept blacks as members. In the Bootheel, federal assistance actually hurt sharecroppers. Landowners turned them into day laborers so they would not have to share government payments and fired them when the government asked them to cut production to boost prices. Owen Whitfield, a black Baptist preacher and sharecropper, led a large protest of eleven thousand sharecroppers camping out beside the highway to show their plight. The action gained national attention and led to more government aid to the region.

Missouri's economy received a shot in the arm in 1933, with the Twenty-first Amendment repealing Prohibition. The breweries of St. Louis and the wineries of the Missouri River valley jumped back into the market, regaining sales almost immediately. Within a year it was as if there had never been Prohibition. Bootleggers went out of business or went legit, and speakeasies put out signs and no longer required passwords to get through the door. The fears of the Prohibitionists were not realized. There was no surge in crime, except for some understandable public drunkenness the first few nights, and in fact crime went down as something so many people were already doing suddenly became legal again.

Through his connections in Washington, Pendergast brought many federal projects into Kansas City. His efforts sheltered the city from the worst of Depression, and voters tended to ignore the fact that he rigged elections and made sure patronage and city contracts only went to him and his friends. In 1934, Pendergast tried to extend his reach by getting Harry S. Truman, an administrator at the Jackson County Court and Democratic Party leader, elected to the Senate. A World War I hero and former farmer, Truman was a popular figure who managed to distance himself from Pendergast and maintain a reputation for honesty and impartiality.

The governor from 1937 to 1941 was another Pendergast man with wide appeal, Lloyd Stark. He advocated big government to see the state through its troubled times and got the Democrat-dominated legislature to raise the sales tax to fund several projects, including aid to the aged, unemployed, and children. He established the state Conservation Commission to manage and improve wilderness and wildlife. Together with the Civilian Conservation Corps, it employed tens of thousands of Missourians to create state parks and plant 11 million trees. They also built forty-seven thousand check dams, an incredible number, to conserve soil.

The Democrats were at the height of their power, but it was not to last. A bipartisan reform movement led by federal district attorney Maurice Milligan challenged the Pendergast machine. It was not the first time reformers tried to bring down the boss, but Milligan had the FBI and the attorney general on his side. A federal investigation found massive fraud in the 1936 elections, and seventy-eight members of the machine went to jail. Truman defended the machine in the Senate, saying the investigation was biased against Democrats, but it did little good. Governor Stark turned against his former patron and put non-machine men on the Kansas City election board. Milligan had more than sixty thousand invalid names struck from the registration lists. Despite losing his ghost and repeat voters, Pendergast's machine won in the 1938 municipal elections on the strengths of its past accomplishments. Milligan realized the machine could be stopped only by getting rid of its operator.

Stark clamped down on gambling, a major source of power for Pendergast and his favorite pastime, and gained control of the Kansas City police force. He and Milligan also got the Treasury Department to investigate Pendergast's personal finances. In 1939, Pendergast was convicted of income tax evasion, given fifteen months in prison, and was forever banned from engaging in politics.

The machine crumbled, and with it went a major source of Democratic power. Pendergast had been an important party organizer, not just in Jackson County but statewide as well. Free from the scandals rocking their rivals, the Republicans won the governorship and the St. Louis mayor's office in the 1940 elections. Truman, faced with claims that he was just as corrupt as Pendergast, barely held onto his seat.

Regular Missourians were heartened by a slowly improving economy. The Depression bottomed out in 1933, and with the implementation of New Deal policies, the country was slowly on the mend. The state had not regained 1929 levels of production, but unemployment fell and the banks remained stable. But rural areas still languished in primitive conditions. By 1940, most farms were still on dirt roads and lacked electricity and internal plumbing.

While things looked better for the state and the nation, Missourians feared being pulled into another global problem. They watched with growing worry as Japan, Germany, and Italy became increasingly belligerent. Japan invaded China, and Italy attacked Ethiopia. In Spain, civil war erupted as the fascist general Francisco Franco overthrew the elected socialist government with German and Italian help. In 1938, Hitler absorbed Austria and the Sudetenland region of Czechoslovakia into the Third Reich.

As in the previous war, Missourians were generally isolationist. The country, they said, had enough troubles. The federal government passed a series of Neutrality Acts banning arms shipments to nations at war, but by 1939 this was becoming an unpopular position as people objected to Hitler's politics. The Jewish community urged the government to put a stop to Hitler's anti-Semitic pogroms, which saw Jews forced into ghettos and, eventually, concentration camps. Gypsies, blacks, socialists, born-again Christians, and anyone else who did not swear full loyalty to the Third Reich, or fit the Nazi ideal of Aryan racial "purity," found themselves in camps as well. Truman warned that the United States would be dragged into a world war sooner or later, and it was better to be prepared. After Hitler invaded Czechoslovakia and Poland in 1939, the bulk of the nation shifted to support prepared (and partial) neutrality. The United States began to sell arms to Great Britain and its allies. Many Missourians hoped they could avoid any further entanglement in the world's troubles, but they would soon be disappointed.

CHAPTER 8

INTO THE MODERN ERA

(1941–2006)

When the Japanese launched a surprise attack on Pearl Harbor on December 7, 1941, they struck close to home; Second Lieutenant George Whiteman, a fighter pilot from Sedalia, was the first Missourian to die in the war when his plane was hit while he was trying to take off.

The next day the *Sedalia Democrat* ran the following editorial:

> Momentary paralysis from the first stunning blow of the treacherous Japanese onslaught has passed. The nerve-strain of dread over what appeared to be an unavoidable and inevitable conflict has ceased. There is a reaction of relief. The die is cast; a job's to be done.
>
> Repugnant, bloody, filthy war is at the door of a nation that desires peace at home and peace abroad. It is a far cry from the tranquil rolling prairies of mid-western Missouri to the mid-Pacific Island of Oahu, yet Sedalia has suffered its initial shock of sacrifice at the very first blazing of guns and bombs in the death of Lieut. George Whiteman.
>
> Tragedy perpetrated by treachery quickly brings unity out of discord. And so today, Central Missourians, poignantly conscious of a personal loss, join with their fellow countrymen in condemnation of a world nurtured on deceit and brutality.
>
> From this moment the states of America are united in support of their commander-in-chief, President Franklin D. Roosevelt. There shall be a moratorium on political bickering, labor strife, personal and group selfishness and greed.
>
> A job's to be done; let's go to it.

Doing that job would be the biggest impetus for change in Missouri's modern history. Hundreds of thousands of young men enlisted.

Work in war materials factories attracted both men and women to cities, and the massive federal spending on the war effort lifted the country out of the Depression.

Truman became chairman of a special committee to oversee that the war effort be conducted efficiently and cost-effectively. He helped get camps into Missouri, including Jefferson Barracks near St. Louis, Fort Leonard Wood in Pulaski County, and Camp Crowder at Neosho. The government also gave $4.2 billion in defense contracts to businesses in Missouri. After the fighting started, Truman's efforts were helped by Hannibal native Donald Nelson, who directed the War Production Board.

But life was not easy. The government strictly rationed gasoline, heating oil, sugar, meat, and many other products to save as much as possible for the war effort. Many women had to adjust to working outside the home when their husbands went off to fight. While there had always been women workers, they were mostly confined to light industry and services. Now they worked in iron foundries and assembly lines.

The federal government encouraged farmers to increase production of livestock and food crops. It also tried to modernize rural areas through the Rural Electrification Administration, raising the amount of farms on the grid from 17.7 percent in 1940 to 31.5 percent by 1945. This was tied with an increase in the size and technical sophistication of farms. High wartime prices meant good times for farmers, just as they had during World War I.

Cities did well, too. St. Louis made a wide variety of war materiel, especially ammunition, bombs, and airline parts. McDonnell Aircraft Corporation, which had just arrived in St. Louis in 1939, won major contracts and soon employed thousands. By 1962, it was the largest private employer in the state and became famous for making the *Mercury* and *Gemini* space capsules. It was later known as the McDonnell-Douglas Aircraft Corporation, but it merged with the Boeing Corporation in 1997.

Emerson Electric Company of St. Louis, which manufactured electric fans and motors, saw its fortunes turn around because of the innovative direction of Stuart Symington, who took over the nearly bankrupt company in 1938 and saved it by fixing longstanding disputes between labor and management. The War Department sent him to England in 1941 to study the construction of movable gun turrets for aircraft. Emerson Electric was awarded the largest contract in the United States for the manufacture of the turrets, and Symington's fortune and reputation were firmly established. Anheuser-Busch's sales jumped, too, showing that

Missourians still had time to relax. Kansas City produced bombers, bullets, and other products.

Most government contracts went to the two big cities, but small towns received some, too. Waynesville, in Pulaski County, benefited from the establishment of Fort Leonard Wood. The influx of thousands of soldiers and millions of dollars changed the town forever. In his memoirs of growing up in Cassville, Barry County, during the war, Howard Ray Rowland remembers that the Ozark Theatre, a popular hangout for him and his friends, offered free admission to anyone who presented fifty pounds of recycled paper to the box office.

The war industry accelerated the move from small towns to big cities and regional centers as well as the shift from agriculture to manufacturing and service industries. St. Louis and Kansas City expanded their suburbs as people bought houses with their new wealth; some factories, for lack of space in the city center, located themselves at the edges. Suburbs were not a new thing to Missouri. At the beginning of the century, residents in Kirkwood could commute to St. Louis on the train, but the rise of the automobile helped fuel the expansion. When gas rationing ended at the close of the war, the suburbs grew even more quickly.

The war also increased opportunities for black Missourians. The government offered jobs, and community activism opened up some factories. Fighting against Nazi Germany, with its racist ideology, made some whites rethink their ideas. St. Louis University integrated in 1944 as a result of a change of thinking within the Catholic community. George Washington Carver's birthplace became a national park.

As with World War I, Missourians rose to important posts. General Omar Bradley of Clark, Randolph County, was an important commander during campaigns in North Africa, France, and Germany and helped shape the overall strategy that won the war. The town of Lamar, in Burton County, produced three admirals: Thomas Combs, Charles Lockwood, and Freeland Daubin.

Missourians fought in all theaters of the war, serving on ships in the great naval battles of the Pacific, making landings at Iwo Jima and Normandy, and fighting at Anzio and the Battle of the Bulge. They found that war was indeed "repugnant, bloody, and filthy." About 450,000 Missourians went off to fight, and more than 8,000 did not come back.

After what the war put them through, Missourians felt vindicated when the formal Japanese surrender took place on the battleship USS

The old Blue Springs School in Jackson County in the 1940s. Mrs. Hazel Montgomery, seen here, was the last teacher at this school. COURTESY BLUE SPRINGS HISTORICAL SOCIETY ARCHIVES.

The old Blue Springs School in Jackson County in the 1940s. Note the war poster on the blackboard and the antiquated heater. COURTESY BLUE SPRINGS HISTORICAL SOCIETY ARCHIVES.

The Japanese surrender on the USS Missouri, *on September 2, 1945, ending the Second World War.* COURTESY OF THE UNITED STATES ARMY.

Missouri on September 2, 1945. The ship saw action in the Pacific and bombarded the islands of Iwo Jima and Okinawa, helping soften up Japanese defenses before the soldiers landed. The USS *Missouri* was the last battleship to be produced by the United States; it served in the Korean and Persian Gulf Wars before becoming part of the memorial museum at Pearl Harbor.

While Missourians were captivated with international affairs during World War II, they were still concerned with politics back home. They considered the state constitution of 1875 to be out of date, and in 1942 voted to hold a constitutional convention. The new constitution, adopted in 1945, allowed women to sit on juries, guaranteed the right of non-government employees to unionize, extended free speech protection to radio, and promoted public libraries and state parks. It also streamlined government by consolidating nearly ninety agencies into only five executive departments (Revenue, Education, Highways, Conservation, and Agriculture), although the legislature added more (Public Health and Welfare, Business and Administration, Corrections, and Labor and Industrial Relations) the following year.

The governor got the extra power of hiring and firing the revenue and budget directors and kept his line-item veto in most cases. But the governor was still limited in his influence, and much of the decision making remained in the hands of the "little governors"—the lieutenant governor, secretary of state, attorney general, treasurer, and auditor. All of these important posts are elected and often operate quite independently of the governor's office. One "little governor" post, the superintendent of schools, was done away with in the 1945 constitution and replaced with a board appointed by the governor. The state supreme court gained the additional power to establish rules of practice and procedure for the lower courts and a wider ability to review decisions made by courts of appeals.

In all, it was a detailed but fairly conservative constitution that improved, but did not radically change, the one it replaced. It did take some steps to emphasize a more progressive and inclusive social policy. The delegates were reaffirming Missouri's democratic freedoms in the face of fascist enemies overseas.

The following year, British Prime Minister Winston Churchill gave a lecture at Westminster College in Fulton titled "The Sinews of Peace." In it he coined one of the enduring terms of twentieth century history when he said, "from Stettin in the Baltic to Trieste in the Adriatic an iron curtain has descended across the Continent." He meant, of course, the Soviet Union and her satellite states. The struggle against Soviet authoritarianism would embroil the United States and her allies for the rest of the century. Truman's call for containment of Communism became the cornerstone of U.S. foreign policy for the next forty years.

While fear of a nuclear war affected many Americans in all parts of the country, they were buoyed up by a great increase in personal wealth. The end of the war led to an unprecedented expansion of the national economy. The old European powers, such as France and Great Britain, were exhausted from the war and busy rebuilding their countries. The Soviet Union was now a superpower, but the Nazi invasion had killed 25 million of its people and destroyed several major cities, severely retarding its development. Japan was a defeated and occupied country. Into this power vacuum stepped the United States. The New Deal and the war effort had pulled the country out of the Depression and the United States, already a major exporter, took over an even greater share of the international market.

The middle class grew at a rapid pace. More and more families found they could own a house in the suburbs and fill it with consumer items such as washing machines and televisions. This latter invention created major social changes. There had been a few experimental TV stations before the war. Starting in 1932, W9XAL in Kansas City made daily broadcasts for nearly two years, despite there only being about fifty TVs in the entire city. The new medium did not catch on immediately, as Rowland's Cassville memoir points out. "In February of 1939 a new invention called television is demonstrated at a school assembly. It is an interesting novelty but seems to have no practical value."[1]

Television all but disappeared during the war, but in 1947, KSD-TV Channel 5 in St. Louis began broadcasting sports, a dance show, and news. In good weather, their signal carried 125 miles, bringing in viewers in Illinois and central Missouri. By the mid 1950s, there were more than a dozen stations in Missouri and half of all families owned a set. When KOMU-TV Channel 8 began operations in Columbia in 1953, the *Columbia Missourian* issued a set of instructions to "save the viewer's eyes."

> Don't sit too close to the screen.
> Don't view at an angle.
> Don't stare continuously.
> Don't think you're at the movies.
> Don't permit dark surroundings.
> Don't let your set get out of adjustment.[2]

There is no record of how much early TV watchers followed these directions, but they certainly took to the new medium, and soon it became more popular than radio or the movies. Missourians, like other Americans, found themselves spending more time at home in order to catch their favorite shows. In the days before syndication, much of the programming was produced at the station, and the hosts became local celebrities. One favorite type of program that started in the 1950s was

---

1. Rowland, p. 23.
2. *Columbia Missourian*, December 21, 1953.

the late-night Creature Feature, where hosts dressed as witches or mad scientists would present science fiction and horror movies. The quality of the films was often atrocious, but in the days before gratuitous gore, they were scary enough. Kansas City's KMBC Channel 9 featured "Gregory Grave," played by Harvey Brunswick, whose darkened eyes and disheveled hair made him look like a zombie as he introduced the *Shock Theater* every Saturday night with the lines, "Ghoul evening, fright fans!" Thomas Winegar was a young boy at the time and was captivated by the show.

> While my Mom and Dad watched the news, which by the way lasted only 15 minutes in those days, I would be fever-ishly at work gathering all of the cushions and pillows in the living room in order to build a fortress so that my flanks and back side would be protected from a mad monster attack. After the bastion had been hastily assembled, I would then stock my anti-monster creation with pop, chips and any other sup-plies that I may need to defeat the coming onslaught from the underworld. My parents would then depart the living room for bed with some clever remark about not scaring myself too much. They totally missed the point of the exercise. I wanted to be completely horrified by the evening's end.[3]

The war years saw the political ascension of Missouri's most famous politician, Harry Truman, who had become nationally prominent in his capacity as the chairman of the Committee to Investigate National Defense Programs. President Roosevelt picked him as his vice presidential candidate in the 1944 elections, which the pair easily won. When Roos-evelt died in 1945, Truman became the first president from Missouri.

Truman's administration continued the New Deal policies of his predecessor and the Pendergast tradition of listening to the concerns of the black community, desegregating the armed forces shortly after the war. He won a narrow victory for reelection in 1948. His two terms in office were among the most eventful of those of any president. He saw the defeat of the Axis powers, the start of the Cold War, the Mar-shall Plan to help Western Europe rebuild, the founding of the United Nations and NATO, and the start of the Korean War. He was a strong

---

3. Winegar, pp. 59–60.

advocate for the containment of Soviet authoritarianism and forging bonds with democratic nations.

Back in Truman's home state, the Democrats had trouble keeping in power. They lost both houses of the General Assembly in the 1946 elections but regained ground two years later with the help of Truman's presidential campaign. Truman's executive orders banning discrimination in federal jobs and the military helped bring in the black vote, while farmers voted Democratic after being disappointed with lack of action for their concerns from the Republican-dominated Congress. The Democrats took over the legislature and virtually all other offices.

This ushered in a period of Democratic rule in Missouri lasting twenty years. The party controlled every statewide office. The 1952 state elections resulted in the first Republican-dominated House in the General Assembly since 1940, but they did not gain the Senate and lost the House again in 1954. The House and Senate would remain in Democratic hands for the rest of the twentieth century. The Democrats also held most of the state's seats in the U.S. Congress.

One of the most influential senators from Missouri was Stuart Symington, who served from 1952 to 1976. He had achieved notoriety by becoming the first secretary of the Air Force in 1947. He resigned from that post in 1950, because he felt the Air Force was not getting a proper share of funding. Symington strongly felt that air power would be the primary factor in any modern war, an idea that has since proven to be true but was less obvious at the time. During his tenure in the Senate he served on the Foreign Relations and Armed Services committees and helped shape U.S. policy during the Cold War. He also spoke out against the Vietnam War and consistently voted for bills benefiting labor and civil rights.

Democratic dominance did not lead to the process for change that it could have. Missouri Democrats did not use their secure position to promote a fundamentally different agenda. Most politicians of both parties were middle of the road economically and conservative socially, so there was little call for serious change from within the government. Lobbyists, however, played an increasing role throughout the second half of the twentieth century and into the twenty-first. In 1967, the first year a count was made, there were fewer than three hundred lobbyists in Jefferson City. By 2005, there were more than two thousand. They came from all sorts of groups, not the least of which were state agencies such as the University of Missouri, which saw major expansion in 1963 when it took over the previously private University of Kansas City and opened a branch in St. Louis. The next year, university administrators made the mining school at Rolla into a full campus. Missouri now had a statewide public university system.

One of the great social movements of the postwar years was for civil rights. During the war, black soldiers had been inspired by the "Double V" movement, standing for "victory abroad and victory at home," meaning that although they had to fight for freedom in a segregated army, they would not give up the struggle for equality. Back home, civil rights groups protested the fact that arms factories often hired blacks only for menial jobs. In 1943, two hundred citizens called for the hiring of black telephone operators at Southwestern Bell by going to the St. Louis office and paying their bills with pennies. Inundated with coins, the company got the message and opened an office in a black neighborhood with black employees. Although this was not desegregation, it was at least employment. During the war, black leaders were divided over how much to protest at a time of national emergency, but after the war they had no such qualms and launched a major drive for equality. The first major victory came with the 1954 Supreme Court decision of *Brown v. the Board of Education of Topeka*, which ruled that segregated schools violated the Constitution.

The ruling stated that schools must integrate "with all deliberate speed," a phrase open to interpretation. Missouri, like many other states, proceeded cautiously. Conservative areas such as the Bootheel and smaller regional centers stayed segregated well into the 1960s, but other outstate districts were among the first to integrate, as indeed a few already had. They could save money by closing the small black schools and bussing the children to white schools. In St. Louis, the Catholic community had started desegregation in their schools seven years before the Supreme Court ruling. After 1954, secular schools in the city quickly followed suit. This did not solve the problem, however. In St. Louis and Kansas City, as with many large cities across the nation, white families moved out of mixed neighborhoods and into the growing suburbs so that their children would not be in a mixed classroom. "White flight" became a major factor in the rise of suburbs and the abandonment of city centers. Government money followed and inner cities languished, a problem that has been only recently, and incompletely, addressed.

A small but active number of blacks got elected to the General Assembly and became instrumental in passing legislation protecting civil rights in employment, business, and housing. In 1968, William

Clay became the first black Missourian elected to the U.S. Congress. He stayed in the House of Representatives for thirty-two years and helped organize the Congressional Black Caucus. His son, William Lacy Clay Jr. took over his seat in 2000.

The experience of women in Missouri politics paralleled that of blacks. They, too, were mostly Democrats, and while their numbers were small, they were visible and vocal. In 1952, Leonor K. Sullivan became the first Missouri woman elected to the U.S. House of Representatives, holding that seat until she retired in 1976. Among the measures she fought for were the Consumer Credit Protection Act, which gave borrowers more information about interest rates on loans, and the creation of the Food Stamp plan.

White flight was only one reason for the growth of the suburbs. Car ownership skyrocketed after the war as gas, oil, and tire rationing ended and the economy boomed. People who once walked or took the streetcar now drove to work. The Federal Housing Administration and the Veterans Administration helped out with loans. Sadly, when blacks tried to buy homes in these new developments, they were usually told there were none available.

The rise in auto tourism that started in the 1920s gained momentum after the war. All regions benefited from this, but the ever-popular Ozarks perhaps most of all. More and more tourist facilities grew up along the shores of the region's various lakes. At Marvel Cave, which had been open for visitors since 1894, developers restored some old cabins, built new "old" buildings, and opened up Silver Dollar City in 1960. It

Missouri is home to hundreds of caves. They provided shelter to prehistoric Missourians and in historic times were used as everything from gunpowder mills to tourist attractions. Marvel Cave in Taney County became popular for square dances. COPYRIGHT SILVER DOLLAR CITY, USED WITH PERMISSION.

soon expanded into a full-scale replica of a frontier town, complete with costumed townspeople and traditional crafts. The site became extremely popular and is a major tourist draw to this day. The expansion of tourism in the Ozarks made some worry about the environmental impact on the region. In the 1960s, environmentalists teamed up with local landowners to keep the Army Corps of Engineers from putting a dam on the Meramec River. The long fight ended in 1978, when the issue was put on a nonbinding referendum and 64 percent of the voters rejected the dam. Although the vote was not legally binding, it was enough to make the federal government eventually stop the project. Another environmental victory came in 1964, when Congress voted to protect 134 miles of the Current and Jacks Fork rivers as Ozark National Scenic Riverways, protecting about eighty thousand acres on both banks of the rivers as a natural preserve.

On the political level, the 1950s and early 1960s saw an expansion of state government funded by higher taxes. Missouri politicians tended to resist federal programs offering matching funds. James Blair, Democratic governor from 1956 to 1960, typified this attitude. He once told a congressional subcommittee that while most federal programs were worthwhile, "it is simply naïve to expect state governments, or local governments, to maintain autonomy while casting more and more dependence for financing upon a higher level of government."[4] This attitude did not stop Blair and other governors from taking advantage of some federal funds, but they did not use them as much as many other states.

In 1961, St. Louis watched with interest as construction began on a giant steel arch, symbolizing the "Gateway to the West." The Gateway Arch had originally been proposed in the Depression as a make-work project but never got underway. When it was finished in 1968, it stood 630 feet high, a powerful symbol of Missouri's heritage and a huge tourist draw.

Another attraction was Busch Stadium, the new home for the Cardinals that opened in 1966. The team celebrated by winning the World Series championship the following year, one of four post-war wins for the Cardinals, including victories in 1946, 1964, 1967, and 1982. The city's other major league team, the American League St. Louis Browns, moved to Baltimore in 1953 and became the Orioles. In 1992, St. Louis acquired the Los Angeles Rams, a football team that went on to win the

---

4. Larson, p. 101.

ABOVE: *The Gateway Arch is nearly complete in this 1965 photo. Made up of 142 triangular steel sections, it had to be held up by a horizontal truss until it was finished. Special elevators fitted with cranes brought sections to the top.* COURTESY JEFFERSON NATIONAL EXPANSION MEMORIAL/NATIONAL PARK SERVICE.

BELOW: *On October 28, 1965, the last section of the Gateway Arch was put into place. Firefighters had to hose down one of the legs because it caught more morning sunlight than the other one and became slightly warped, making it a few inches lower. Once the legs were at an even height, the completion ceremony could take place.* COURTESY JEFFERSON NATIONAL EXPANSION MEMORIAL/NATIONAL PARK SERVICE.

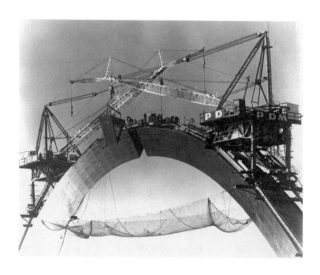

Super Bowl in 1999. On the other end of the state, the Kansas City Royals played its first game in 1969 and defeated the Cardinals in the World Series in 1985, their first series win.

A major shakeup of the General Assembly occurred after the U.S. Supreme Court ruled in 1962 that states must ensure that representatives be apportioned in relation to actual population. Two years later, the federal government determined that Missouri's districting was in violation of the ruling. Before this, each Missouri county got at least one seat in the House, meaning that the state's many small counties actually dominated the General Assembly. Because of the Supreme Court ruling, the state constitution was amended in 1966 to create 163 voting districts of roughly equal population. This swung the balance of power toward the urban vote, incidentally giving black voters in major cities extra clout.

The 1964 election saw the Democrats with a comfortable majority in both houses of the General Assembly and their candidate, Warren Hearnes, elected governor. It would not all be business as usual, however. The country's increasing military involvement in Vietnam was beginning to show the fault lines in American society. The killing by the National Guard of four antiwar protestors at Kent State University sparked protests across the nation. When more than five thousand students gathered at the University of Missouri at Columbia, Hearnes criticized the antiwar protestors as unpatriotic. When a few students at a University of Missouri–Kansas City commencement ceremony flashed the peace sign, the school threatened to withhold their diplomas, causing the American Association of University Professors to blacklist the University of Missouri system for several years.

Race relations also deteriorated as black Missourians questioned why they were being disproportionately sent off to yet another war while still facing discrimination at home. Black and white activists pressed for full integration by ignoring "whites only" and "colored" signs at lunch counters and retail outlets. This struggle had been going on for many years, but it gained added momentum in the politically active atmosphere of the 1960s.

Matters came to a head on April 9, 1968, the day slain civil rights leader Martin Luther King Jr. was to be buried. The Kansas City school board decided to hold classes that day, but black students in three inner city schools staged a walkout. Soon the students formed into a protest march and headed for City Hall as community leaders and other black residents joined them. By the time they made it to City Hall, they numbered more than a thousand and came face to face with a force of police in riot gear. The marchers, who until this time had been peaceful, began to get angry and shout at the officers. Others left to attend a dance at the Holy Name Catholic Church.

The tense situation disintegrated when a teargas canister went off. The police claimed it was thrown by the crowd but could not explain how they had been able to get a hold of it. The protestors began to pelt the police with rocks and bottles and the police pushed them back by spraying teargas. Soon the city had a full-scale riot on its hands. Police chased the rioters down the streets as they looted and destroyed property. When the police discovered a large congregation of black teenagers dancing at the Holy Name Catholic Church, they assumed they had found a group of rioters and gassed them, too.

What had started as a peaceful display of mourning degenerated into mass violence lasting four days. Rioters burned and looted white-owned businesses while police and National Guard units struggled to keep order. By the time it was over, millions of dollars of property had been destroyed, hundreds of people arrested, and six people, all black, lay dead.

Governor Hearnes appeared on the scene to show himself as a "law and order" candidate. It was an election year, and voters had approved a bill abolishing the one-term limit for governors. Despite being booed by black delegates at the Democratic convention, he won easily and became Missouri's first two-term governor.

The next governor, elected in 1972, was Christopher "Kit" Bond, the first Republican to hold that office since 1945. The GOP got more candidates elected to the position thereafter, thanks in great part to Bond's popularity and charisma. Bond, only thirty-three when he took office, is the youngest governor in Missouri history. His main achievement was getting the General Assembly to pass the Omnibus State Reorganization Act of 1974. The state government had grown steadily since the constitution of 1945, and this act reorganized the state's many departments into thirteen larger ones and an Office of Administration, reducing cost and bureaucracy.

In the 1976 election, voters approved a one-eighth of a cent sales tax to fund the Missouri Department of Conservation. Taking their case directly to the people was an unusual step for the department. It wanted more dependable funding than what the often unsympathetic state legislature

The governor's mansion, built in a French-Italian style and completed in 1871.
COURTESY MISSOURI STATE HISTORIC PRESERVATION OFFICE.

provided. One the main advocates for getting the referendum on the ballot was Jim Keefe, head of the department's information section. Over a long career he published numerous articles and books, made half a dozen films, and turned the *Missouri Conservationist* into a major statewide magazine. His wife Doris "Dink" Keefe organized the campaign as a full-time volunteer. The tax now brings in about $80 million annually to help preserve Missouri's rich natural spaces. For their efforts both Jim and Dink Keefe were inducted into the Missouri Conservation Hall of Fame.

Bond lost the 1976 governor's race to the colorful Democrat Joseph Teasdale, who earned the nickname "Walking Joe" for his cross-state hike in a previous campaign. Teasdale knew just how to get media attention and understood the growing power of television. He launched a negative ad campaign that, while all too familiar to today's voters, was considered shocking at the time. Teasdale had less success manipulating the media once he was in office. He was criticized as a showman and created a scandal when he used the Highway Patrol to deliver his meals. His "meals on wheels," as *the Kansas City Star* called them, was not the last of his problems. He also drew fire for raising the state budget from $2.6 billion to nearly $4 billion in just four years, although to be fair this was not only because of his increased spending but also the runaway inflation of that decade. In response, he supported the Hancock Amendment to the state constitution, named after anti-tax activist Melton Hancock. The amendment required any increase in taxes or fees to be approved by popular vote, and it passed a referendum in 1980.

Teasdale's troubled tenure led to Bond retaking the governor's mansion in the 1980 election. He responded to voter opposition to big government by cutting spending and firing 4,800 state employees. Bond said it was necessary to avert a financial crisis, although Teasdale and his supporters said there was no crisis. Bond's state budget in his final year was only $4.6 billion, not much more than what it had been when he took office, so while he curbed government spending, he did not reduce it. Another landmark move came in 1984, when he appointed Margaret Kelly, auditor of Cole County, to fill the position of state auditor after the previous auditor resigned. Kelly became the first woman to hold a statewide office, and she was reelected several times, serving until 1999. The same year Kelley entered office, Democrat Harriet Woods won the race for lieutenant governor. Women had finally become major players in Missouri state politics.

Bond's return to the state capital marked the beginning of Republican ascendancy in Missouri politics. While the General Assembly remained a Democratic majority, more and more statewide offices and U.S. congressional seats went to the Republicans.

Bond did not run again in 1984, instead becoming a U.S. senator after defeating his own lieutenant governor, Harriet Woods. Republican State Attorney General John Ashcroft moved into the governor's mansion for two terms. A conservative Christian, he refused to serve liquor at formal state functions and often sang gospel numbers to guests. He followed Bond's lead in conservative spending, although he did approve a four cents a gallon gasoline tax and increased funding for universities, roads, bridges, and the fight against drug abuse. In fact, by the time he left office in 1993 the state budget had blossomed to $10 billion. He also passed a welfare reform bill that put recipients into work programs. Like Bond, Ashcroft moved on to become a U.S. senator, winning in the 1994 race that gave Republicans control of Congress for the first time in forty years.

During his time as governor, Ashcroft had to deal with one of the nation's worst environmental disasters. The Environmental Protection Agency evacuated the town of Times Beach, St. Louis County, after it found dangerously high levels of dioxin and PCBs left over from earlier industry. The cleanup cost $110 million and was the largest exposure of dioxin to civilians in U.S. history. The 2,240 residents were never able to go back to their town, and the site underwent a costly cleanup before being converted into Route 66 State Park.

The naming of the park is a reflection of how important highways were to the development of the state. With the rise of the automobile, trains began to lose business. First Route 66 and then the Interstate highway system allowed Missourians to crisscross the state more quickly than ever before. Passenger lines were abandoned and freight lines lost business as trucks took more and more goods on the interstate highway system. The Missouri-Kansas-Texas Railroad, popularly called the MKT, closed in 1986. The federal National Trails System Act ruled that unused lines could be turned into public space, so the line became the Katy Trail State Park. Running across the state from St. Charles to Clinton, the old railway line provides a walking and biking route along which people can see a cross-section of Missouri.

The Democrats regained the governor's mansion with Mel Carnahan in the 1992 contest. One of the major struggles of his first term

Oliver's Deep Rock Service Station, Route 60–63, Willow Springs, Howell County. As the United States became a car culture, businesses sprang up along Missouri's highways. Courtesy Missouri State Archives.

was over school funding. A judge had ruled in 1993 that state funding of the system was illegally low, and ordered the state government to circumvent the Hancock Amendment in order to secure more money. Carnahan secured passage of the Outstanding Schools Act, adding $315 million in school taxes, as well as reallocating funds from other areas. The money created more teaching jobs and gave many schools their first computers. Carnahan also spearheaded a drive for a major expansion of the University of Missouri campuses.

In response, Melton Hancock, now a congressman, got a Hancock II amendment on the ballot. It would have put serious limits on taxes and cut state funding by at least $1 billion. It failed, and Carnahan's more moderate suggestion, that any tax increase of more than $50 million would require voter approval, eventually passed in 1996. By 2000, the state budget was at $19 billion. The boom years of the 1990s meant rich times for state government.

That same year the voters approved term limits of eight years for legislators. The idea was to make government more accountable to the people by keeping vested interests from maintaining the status quo, but opponents countered that those same vested interests could control new legislators more easily than experienced ones. Regardless of the relative merits of these arguments, the bill passed with 75 percent of the vote.

Missouri had more than school funding and entrenched legislators to worry about in 1993. Heavy rains made water levels rise throughout the state. The Missouri River broke levees, closing down parts of Interstate 70 and cutting off towns. A historic cemetery on the flood plain was swept away and old lead coffins, their glass tops showing the bones within, washed ashore downstream. West Alton in St. Louis County was completely inundated. Water levels at Jefferson City reached 38.6 feet on July 30, an all-time record. Much of the capital city was flooded, but the historic capitol building stood on high ground and survived unscathed. The Grand River flooded Pattonsburg in Daviess County, forcing its four hundred residents to move their entire town to higher ground. The town's one industry, a baseball cap factory, relocated to the new town.

Despite the unpredictability of the state's rivers, in 1994 voters decided to try their luck with a new form of revenue, river boat casinos. None of these "river boats" actually go anywhere; they are in fact floating buildings made to look like river boats. Critics point out that the revenue from these casinos is only a modest enhancement of the Missouri budget and brings a host of social ills. A law stipulating that gamblers can only lose up to $500 with each visit has done little to stop gambling addiction.

Carnahan was reelected for a second term as governor but had to deal with an embarrassing incident in 1999 when a photo surfaced of him performing in blackface at a Kiwanis Club minstrel show in 1960. While such performances were common at the time, blacks objected to them then, and by 1999 such things seemed primitive to most whites as well. Abundant apologies and his general popularity kept him in the race against Ashcroft for the Republican's Senate seat, but Carnahan died tragically on October 16, 2000, in a plane crash along with his son and a campaign advisor. His funeral was an official day of mourning in Missouri and was attended by four hundred guests, including Ashcroft, President Bill Clinton, and Vice President Albert Gore.

It was too late to change Carnahan's name on the ballot, so his wife Jean ran in his place. The Carnahans won, beating Ashcroft in a race that drew nationwide attention. She became Missouri's first female senator. Ashcroft's embarrassing loss to a dead man actually ended up working in his favor, because he was free to accept President George W. Bush's offer to make him U.S. attorney general.

After a brief tenure by Lieutenant Governor Roger Wilson, the Democrat Robert Holden moved into the governor's mansion. Holden's main trouble in office was finances. The boom years were over. The dotcom bubble that had largely fueled the wealth of the 1990s had burst. The constriction of the computer industry, tumbling stock prices, corporate corruption scandals, and the movement of industry and jobs overseas all contributed to a serious recession in 2001. The loss of manufacturing jobs to foreign competitors was especially hard on Missouri. The Department of Economic Development noted that between October of 2000 and September of 2001, Missouri lost 24,459 manufacturing jobs, the most of any state.

Holden had a rocky relationship with the General Assembly. The Democrats controlled the House and the Republicans controlled the Senate, and he had a hard time getting his measures passed. Tax revenues dwindled while the people's need increased. Holden cut funding to the university system and other services.

The economic outlook worsened when terrorists from a shadowy group called al-Qaeda hijacked four planes and crashed three of them into the Pentagon and World Trade Center, the fourth plane going down in a field in Pennsylvania. The terrorists were radical Islamists from Saudi Arabia, Lebanon, Egypt, and the United Arab Emirates. President Bush responded by attacking Afghanistan, where al-Qaeda's leader, Osama bin Laden, was believed to be hiding, and continuing his father's war on Iraq. Missourians in the Reserve and National Guard units found themselves called up alongside the regular military. Advanced B-2 Stealth bombers flew missions from Whiteman Air Force Base, flying all the way to the Middle East and back without landing.

The end of the twentieth century saw some changes in Missouri companies. Payless Cashways, a major employer, went bankrupt in 2001, and Farmland Industries followed suit in 2002. McDonnell-Douglas was bought by Boeing in 1995, and TWA was bought by American Airlines in 2001.

Natural disaster struck again on May 4, 2003, when a tornado killed eight people in the southern part of the state. Two of them died in Pierce City, Lawrence County, which also lost much of its historic downtown. President George W. Bush visited the town on May 13 to express his condolences. Tornados have always been a danger in Missouri, and the increase in population has made fatalities from the storms' meandering courses over the landscape more likely.

In 2005, the governorship once again fell into Republican hands with the election of Matt Blunt. A fiscal conservative and member of the American Legion, Blunt reflected the new conservativism that gave Bush a second term in the White House. Blunt pushed for welfare reform and increased school budgets. Faced with lackluster tax revenues and the reduction of federal funding, he trimmed state expenses by limiting the leasing of office space and the purchase of equipment such as cell phones and vehicles, and closed down Missouri's Washington office on the reasoning that Missouri's congressmen could handle the state's interests in the national capitol.

Missouri entered the new millennium reflecting the trends of the previous fifty years. In the year 2000, 68.7 percent of the population lived in urban areas, defined as population centers with greater than 2,500 people. In 1940, the figure had been 51.8 percent. Since 1970, almost all growth has been in the counties around the two major cities, or those with regional centers such as Boone and Greene counties. The concentration of population has been so marked that the ninety least-populated counties in Missouri experienced an almost zero population growth in the last three decades of the twentieth century. Some of the more agricultural counties, especially to the north of the Missouri River, have actually seen a drop in population.

This reflected not only a move away from farms to big cities and regional centers, but also a move to suburban areas near major cities. Many of the fastest-growing counties are near to, but do not contain, large cities. Middle-class workers have found that for the price of a moderately sized house in Kansas City, they can buy an antebellum brick home in Lexington, in Lafayette County, and commute to work. The trend of the early twenty-first century seems to be increased suburbanization and the filling up of former small towns that happen to be within easy driving distance of larger employment centers. This is helping to preserve old buildings and towns that were otherwise being left to deteriorate for lack of funds. Both native Missourians and newcomers are becoming more in tune with the state's heritage by restoring and researching their towns.

Old downtown areas are being revitalized as well. In St. Louis, a $3 billion redevelopment plan included a new Busch stadium, which opened for the 2006 season with a seating capacity of forty-four thousand. Fans are able to see the Gateway Arch through an opening in the stadium wall and have access to a $300 million "Ballpark Village" with retail, office, and residential space. The stadium itself cost about $350 million. While this brings visitors to downtown, critics say the lavish expense has done little to improve the lives of low-income families in the area.

County population figures from the 2004 U.S. Census reveal some interesting facts about where Missourians live. Of Missouri's 114 counties, only 8 have populations above one hundred thousand. These are Boone, Clay, Greene, Jackson, Jasper, Jefferson, St. Charles, and St. Louis. Boone County is home to Columbia, which boasts a state university campus and several medical centers and is within commuting distance of Jefferson City. Clay and Jackson counties are part of the Kansas City system, as Jefferson, St. Charles, and St. Louis counties are part of the St. Louis city system. Greene County is home to Springfield, Missouri's third largest city, with a population of 150,704. Jasper County is home to the towns of Carthage and Joplin, with populations of 13,003 and 46,830, respectively.

On the other hand, twenty-seven counties have fewer than ten thousand residents. Five of those have fewer than five thousand residents. The smallest of these is Worth County, which in 2004 had only 2,294 people. Set along the Grand River in the northwestern part of the state, it has the distinction of having been formed during the Civil War in 1861, when it separated from Gentry County. Its county seat of Grant City, population 871, is famous for being where a young Glenn Miller learned to play the trombone and performed in the town band. Significantly, none of these sparsely populated counties is along the Missouri River or the Mississippi south of the Missouri. As in frontier days, Missouri's population still tends to congregate around the two major rivers.

Recent figures reveal some of the challenges Missourians will face in the twenty-first century. In the second half of the twentieth century, Missouri's population grew from 4 million to 5.6 million, an increase of 42 percent. While this made Missouri a more urban state, it did not keep up with the national increase of 86 percent. At the beginning of the twenty-first century, Missouri ranked seventeenth among states in population. In 1900, when the population was 3.1 million, it had ranked fifth.

Missouri scores low in other rankings as well. In 2002, it ranked thirty-fifth in median household income with an average household income of $37,934, this despite the fact that Missouri generally has a lower unemployment rate than the national average. The state is still looking for ways to attract lucrative jobs at a time of greater competition in the agricultural sector and the movement of manufacturing and some service jobs overseas.

Missouri's greatest asset, its agricultural base, remains strong. In 2001, Missouri ranked second in the number of farms (108,000), with a total income of $5.56 billion. The state ranked second in the production of hay and cattle, fourth in turkeys, sixth in hogs and rice, and seventh in soybeans. Consolidation and mechanization of farms continued during the second half of the twentieth century. At times this could have an adverse effect on local areas. By the 1960s, most farms in Pemiscot County in the Bootheel were using cotton-picking machines, and the county lost 32 percent of its population. On the other hand, Missouri continued to increase its productivity. In 1939, the average acre yielded thirty bushels of corn; in 1977 it yielded seventy-six bushels. By 1968, soybeans had replaced corn as the number one crop because of high demand for a wide variety of uses, everything from food additives to ink.

Livestock actually accounts for slightly more than half of all farm receipts. Cattle are the most profitable animal (the state ranks ahead of all others, except Texas, in cattle production), followed by hogs. The Ozarks are important for dairy and poultry.

Two older industries, wine and beer making, are both doing well. The German settlements in central Missouri have become tourist destinations, as well as wine producers. The Anheuser-Busch brewery has worldwide distribution, and Budweiser is one of the country's best-known products.

While the heyday of the timber industry has passed, Missouri still produces $3 billion in wood products a year. The rough hills of the Ozarks also produce a large crop of walnuts that are used for food and turned into tableware.

Mining has had its ups and downs in Missouri. Lead, which was the impetus for some of the region's earliest European settlement, remains a major industry. In 1955, the discovery of a rich lead vein in Viburnum, Iron County, helped the state become the preeminent supplier for lead in the United States, offsetting the effects of other mine closings in the 1950s and 1960s. Demand for lead has gone down, however, as its adverse health effects have caused it to be banned from gasoline and many household items. Another hope for Missouri's mining industry, zinc, has seen increased competition from mining regions outside the state. Despite these troubles, Missouri still provides more than 80 percent of the nation's lead production and 30 percent of its zinc. Another important mineral resource is coal. About a third of the state is underlain by bituminous deposits. Coal is one of the main power sources for the state, although the large strip mines used to extract it are a sad blight on the landscape. Other useful minerals include silica sand, used for glassmaking in the famous Crystal City, limestone for cement, and fireclay for brick making.

Manufacturing is still important, employing more than 320,000 people. World War II kicked off a great expansion in electronics, chemicals, aircraft, aerospace, defense, research, and development. While the boom years of the war are long gone, the manufacturing sector remains strong and diversified and is a major producer of everything from greeting cards to automobiles.

Hallmark Cards, which sells about half the greeting cards in the United States, has its corporate headquarters in Kansas City and employs about 4,500 people. Hallmark donated its photographic collection of 6,500 images to the Nelson-Atkins Museum of Art. This collection spans the history of photography, from 1839 to the modern day, and includes works by many famous photographers. Kansas City is a financial center as well. In 1955, Henry and Richard Bloch founded H & R Block, after the Internal Revenue Service started charging for filling out tax returns. The company has since become the largest personal finance management and tax-preparation company in the United States.

Missouri is also responsible for making more automobiles than any other state except Michigan. Besides these newer industries, the two big cities have kept some of their traditional ones. Kansas City is the second largest grain-milling center, processing grain from the vast plains just to the west, and continues to do a large amount of meat processing. St. Louis is still home to the country's largest brewery and has a wide variety of other manufacturing operations.

Non-manufacturing jobs, such as the service and building industries, are doing well because of the continued growth of suburbs. In the 1960s, the service industry replaced manufacturing as the largest employer. This is a trend reflected across the country. Unfortunately, service jobs are often underpaid and provide poor benefits. To maintain a strong economy, both the state and the country will need to keep producing products, not just selling them.

Tourism is another strong industry that has had steady growth throughout the century. Tourists spend an estimated $13 billion a year in Missouri, helping local economies, filling government coffers, and employing a quarter of a million people. The Ozarks have seen the greatest development of tourism. Once a rural backwater, Harold Bell Wright's books and the lakes created during the Depression made the Ozarks a major tourist destination. The Lake of the Ozarks started as a quiet fishing spot, but now fishermen have to compete for space with powerboats, private homes, resorts, and marinas. Branson, in Taney County, draws six million people a year to hear country music and enjoy the Silver Dollar City theme park, making it the largest live music attraction in the country. Hannibal, in Marion County, has become a successful tourist attraction through its ties to Mark Twain.

The key to Missouri's economy has always been its diversity. The state has been rated by the Missouri Economic Research and Information Center as the fifth most diverse economy in the country. Low taxes, especially for businesses, have also helped attract investment, although this has had an adverse effect on state development. The U.S. Census Bureau rates Missouri as forty-eighth among the states in business tax burden per worker.

The end of the twentieth century saw an increase in a new immigrant group, Hispanics. Some had arrived along the Santa Fe Trail in the nineteenth century and settled in Kansas City and other western Missouri towns. Currently, they come to Missouri to get jobs in the meat processing, building, and service industries. In 2000, there were 118,592 Hispanics in the state, almost double the figure of ten years before. The actual number is higher, however, as many do not have immigration papers and therefore do not appear on the census. As with other states, the cheap labor and sales tax revenue these new workers provide helps local economies and leads the government to look the other way. Illegal immigrants still have to worry about the police sending them back to their home countries, but their main concern is unscrupulous bosses who force them to work long hours at low wages.

Other immigrant groups came to Missouri as well. Bosnians moved to the state during the war in former Yugoslavia in the 1990s. Most of them settled in St. Louis, and by 2001 the city had a Bosnian population of 30,500, which was the largest Bosnian community outside Europe. Refugees make up a significant portion of the city's population; there are more than forty-five thousand living in the metro area.

South Asian families bought up many of the hotels and motels, while Arabs opened cafes, grocery stores, and other businesses. The Little Dixie town of Columbia has its own mosque with worshippers from nearly fifty countries, as well as Indian, Middle Eastern, and Latino grocery stores. Because of its major research university, Columbia is home to scientists and academics from around the world.

Missouri's original inhabitants, the various Indian tribes pushed out by European settlement, still maintain their culture and history. The Osage were given a strip of land in Kansas in 1825, but they were again pushed out by white settlement. In 1871, they moved to a region in northeast Oklahoma where most still live today. The buffalo had almost disappeared by then, and the last hunt took place in 1876. The money they received for their Kansas reservation kept them going until oil was discovered on their new land in 1897. Income from this and other mineral resources is shared out among the tribe. Osage also work a variety of jobs in the local area.

The fate of the Otoe-Missouria was similar to the Osage. Pushed into southeastern Nebraska, they watched their land dwindle throughout the nineteenth century until they were moved to the Red Rock region in northeastern Oklahoma in 1881. While they did not find oil on their land, they successfully sued the U.S. government in the 1960s for being cheated out of their original territories in the removals of 1830, 1833, and 1854. Like the Osage, they have held onto their culture. Both groups have built museums and cultural centers and strive to teach their children where they came from. While they have not lived in the state for more than a century, they are fully aware that they are Missourians.

As the face of Missouri continues to change, ties to the past remain strong. Missouri is still a conservative state, suspicious of any radical political or social change, but this also translates into an appreciation of its unique heritage. In Lexington, locals point out where a cannonball from the Civil War battle is still lodged in a pillar in the courthouse. Nevada celebrates its heritage with an annual "Bushwhacker Days" celebration, and since 1898 has been home to the W. F. Norman Corporation, one of the nation's few producers of ornamental metal ceiling panels. Using period machinery, it continues a style of decorating more than a century old. In Columbia, the Historic Avenue of the Columns connects the four columns still standing after the razing of the old courthouse in 1909 to the six columns that survived the Academic Hall fire on the University of Missouri campus in 1892.

A reenactor demonstrates frontier cooking in the Sharp-Hopper Cabin, built in 1835 and located in Harrisonville, Cass County. Living history festivals have become an increasingly popular way to learn about the state's past. COURTESY CASS COUNTY HISTORICAL SOCIETY.

One of the best symbols of Missourians' endurance and respect for the past comes from one of its smallest towns. Huntsdale, in Boone County, was founded in 1817, making it the second oldest community in the county. Originally called Terrapin Neck, this Missouri River town became important as a shipping-off point for local produce on the steamboats that plied the river. The town managed to survive the decline of the steamboat trade when, in 1892, Burch Hunt, a leading wheat farmer and descendant of some of the earliest settlers to the area, platted a town along the MKT railroad. The town was incorporated in 1906 and by that time was a popular stop along the railway for visitors and businessmen. But once again times changed and the trains came less and less often. The depot was torn down and a smaller one, used only for mail and freight, was put up in its place. Eventually the trains stopped coming altogether, and the town, never very large, began to shrink. The townspeople had already stopped having elections in 1929, and their status as a town ended. The town managed to survive the great flood of 1993, but the oldest local resident, a burr oak, estimated to be more than 350 years old, was inundated for more than thirty days. Luckily, it survived the flood. By the beginning of the twenty-first century, the town had only a couple dozen residents, but they were eager to join in the bicentennial festivities celebrating Lewis and Clark, who had stopped nearby. It was then that the locals realized they no longer had an official town because they had not had an election for seventy years, and were therefore not eligible for federal funding.

A drive to get the town reinstated succeeded in 2002, and elections were held the following year. In 2004, the town held its first annual Huntsdale River Days, hosting a crew of re-enactors who retraced the journey of Lewis and Clark. While Huntsdale still has a population of less than two dozen, it has gained a new lease on life by catering to people using the river and the MKT trail. Huntsdale has survived two hundred years of economic changes and natural disasters and has maintained its character as a friendly Missouri town.

For those interested in finding out more about Missouri's rich heritage, the state is home to two statewide historical societies and the nationally known Western Historical Manuscripts Collection. Every county and many towns have their own local historical societies and museums. As with Huntsdale, even the smallest towns have a fascinating past. Hopefully, the state's many newcomers will continue to learn about the history of their new home and join in the struggle to preserve and research it. If they do, their stay in Missouri will be all the richer.

ABOVE: Most of the population of Hunstsdale, Boone County, in the 1970s. Many of Missouri's smallest towns are among its oldest. Huntsdale was founded as Terrapin Neck in 1817. COURTESY OF THE COLUMBIA MISSOURIAN.

BELOW: Most of the residents of Huntsdale in 2006. While the population has remained small, the town has survived war, flooding, and loss of its status as a town. Now reinstated, it hosts an annual festival and is popular with people using the MKT Trail. PHOTO BY SEAN MCLACHLAN.

BIBLIOGRAPHY

Atherton, Lewis. "Missouri's Society and Economy in 1821," in *Missouri Historical Review*, vol. LXV, No. 4, pp. 450–472, July 1971.

Bailey, Garrick. "Osage," in *Handbook of North American Indians*, vol. 13, No. 1, William C. Sturtevant, general editor. Washington, DC: Smithsonian Institution, 2001.

Bailey, Garrick, and Gloria A. Young. "Kansa," in *Handbook of North American Indians*, Vol. 13, No. 1, William C. Sturtevant, general editor. Washington, DC: Smithsonian Institution, 2001.

Beights, Ronald. *Jesse James and the First Missouri Train Robbery*. Gretna, LA: Pelican Publishing Company, 2002.

Botkin, B. A. *A Treasury of American Folklore: Stories, Ballads, and Traditions of the People*. New York: Crown Publishers, 1944.

Bowen, Elbert. *Theatrical Entertainments in Rural Missouri before the Civil War*. University of Missouri Studies, Vol. XXXII. Columbia: University of Missouri Press, 1959.

Brown, A. Theodore. *Frontier Community: Kansas City to 1870*. Columbia: University of Missouri Press, 1963.

Castel, Albert. *General Sterling Price and the Civil War in the West*. Baton Rouge: Louisiana State University Press, 1968.

Chapman, Carl and Eleanor. *Indians and Archaeology of Missouri*. Columbia: University of Missouri Press, 1983.

Christensen, Lawrence, William E. Foley, Gary R. Kremer, and Kenneth H. Winn. *Dictionary of Missouri Biography*. Columbia: University of Missouri Press, 1999.

Christensen, Lawrence. "Black Education in Civil War St. Louis," in *Missouri Historical Review*, Vol. XCV, No. 3, pp. 302–316, April 2001.

Christensen, Lawrence, and Gary Kremer. *A History of Missouri. Volume IV: 1875 to 1919*. Columbia: University of Missouri Press, 2004.

Clamorgan, Cyprian. *The Colored Aristocracy of St. Louis*. Edited with an introduction by Julie Winch. Columbia: University of Missouri Press, 1999.

Clark, Kimball. "The Epic March of Doniphan's Missourians," in *Missouri Historical Review*, Vol. DXXX, No. 2, pp. 134–155, January 1986.

Clevenger, Martha, editor. *"Indescribably Grand"—Diaries and Letters from the 1904 World's Fair*. St. Louis: Missouri Historical Society Press, 1996.

Constantin, M. M. *Sidestreets St. Louis*. St. Louis: Sidestreets Press, 1981.

Cuoco, Lorin, and William H. Gass, editors. *Literary St. Louis: A Guide*. St. Louis: Missouri Historical Society Press, 2000.

Daly, Gale, and Linda Brown. *History of Huntsdale*. Huntsdale, MO: privately published, 2005.

Dains, Mary. "The Congressional Campaign of Luella St. Clair Moss," in *Missouri Historical Review*, Vol. LXXXII, No. 4, pp. 386–407, July, 1988.

Denny, James. "Running the Lower Missouri River Gauntlet: The First Trial of the Lewis and Clark Expedition," in *Missouri Historical Review*, Vol. XCVIII, No. 4, pp. 283–313, July 2004.

Dickey, Michael. *Arrow Rock: Crossroads of the Missouri Frontier*. Arrow Rock, MO: The Friends of Arrow Rock, Inc., 2004.

DuBois, W. E. B. *John Brown: A Biography*. New York: M. E. Sharpe, 1997.

Duden, Gottfried. *Report on a Journey to the Western States of North America*. James Goodrich, general editor. Columbia: State Historical Society of Missouri and University of Missouri Press, 1980.

Evans, Clement Anselm, editor. *Confederate Military History; a library of Confederate States history, in twelve volumes, written by distinguished men of the South, and edited by Gen. Clement A. Evans of Georgia*. New York: Thomas Yoseloff, 1899.

Faherty, S. J., William Barnaby. *The St. Louis Irish: An Unmatched Celtic Community*. St. Louis: Missouri Historical Society Press, 2001.

Fannin, William. *Defenders of the Border: Missouri's Union Military Organizations in the Civil War*. Jefferson City: Mid-Missouri Genealogical Society, 1982.

Ferrell, Robert. *Collapse at Meuse-Argonne: The Failure of the Missouri-Kansas Division*. Columbia: University of Missouri Press, 2004.

Finkelman, Paul. *Dred Scott vs. Sandford: A Brief History with Documents*. Boston: Bedford Books, 1997.

Foley, William. *A History of Missouri. Volume I: 1673 to 1820*. Columbia: University of Missouri Press, 1971.

———. *The Genesis of Missouri: From Wilderness Outpost to Statehood*. Columbia, University of Missouri Press, 1989.

———. "Friends and Partners: William Clark, Meriwether Lewis, and Mid-America's French Creoles," in *Missouri Historical Review*, Vol. XCVIII, No. 4, pp. 270–282, July 2004.

Gerteis, Louis. *Civil War St. Louis*. Lawrence: University Press of Kansas, 2001.

Giffen, Jerena, "'Add a Pinch and a Lump'—Missouri Women in the 1820s," in *Missouri Historical Review*, Vol. LXV, No. 4, pp. 473–504, July 1971.

Gilbert, Joan. *The Trail of Tears across Missouri*, Missouri Heritage Readers. Columbia: University of Missouri Press, 1996.

Gilmore, Robert. *Ozark Baptizings, Hangings, and Other Diversions: Theatrical Folkways of Missouri, 1885–1910*. Norman: University of Oklahoma Press, 1984.

Hartman, Mary, and Elmo Ingenthron. *Bald Knobbers: Vigilantes on the Ozarks Frontier*. Gretna, LA: Pelican Publishing Company, 1988.

Hyslop, Stephan. *Bound for Santa Fe: The Road to New Mexico and the American Conquest*. Norman: University of Oklahoma Press, 2002.

Kirkendall, Richard. *A History of Missouri. Volume V: 1919 to 1953*. Columbia: University of Missouri Press, 1986.

Knipmeyer, James, "Denis Julien: Midwestern Fur Trader," in *Missouri Historical Review*, Vol. XCV, No. 3, pp. 245–263, April 2001.

Krone, Charles. "Recollections of an Old Actor," in *Missouri Historical Society Collections*, Vol. 3, pp. 275–306, April 1908.

Larsen, Lawrence. *A History of Missouri. Volume VI: 1953 to 2003*. Columbia: University of Missouri Press, 2004.

Latrobe, Charles Joseph. *The Rambler in North America: 1832–1833*, vol. I. London: R. B. Seeley and W. Burnside, 1836.

Lexington Historical Association. *The Battle of Lexington*. Lexington, MO: Lexington Historical Association, 1999.

March, David. "The Admission of Missouri," in *Missouri Historical Review*, Vol. LXV, No. 4, pp. 427–449, July 1971.

Matthews, George, and Sandra Marshall. *St. Louis Olympics 1904*. Chicago: Arcadia Publishing, 2003.

McCandless, Perry. *A History of Missouri. Volume II: 1820 to 1860*. Columbia: University of Missouri Press, 1972.

McQueen, Kevin. "Carrie Nation: Militant Prohibitionist," in *Offbeat Kentuckians: Legends to Lunatics*. Kuttawa, KY: McClanahan Publishing House, 2001.

Monaghan, Jay. *Civil War on the Western Border, 1854–1865*. New York: Bonanza Books, 1960.

Moulton, Gary, editor. *The Journals of the Lewis & Clark Expedition August 30, 1803–August 24, 1804, Vol. 2*. Lincoln: University of Nebraska Press, 1986.

Nagel, Paul. *Missouri, A History*. Lawrence: University Press of Kansas, 1988.

O'Brien, Michael, and W. Raymond Wood. *The Prehistory of Missouri*. Columbia: University of Missouri Press, 1998.

Osage County Historical Society. "World War I . . . Lest We Forget," in *Osage County Historical Society Newsletter*, Vol. 18, No. 7–9, July–September 2003.

Parkin, Robert. *The Revolution in the Environs of St. Louis.* St. Louis: St. Louis Genealogical Society, 1993.

Parrish, William. *A History of Missouri. Volume III: 1860 to 1875.* Columbia: University of Missouri Press, 1973.

Parrish, William, Charles Jones Jr., and Lawrence Christensen. *Missouri: The Heart of the Nation*, 3rd edition. Wheeling, IL: Harlan Davidson, 2004.

Payton, Leland and Crystal. *See the Ozarks: The Touristic Image.* Springfield, MO: Lens and Pen Press, 2003.

Peterson, Charles. *Colonial St. Louis: Building a Creole Capital*, 2nd ed. Tucson: Patrice Press, 1993.

Piston, William Garrett. "'Springfield Is a Vast Hospital': The Dead and Wounded at the Battle of Wilson's Creek," in *Missouri Historical Review*, Vol. XCIII, No. 4, pp. 345–366, July 1999.

Porchey, James. *A Historical Survey of Broadcasting in Missouri.* Unpublished Master's thesis, University of Missouri–Columbia, 1969.

Pryor, Jerry. *Southwest Missouri Mining.* Chicago: Arcadia Publishing, 2000.

Randolph, Vance. *The Ozarks: An American Survival of Primitive Society.* New York: The Vanguard Press, 1931.

Randolph, Vance. *Ozark Magic and Folklore.* New York: Dover Publications, Inc., 1947.

Reddig, William. *Tom's Town: Kansas City and the Pendergast Legend.* Columbia: University of Missouri Press, 1986.

Renner, G. K. "Prohibition Comes to Missouri, 1910–1919," in *Missouri Historical Review*, Vol. LXII, No. 4, pp. 363–397, July 1968.

Rhodes, James Ford. *History of the Civil War, 1861–1865.* New York: Macmillan Co., 1917

Rowland, Howard Ray. *Big War, Small Town: How World War II Changed Cassville: A Personal Account.* St. Cloud, MN: North Star Press of St. Cloud, 2003.

Ryan, William James. "Which Came First? 65 Years of Broadcasting in Kansas City," in *Missouri Historical Review*, Vol. LXXXII, No. 4, pp. 408–423, July 1988.

Schweitzer, Marjorie. "Otoe and Missouria," in *Handbook of North American Indians*, Vol. 13, No. 1, William C. Sturtevant, general editor. Washington, DC: Smithsonian Institution, 2001.

Shoemaker, Floyd. "Pioneer Dentists Did Big Job with few Tools," in *Missouri Historical Review*, Vol. XLVI, No. 2, pp. 145–147, January 1952.

———. "David Barton, John Rice Jones and Edward Bates: Three Missouri State and Statehood Founders," in *Missouri Historical Review*, Vol. LXV, No. 4, pp. 527–543, July 1971.

Snead, Thomas L. *The Fight for Missouri.* New York: Scribner's Sons, 1886.

Stevens, Walter. "The Missouri Tavern," in *Missouri Historical Review*, Vol. XV, No. 2, pp. 241–276, January 1921.

Strickland, Arvarh. "Aspects of Slavery in Missouri, 1821," in *Missouri Historical Review*, Vol. LXV, No. 4, pp. 505–526, July 1971.

Sunder, John. "St. Louis and the Early Telegraph, 1847–1857," in *Missouri Historical Review*, Vol. L No. 3, pp. 248–258, April 1956.

Thompson, Henry. *Our Lead Belt Heritage.* Marceline, MO: Walsworth Publishing Company, 1992.

Traylor, Richard. "Pulling Missouri out of the Mud: Highway Politics, the Centennial Road Law, and the Problems of Progressive Identity," in *Missouri Historical Review*, Vol. XCVIII, No. 1, pp. 47–68, October 2003.

Wedel, Mildred Mott. "Iowa," in *Handbook of North American Indians*, Vol. 13, No. 1, William C. Sturtevant, general editor. Washington, DC: Smithsonian Institution, 2001.

Williams, Stephen, and John Goggin. "The Long Nosed God Mask in Eastern United States," in *The Missouri Archaeologist* 18(3), 1956.

Winegar, Thomas, "Monster Memories of Gregory Grave," in *Scary Monsters* 10, pp. 59–60, March 1994.

Wolferman, Kristie. *The Osage in Missouri,* Missouri Heritage Readers. Columbia: University of Missouri Press, 1997.

Wood, Larry. "Harry Truman: Federal Bushwhacker," in *Missouri Historical Review*, Vol. XCVIII, No. 3, pp. 201– 222, April 2004.

Wood, W. Raymond. *Prologue to Lewis and Clark: The Mackay and Evans Expedition.* Norman: University of Oklahoma Press, 2003.

Wright, Harold Bell. *The Shepherd of the Hills.* Gretna, LA: Pelican Publishing Company, 2001.

INDEX

Page numbers in **bold** refer to text graphics.

Also available . . .

California: An Illustrated History
Robert J. Chandler
252 pages · 5½ x 8½ · $14.95pb · 0-7818-1034-5 · (583)

Florida: An Illustrated History
Robert A. Taylor
238 pages · 5½ x 8½ · $14.95pb · 0-7818-1052-3 · (36)

New Mexico: An Illustrated History
Patrick Lavin
200 pages · 5½ x 8½ · $14.95pb · 0-7818-1053-1 · (51)

Virginia: An Illustrated History
Deborah Welch
220 pages · 5½ x 8½ · $14.95pb · 0-7818-1115-5 · (375)

Prices subject to change without prior notice. **To purchase Hippocrene Books** contact your local bookstore, call (718) 454-2366, or write to: HIPPOCRENE BOOKS, 171 Madison Avenue, New York, NY 10016. Please enclose check or money order, adding $5.00 shipping (UPS) for the first book, and $.50 for each additional book.